THE DECLINE OF LEARNING
IN AMERICA

THE DECLINE OF LEARNING IN AMERICA

CHARLES T. STEWART, JR.

Nova Science Publishers, Inc.
New York

Copyright © 2008 by Nova Science Publishers, Inc.

NOTICE TO THE READER

LIBRARY OF CONGRESS CATALOGING-IN-PUBLICATION DATA

Stewart, Charles T., 1922-
  The decline of learning in America / Charles T. Stewart, author.
     p. cm.
  Includes bibliographical references and index.
  ISBN 978-1-60456-223-1 (hardcover : alk. paper)
  1. Educational change--United States. 2. Education, Secondary--United States. 3. High school teachers--Training of--United States. I. Title.
LA222.S68   2008
370.973--dc22
                                                                                        2007048709

Published by Nova Science Publishers, Inc. ✦ New York

CONTENTS

PREFACE

This book offers a complete and coherent analysis of the interrelated problems of student achievement at every level, the supply of scientific and technical manpower, its contribution to the nation's economic future, and the diverse policies directed at improving school achievement and the quality of labor supply.

Chapter 1 - Our public high schools are widely perceived to be in crisis. In a big country, one can find examples of everything, from public schools that successfully compete with elite private schools for able students and dedicated parents to child care institutions that churn out high school dropouts. One perception is that the quality of education - the average performance of schools - has declined. The unsatisfactory achievement of high school graduates is widely recognized, notably in the sciences and math, but in history, geography and other fields as well. This is an old story. Whether or not achievement has declined, it does not rank high in international comparisons, nor in the judgment of employers. A third perception is that inequality in educational achievement has increased.

Chapter 2 - Whatever the facts on quality of education, and whatever the allocation of causes, one thing is clear: schools are having great difficulty in recruiting good teachers, and many teachers are teaching subjects in which they are poorly qualified. The retirement of a large number of teachers is expected in the decade ahead; they need to be replaced. In the 1950's the baby boom generation entered elementary schools, prompting a hiring binge for elementary school teachers. The 1960s was the decade for hiring high school teachers, as baby boomers aged and an increasing proportion completed high school. The number of public school teachers (in thousands) rose from 1,014 in 1950 to 1,408 in 1960 and 2,059 in 1970. There was little further increase till the 1990s; the number rose to 2,979 thousand by 2001, in response to smaller average class size and a slight increase in enrollments. As a result the median years of teacher experience declined from 11 in 1960 to 8 in 1970, but has been increasing since, to 12 in 1980, 15 in the 1990s, down to 14 in 2001 as retirements increased. The average age of public school teachers is increasing, from a low of 33 in the mid-1970s to 46 in 2001.

Chapter 3 - This chapter is concerned with the content of instruction and the methods of instruction as determinants of student achievement. It focuses on public elementary and secondary schools.

Chapter 4 - "...here are college graduates, many of them cannot read accurately or write clearly, cannot do fractions or percentages without travail and doubt, cannot utter their thoughts with fluency or force...cannot trust themselves to use the foreign language they have studied for 8 years, and can no more range conversationally over a modest gamut of intellectual topics than they can address their peers consecutively on one of the subjects they have studied." [1] This is the admittedly elitist verdict of Jacques Barzun nearly half a century ago, after the large increase in college enrollments following World War II, but before the even larger increase by the baby boom generation and the dramatic decline in standard test scores of high school graduates. Chapter 4 will examine the consequences for colleges of admitting high school graduates who are ill-prepared for college work, and how colleges have adjusted to a combination of decline in entering student achievement and increase in college enrollments.

Chapter 5 - Too many people are going to college in terms of the needs of the economy. Not enough are graduating with the skills needed for maintaining its forward motion. Our ability to in-source highly qualified foreigners to fill our gaps in human capital is eroding. The failure of our educational system places our future at risk.

This unhappy situation is the inevitable result of primary and secondary education in this country and its impact on colleges. Since anyone can get into some college these days (and two thirds of high school graduates do), the problem of poorly educated high school graduates is not college admission, it is debasement of the college curriculum and degree, and mismatch between education and labor market needs.

When college students graduate and seek employment, they face a discontinuity between the universe of education and the labor market. Competitive capitalism is meritocratic; employers are selective in job offers, and discriminate in pay and promotion on the basis of performance. Grade inflation in college and debasement of standards for graduation simply defer the consequences to the labor market, they do not prevent them. Egalitarianism in higher education complicates the employer's hiring efforts: how to distinguish between applicants with similar grades and recommendations. Prospective employers who have unreliable information on individual students may adjust by choosing schools before considering individuals (this is not new, but now more prevalent); and by upgrading minimum educational requirements (college, where high school was good enough in the past). Choosing schools, before selecting individuals from those schools makes sense if graduation from a particular school, its grades or its recommendations are credible indicators of competence. Increasing educational requirements is more of a shotgun approach toward narrowing the pool of eligible candidates.

Employers will make more mistakes than in the past; there will be greater need to terminate new employees who don't pass muster. This will prove highly frustrating to graduates who on the basis of their college records thought they were very able and highly qualified. More money, time and effort will have to be devoted to on-the-job training and remedial education.

One can foresee growing efforts to export the egalitarian norms from school to office and factory, making it very difficult and expensive to terminate workers, as in some European nations. The result has been a combination of great reluctance to hire at all, with persistent high rates of unemployment, or the expansion of an underground economy violating or circumventing regulations: a dual labor market. The former response is prevalent in France and Germany, the later in Spain and Italy. These nations do not suffer from the burden of egalitarian college education or pre-college education largely dissociated from future employment opportunities, or nowhere to the same extent as American high schools and colleges. Still they are paying a high price for limiting the role of worker performance in labor retention decisions.

Chapter 6 - Why are our schools so bad, and what can be done about it? One should recognize that comparisons of high school student achievement today with 50 years ago are imperfect, for two reasons: 50 years ago, most never finished high school; graduating classes on average were abler than they can be today. (This does not apply to elementary school.) However there is no weaseling out of the fact that American students at various ages score poorly in comparison with students in other nations with universal elementary school attendance and rates of high school graduation near or exceeding our own. Second, curricula have changed, or at least curriculum requirements should have changed. There were no computers, they are ubiquitous now. Knowledge of foreign languages was considered more important than it is today despite all the promotion of multiculturalism. Needs for mathematical competence have grown.

There is much concern about the quality of education and much controversy about causes and cures. Many perceive that education is in crisis. Americans believe that all problems have solutions. Many are addicted to single causes and simple solutions. What about class size and teacher pay? Are they self-serving proposals or important policies?

Chapter 7 - What if anything should be done? People of many points of view agree that something should be done, although they may disagree on why and on what. Promoters of self-esteem should recognize that self-esteem is a consequence, not a cause of achievement. Teaching methods that focus on learning do more for self-esteem than those that stress self-esteem. Egalitarians should support change, because the current egalitarian agenda has actually increased inequality of achievement by lowering standards and stakes. Underperforming pedagogies should be abandoned. Only those whose interest in education is the promotion of ideologies and secular religions might resist change, for their agenda has had some success and any alternative would pose a threat.

But what change, and how much change? On this there is bound to be disagreement, deriving from different concepts of the purpose of public education. At the heart of controversy is the choice between meritocracy and egalitarianism. It is also a choice between public wants and private needs, between democracy and a competitive economy. Democracy is egalitarianism unqualified. A competitive economy only thrives on the selective principle of meritocracy. For what are public schools preparing students? Not for citizenship - civics is grossly neglected and history is badly taught. Not for economic success - the basic learning tools of language and numbers, in both of which performance has lagged. I see no reason why public schools cannot do both; the adult is both a citizen and a worker.

To speak of solutions one must define the problem. There is no consensus on what schools and students should accomplish, nor on the adequacy of current achievements. Millions, in particular those engaged in the industry of education, see little need for higher achievement, or what is the same thing, see no problem that cannot be solved by pouring more money down a bottomless maw: higher salaries, smaller classes, computers for all. They oppose every other proposal to change the status quo. Most do see a problem, but there is a variety of views, disagreements, on the proper content of achievement, on the desired level of achievement, even on achievement for whom.

In this chapter I assume that the purpose of educational reform is to improve learning to empower the individual as a worker, and maintain national economic growth via economic efficiency and leadership in innovation. This is not, never has been, the only purpose. Some may care nothing about economic prospects for students or for society; they may prefer other purposes and propose a different set of reforms. Accordingly the following proposals should be viewed as possible components of diverse strategies for raising achievement, however defined, rather than "solutions" to a "problem". They are diverse: some refer to incentives, others to penalties, yet others to quality and efficiency concerns, to competition, to information.

Americans like single 'causes' and simple solutions, and prompt, even immediate results. The failures of our schools started early in the twentieth century, those of our colleges go back a half century. There is no way of reversing course in a decade, of restoring a healthy system of learning in just a single generation. Some policies can yield prompt results, others require a generation or two. Both are needed.

We know that there are many factors influencing outcomes, that some of them are beyond the control or perhaps even the influence of school systems and teachers and outside their responsibility. Some factors are interdependent, so that looking at just one cannot tell us the magnitude of its contribution. It is possible that the popular variables are not important; they are superficial at best. Factors not measured by class size or teacher pay or spending per student, such as teacher quality, are more fundamental. And not much improvement in teacher quality is possible in the short run; it is nearly impossible to terminate bad or mediocre teachers, and impossible to hire large numbers of superior teachers in some subjects, even with substantial increase in salaries; the supply isn't there.

The large number of proposed policies to improve learning in public schools are not a menu; they are not alternatives. They serve different purposes. Most policies have unintended consequences; some are quickly implemented, others take a long time. There is an optimal sequence of policies. The first is information.

How can radical improvement be brought about? Many things need to be done. But what are the priorities? What is the sequence? To hire and retain much better teachers it is necessary to bypass schools of education and teachers unions. A salary scale that reflects the market and rewards merit must be instituted, over the opposition of the teachers unions. Curriculum and pedagogical reform can only follow from staffing schools with teachers who were not mindwashed by schools of education. Vouchers and other means of compelling performance from public schools are likewise adamantly opposed by the industry itself. Under these conditions the proper strategy is to concentrate on information. Parents, and students, must be made acutely aware of the failings of their schools, in providing basic learning skills, in preparing them for college, for jobs. At present too many parents of students in failing schools are pleased with their children's' high grades and many honors. Freedom of information is the necessary condition for genuine reform. Without information there is not enough pressure to adopt a reform agenda; even if such an agenda were adopted, it would not be implemented.

I consider first, the key obstacles to reform of public schools, which are the monopoly of public education, the teachers unions, and the schools of education. Then I focus on the substance of reform, its core objectives, which are better teachers and a radically improved curriculum, which combined imply pedagogic reform as well. Only then can the numerous policies be considered, together with their interaction and appropriate sequence.

Many private schools suffer from the same handicaps and shortcomings that beleaguer the public school system. But they are only one tenth the enrollment, parents have a choice of schools, and change must come one school at a time, whereas in the public school system much change can be at the district and state level, and some at the national level.

Chapter 8 - How to attract able and well-prepared individuals into high school teaching? It will take time in the best of cases - a generation or two. As indicated previously, not enough college students have been majoring in some scientific fields to supply the needs of the economy and of schools, even with a substantial pay increase. How do we persuade abler students to teach in elementary schools? How will we persuade more majors in fields other than education to enter high school teaching? Pay isn't everything. It alone will not buy the occupational prestige needed to attract more and abler college graduates into teaching.

In many other countries, teachers, high school teachers especially, are held in great regard. Their status is comparable to college professors in this country. No wonder students do better than ours. Nations whose students do best are distinguished not by high salaries but by high standards for teachers. The fact that high school completion was the exception and college attendance rare elsewhere until very recently may be a factor. But history and culture may be a more important explanation. Our tradition is the frontier, a nation of immigrants. We never looked up to an aristocracy; we never had one. Many of those we admire were self-made. We valued enterprise and hard work more than intellect and higher learning. Many of our presidents before the twentieth century were high school dropouts or less. Education was not the main path to success. Conditions have changed, people are becoming aware of the importance of education for individuals and for the society. The widespread concern with the status of our schools and colleges is one result. In time this revaluation of education in the public mind should upgrade the status of teachers.

Chapter 1

INTRODUCTION

"The race which does not value trained intelligence is doomed"
A. N. Whitehead

Our public high schools are widely perceived to be in crisis. In a big country, one can find examples of everything, from public schools that successfully compete with elite private schools for able students and dedicated parents to child care institutions that churn out high school dropouts. One perception is that the quality of education - the average performance of schools - has declined. The unsatisfactory achievement of high school graduates is widely recognized, notably in the sciences and math, but in history, geography and other fields as well. This is an old story. Whether or not achievement has declined, it does not rank high in international comparisons, nor in the judgment of employers. A third perception is that inequality in educational achievement has increased.

CHANGING ROLE OF EDUCATION

The aims of education have changed. Once only the children of a tiny elite went to college; not many more completed secondary school education. Many of them had the benefit of tutors. Most of them were wealthy by inheritance, a "job" was theirs for the taking, should they want one. Many did not need one. They were trained to be cultured members of society and the polity, not for jobs and occupations. Schools were aging vats, stir-mixing socialization institutions, media for acculturation. The Hundred Great Books approach is a direct descendant of the elite education of past centuries. It prepares students to be philosopher kings, leaders in a hierarchical society. It is a throwback, fixated on past greatness, not oriented toward an unknown future. For the majority, elementary school was the end of formal education. Other than literacy, it was meant to build character and to instill civic virtues.

Until shortly after the Civil war the majority of workers were farmers. Many of the rest were self-employed. They acquired occupational skills by informal apprenticeship, largely from the older generation; occupations and work were inherited to a considerable extent. Workers had little schooling and received little if any formal training. The United States never had a guild system. Few jobs and occupations had specific educational requirements. Most women worked in the farm and household and nowhere else.

The modern situation is radically different. As recently as 1920, one quarter of workers were engaged in farming; now it is two percent. With urbanization and rapid change in occupational structure in recent generations, most young people came to need jobs to live, and most of them could no longer inherit jobs or even occupations from their parents. The vast majority are employees, women included. Very few own a job. Most do not own an occupation, as guild members once did (and as doctors and lawyers do still). Preparation for employment became a central purpose of education. Formal education and training gradually acquired a monopoly of access to an increasing proportion of jobs and occupations [1]. In many cases there were specific requirements: medical school, law school, and qualifying exams. In others, additional education became a dominant advantage in competing for jobs. Truman was the last president who did not go to college. Bill Gates, college dropout, is a rare exception in big business. (These are not success stories that can be generalized. Most of the success stories of high school and elementary school dropouts refer to entrepreneurs who create their own jobs.)

There were many reasons for this trend: geographic mobility limiting information based on personal contacts, placing a premium on impersonal qualifications; the decline of the family business limiting the role of informal apprenticeship; growth of large organizations in every field faced with high turnover that have to decide among numerous applicants; the growing technical complexity of many jobs and occupations; and more recently, the fear of lawsuits by or in behalf of rejected applicants. Whatever the explanation, the fact remains that educational accomplishments have become crucial in competing for jobs. Whether educators like it or not, schools are perceived as preparation for jobs and occupations as well as citizenship.

Meanwhile, literacy and elementary school attendance became nearly universal. More recently enrollment in secondary schools rose rapidly. Average school attendance for children 5 to 17 years old was only 78 days in 1870, rising to over 99 in 1900, 143 in 1930, then to 162 in 1970, about where it has been since [2]. Once secondary school completion became a universal goal, and attained by the great majority, college attendance became the goal. Specific job-related education and training in high school has diminished, on the implicit assumption that everyone will go to college. Availability of occupational training expanded after high school, primarily in community colleges.

While formal education has become the dominant entrée to jobs and occupations, public schools have defaulted on their responsibilities. One would have expected that greater focus on preparation for college would have improved academic performance, but no such thing happened. Neither their curricula nor their standards have adjusted to the needs of students, the economy or the society. The amount of school time devoted to academic preparation has declined, and the level of expectations and achievement has fallen. The deemphasis on literacy and numeracy (call it what you wish, it is deemphasis) which are prerequisites for most jobs, disadvantage both those seeking job-specific skill training in community colleges and those pursuing more traditional college careers in four-year colleges and universities. Other concerns and activities have gained ground. The preparation for employment of the large number of students who are not college-bound has been neglected. The hunger for equality underlay this change of function and direction.

As four year colleges and universities expanded greatly in enrollment, they assumed many of the tasks formerly borne by high schools. Remedial course work in basic subjects: English and math, grew rapidly. The task of specific training for the jobs held by much of the labor force fell largely in the hands of community colleges, leaving untrained many of the age group that never finished high school or never went beyond high school.

College education, once intended to produce well-rounded and informed elite citizens, was now expected to prepare students for preferred employment by choice of majors. Courses in a variety of spheres of knowledge which educated graduates for specific occupations came to be expected for access to jobs in these occupations. But universities have never viewed themselves as training schools, except for some professions, such as theology and law, more recently a growing range of scientific and technical occupations such as engineering and medicine. Specific course distribution requirements for graduation have been reduced or eliminated, and the student became free to pick and choose from a large and diverse curriculum menu. New majors were established offering little prospect of related jobs or occupations. A college degree no longer implies any common core of knowledge or competence.

Thus first in primary and secondary school, and then in college, the aims of education held by the educational establishment, as implied in its offerings, have diverged widely from the expectations of the public and the needs of the economy. The failure of public education may have become apparent from the early 1960s, when SAT and other test scores taken by high school seniors started plunging. But its beginnings are much older. The decline in learning in earlier grades would have become significant in the 1950s. The writers on education who revolutionized the practice of teaching. among them John Dewey and William Kilpatrick, wrote in the first two quarters of the 20th century [3]. The major impact of the new doctrines was long delayed for two reasons: initially most high school teachers were not education majors, and experienced elementary school teachers had not been indoctrinated in the new pedagogy. It takes some forty years to turn over the teaching faculty. During the great depression schools attracted better people into teaching than would have entered the field under normal economic conditions, and many of them did not retire until the 1960s. It was in the 1960s also that the teachers unions came to include most public school teachers and schools of education came to dominate the profession. Their doctrines became the vested interests of the unions and of most of the school of education graduates making teaching their profession. But doctrines which were initially well-intended and often helpful have since proven detrimental to schools and students. Opportunity has become the equality of lower expectations; tolerance of differences has become an encouragement of separatism, and education has become indoctrination.

The decline in performance of public schools is grossly understated because it does not reflect 1. the increase in the average number of school days attended, from in 99 days in 1900 to 162 in 1970 and after; 2. the large increase in proportion of students who are in special education, from 8.3% in 1976, the first year after passage of the Education for Handicapped Children Act, to 13.8% in 2005-6. They do not take the tests that indicate achievement of students and school systems, inflating average test scores. There is substantial variation in the proportion by state, the lowest being California at 10.5, the highest Rhode Island at 20.1%, followed by Maine 18.7 [4]. I suspect that interstate variation is partially explained by differences in academic standards and curriculum requirements. 3. The increase in number of years of education at every grade level. At one time almost no public school students went to preschool, few to kindergarten; now almost everyone goes to kindergarten, and the proportion of 3 and 4 year olds enrolled in school has risen from 10.6% in Fall 1965 to 54.6% in Fall 2005. For 5 year olds, the increase was from 60.6% to 86.4% [5]. Kindergarten enrollment has been 93-95 % of first grade public school enrollments in successive years for some time At the fourth grade level we are comparing students several decades ago who had completed three years of previous schooling with current fourth graders who will average 4 and two-thirds years of previous schooling. Many high school seniors graduate with 14 years of schooling, not the 12 of long ago. The decline in achievement coincided with substantial increases in real dollars spent per student, in educational attainment of teachers, and decreases in average class size.

How far we have fallen since the early 1960s, how much we have recovered in recent years is hard to say. The standardized tests taken by high school seniors which serve as indicators have been revised, re-entered, i.e., dumbed down. Ultimately comparisons with an ever more distant past do not matter; what does matter is current achievement compared to the needs of the economy and society. The economy has changed with the growth of technology in the workplace, and schools are not keeping up. Nor are they meeting the demands of the society in which we live.

INTERNATIONAL COMPARISONS

The international comparisons which have cast such a bad light on American students are recent in origin. Curricula differ among nations for a variety of reasons. Thus comparisons of student achievement must be made with care and reservation. It is in science and mathematics that one expects minimal differences in subject matter, although the sequence in which various topics are taught does vary between schools, as well as nations, and so does the amount of time devoted to them. It is precisely in these subjects that there are international comparative data.

The Third International Mathematics and Science Study (TIMSS) tested fourth and eighth graders in math and in science in 2003 [6]. Earlier tests had been conducted in 1995 and 1999. Between 1995 and 2003 there was no change in the performance of fourth graders in math, some decline in science, and some decline in both relative to the performance of the 14 countries in both reports. But eighth graders improved in performance and in relation to the 21 other nations participating: 8th graders rose from 28th to 15th in math, from 17th to 9th in science. Fourth graders remained no. 12 in math, dropped from 3rd to 6th in science.

American fourth grade students do very well in science, but it has been suggested that their performance is more due to out of school exposure to scientific materials than to study in school. This in turn could be attributed in part to the high proportion of 4, 5, and 6 year olds in preschool and kindergarten as well as exposure to educational TV, museums, science magazines [7]. As they move up to the 8th grade, their relative scores decline, a reflection of unsatisfactory performance of public elementary schools and middle schools. The US is the only nation showing a significant drop in achievement as students age [8].

The Program for International Student Assessment (PISA), in collaboration with the OECD, has conducted two surveys of performance of 15 year olds. The first, in 2000, stressed literacy and reading; the second, 2003, stressed mathematics; the latest, in 2006, stressed science. U.S. 15-year olds in 2000 ranked 19th in math, 14th in science, and 15th in reading. [9]. In 2006, they ranked 24th in math and 18th in science. Thus their performance, below average in both years, declined relative to other OECD nations.

The 2003 survey focused on several content areas in mathematics and on problem-solving. In every area the United States had a higher percentage of students in the lowest proficiency levels than the OECD mean, and a lower percentage in the highest proficiency levels. The 2003 reading literacy and science literacy results were little different from 2000; reading was at the mean, science somewhat below it [10].

There are problems with international comparisons. First, what is important is whether our students are learning what they should know, and doing it well, not how they compare with other nations with different conditions and perhaps somewhat different needs. Second, the comparisons are flawed, according to Iris Rotberg [11]. Countries differ significantly in the proportion of an age group completing secondary school; in the average age of students participating in the tests, in school curricula, and in the sample of students and schools represented. These differences are important for seniors, but much less significant for elementary school students. The examiners attempt to allow for them but cannot be sure they have fully succeeded. The excuse that American schools have more ethnically diverse student bodies is contradicted by their good performance in the early elementary years. And there are other countries with diverse student bodies which do better [12]. Several have higher rates of high school graduation than the United States.

Deconstruction of international comparisons does not imply that American students are doing well or doing better. Ultimately we need to know whether high school graduates are well prepared for postsecondary education, for the labor market, for citizenship, whether they be 16, 18, or 20 years old. Past performance and international comparisons are helpful indicators, no more.

On the whole, looking at literacy, math and science scores, American students are not doing terribly internationally; they are about average or a little below average for the OECD countries, all advanced or semi-advanced nations. That is not good enough, not because we want to be number one, but because the United States was first in near-universal secondary school education, and in mass college education. One would expect an educational system that achieved a steady state a generation or two ago to perform better than systems which have just attained or are in the process of attaining the same levels of mass education. There is another more compelling reason. The United States is the technological leader, in invention and innovation, in the demand for new and changing skills and capabilities. The structure of the economy, and its rapid change, require better than an average performance from its educational system, especially in math and science. What is terrible is the great inequality in achievement between schools and school districts, itself a major explanation for the mediocre average.

INEQUALITY IN PUBLIC SCHOOLS

Within living memory, typical school-leaving age was 14, eighth grade, then rose to 16 with the rise in minimum age for work, now it is 18, high school graduation, attained by some 72% of the age group according to official statistics (half the remainder graduate or obtain high school equivalency degrees eventually), and two thirds of high school graduates enter college. Education is compulsory to age 18 in 13 states and 17 in 8 states; to 16 in the rest. High school graduation is accepted in lieu of a maximum age in most states [13]. Thus school-leaving age exceeds the minimum age for labor force entry in 20 states.

Inequality in number of years of schooling completed has fallen dramatically. But there remains great inequality in the quality of schooling at every level. Egalitarian practices have not prevented great inequalities in opportunity and achievement. Years of educational attainment is an insufficient indicator of investment in human capital. Since abler students are likely to go to better schools and to be taught by better teachers, differences in quality of education magnify differences in ability. Equalization of educational attainment has been achieved partly by social promotion and lower standards. Few are allowed to fail en route to high school graduation, although in fact many drop out. Inevitably the inequality of scholastic achievement increases as students move up grade by grade, within schools as well as between schools. A wide range of achievement, in the absence of tracking, makes teaching more difficult. A high school diploma is no longer a guarantee of literacy, numeracy, or superficial command of any subject.

Differences in performance by school and school system have been accentuated by changes in social structure. Now this is a predominantly urban nation. In recent decades urban areas have become differentiated between suburbs and central cities, with poor and minority populations concentrated in the city, and richer, better educated and predominantly white populations in the suburbs. Growing residential segregation by income level is correlated with parental educational attainment, both of which are correlated with student achievement. This segregation has been facilitated by the rise in cars as the dominant form of transportation, spreading out the population of large urban areas.

Parental income and educational attainment are correlated with private contributions to schools, both in cash and in parental involvement in the education of their children. As a result students in suburban schools on average outperform those in urban schools by a significant margin. Often the better-off areas are also separate political entities with the taxing power to finance superior schools. In general, the suburbs get the better qualified teachers, the more experienced teachers. And to a larger extent than in the past it is these same parents who send their children to private schools, reducing the local tax burdens of public schools. Since the culprit is near-universal car ownership, the process of geographic segregation is unlikely to be reversed.

This inequality in achievement is widely regarded as unacceptable, whatever the average level may be. As one result, the high school diploma has been degraded; who knows what it represents? It is not enough to raise the average; the differential between urban and suburban schools must also be reduced. One consequence is a growing differentiation between graduates on the basis of high school attended. Graduates of private schools are generally held to be better prepared than graduates of public schools. But some public schools are known locally, some nationally, for their selective student body and outstanding achievement, high schools such as the Bronx High School of Science, the Thomas Jefferson High School in Virginia. The value of their diplomas has been enhanced.

One indicator of alarming inequality is that black high school seniors perform on average at the eighth grade level compared to whites - a four-year gap in attainment. The large difference in average performance of schools with white majority enrollment and those with majority minority enrollment cannot be explained in terms of class size, money spent per student, or other observable indicators of school inputs. It does suggest that the influence of peers, parents and community may be more important than school resources or policies. Quality of teachers may be another factor.

Differences in quality can be reduced. Since schooling is compulsory, ideally all students should have access to the same quality of education. But we should not expect too much. Rising educational attainment as an indicator of economic competence has been compromised by Henry Ford, who made possible the geographic segregation by income and incidentally by other characteristics which differentiate urban from suburban schools. It has been weakened by a shift in school agenda toward sports, self-esteem, recreation and cultural indoctrination to the neglect of cognitive skills, an agenda now prominent in many college campuses as well as in lower schools. Attainment as an indicator of achievement has been further weakened by a lowering of standards to permit all to advance in lockstep and to avoid the stigma (or spur) of low grades.

It is odd that the maximum age for compulsory schooling should exceed the minimum age for work in many states. It is odder still that there is so much self-serving pressure from the industry of education to keep people in full-time study to age 21 or older at a time when the number of retirees will be increasing more rapidly than the population of working age. The forecast is that eventually there will be one retiree for every two workers, and one response to this heavy burden on workers is to increase the average age of retirement. Increasing the average school-leaving age would worsen a difficult situation. It needs a serious justification as long as quality remains a serious problem.

Schools are only one factor in achievement. Even the worst schools graduate the occasional over-achiever. Whatever the complaint, one should not simply point the finger at the schools and teachers. The influence of extended family and community may be more important than quality of teachers, or student ability. Single-parent children, two-worker families and latch-key students labor under disadvantage. Peer groups, community values, the culture of poverty, influence what schools can accomplish. These factors are largely beyond the reach of public policy instruments. But their presence does not exclude or exonerate bad teaching or bad curricula nor exempt efforts to improve both. Explanation is no excuse for unsatisfactory performance.

It is not parental income and education that lead to high scholastic achievement. They are mere imperfect surrogates for student effort and commitment, parental values and expectations, and school location and quality. A survey of 15 year olds in 27 OECD nations found that the U.S. was third in total variation in performance; South Korea was last, Japan was third from the bottom. In between-school variation in performance, which is explainable by the socioeconomic status of students, the U.S. was second only to the UK; South Korea again was at the bottom, followed by Finland [14], two nations that score at the top in academic achievement. Most of the other nations surveyed graduate as large a proportion of the age group as the United States. Some of them also have as large or larger immigrant populations. They demonstrate that it is possible to have higher standards with greater equality of academic achievement without sacrificing educational attainment. High expectations do place pressure on students to perform. What is so bad about that? Failure to do so has consequences.

FRAMEWORK OF ANALYSIS

In identifying problems and considering responses or solutions, one should distinguish the inevitable consequences of universal high school education and vastly expanded college attendance and graduation from problems that are soluble. I am assuming that there is no prospect of reversing the great increases in educational attainment of the past half century, attainment measured in years of school completed. Attainment in terms of knowledge and competence is another matter, not determined by years of schooling alone. It is knowledge and competence that needs increasing, certainly not by idiotic simple-minded efforts to put everyone through college with the expectation that all will land skilled high-paying jobs, a current form of the fallacy of composition.

There are many partial explanations and their implicit solutions: class size is too large and should be reduced; teacher pay is too low and should be increased; teacher training and resulting quality of teachers is inadequate; teacher labor unions preclude hiring, promotion, pay on the basis of merit; family breakdown weakens the home learning environment and family support of the schools; peer group values conflict with a culture of learning and discipline. Much can be done about some of these factors, if it can be demonstrated that they really matter; not much can be done about others.

It will be argued that the procedural approaches toward improving education: more pay, smaller classes, computers for all, do not deal with the fundamental problems. Even teacher training is only a partial answer. It is prevailing values and their consequences, not dollars, that matter most. The value of egalitarianism permeates behavior of public education, teachers' unions, teachers' education and much of the community in which schools operate. It has justified a process of leveling down requirements and attainments, although logically it could just as well justify leveling up. A second underlying problem, which is partially a byproduct of egalitarianism, is teacher prestige or status, and its impact on teacher quality. Prestige is low, and its increase is a necessary condition for attracting and holding high quality teachers. A third problem underlying multiple explanations, not a value but a special interest, is the triple monopoly of schools of education, teachers unions, and public education.

Although problems exist at every level of education, there are differences between elementary school education, where the process of learning dominates issues of content in teaching, at least initially, as it should, and high schools, where subject content matters most. The problems of value systems and social dysfunction found at the elementary school level are the same as those evident at the high school level. The primary focus will be on high school education, where issues of what to teach and what to learn become paramount; where concerns about method or process should be subordinated to issues of substance. But high schools can only accomplish so much if entering students are semi-literate and semi-numerate. One must start at the beginning. Affirmative action and remedial course work three quarters of the way from first grade toward a college degree is too little too late.

Education is sequential; shortcomings at every level are visited on the next level. Colleges are not immune. This society no longer regards a high school diploma as the end product; in fact most high school graduates start college. Although not quite a third are completing college, a degree is becoming the goal of education. Thus we shall consider the implications for college education of the deficiencies of the primary and secondary school systems. They have been evident for some time, at least to employers, even though the focus of public attention has been on public elementary and secondary schools. Another reason to glance at college education is that one of the means of improving high school education is to increase the number of college students majoring in the fields in which high school students do poorly, fields in which public schools have great difficulty in hiring.

It is not my intention to pronounce a problem and propose solutions. Instead I describe current conditions, consider their causes, and discuss their consequences. Education has diverse objectives, not fully reconcilable with one another. Americans are of many minds. The only objective that I assume and propose is nurturing of the talents and provision of the skills required to maintain forward momentum in the economy: rising rather than stagnant or declining real incomes per capita. These talents and skills are for discovery, invention, and innovation. They are concentrated in certain occupations, engineering and applied sciences in particular. An educational system that is not adapted to the needs of a dynamic economy is a long term threat to our future. The days of untutored tinkerers are over. We have been living on borrowed human capital: highly educated immigrant workers and entrepreneurs in Silicon Valley and other centers of new technology, researchers in public and private institutions, foreign students and faculty in our schools of engineering. Our economy has been doing well, but it cannot sustain a domestic brain deficit forever and flourish.

Human capital is our most important resource. Its continuous creation and allocation are main determinants of the progress of our economy and society We are not educating enough to maintain momentum in the next generation. How many is enough is an open question. But we do need more high school graduates knowledgeable enough in the sciences and particularly in math to consider majoring in these subjects in college and entering these occupations. There is more than one way to do this: raising standards for most students in elementary school and high school or increasing the numbers in a rigorous academic track similar to advanced placement in these subjects, and many combinations of standards and tracking. I have no personal preference for any particular formula. Beyond providing for economic growth, there are other aims of education, and they too can be pursued in diverse ways. Cause and effect are measured in generations, not years. It took the better part of a century to arrive at our current educational dilemma; it may take generations to work us out of it.

Chapter 2

PROBLEMS OF HIGH SCHOOL TEACHER SUPPLY

RETIREMENT AND RECRUITMENT NEEDS

Whatever the facts on quality of education, and whatever the allocation of causes, one thing is clear: schools are having great difficulty in recruiting good teachers, and many teachers are teaching subjects in which they are poorly qualified. The retirement of a large number of teachers is expected in the decade ahead; they need to be replaced. In the 1950's the baby boom generation entered elementary schools, prompting a hiring binge for elementary school teachers. The 1960s was the decade for hiring high school teachers, as baby boomers aged and an increasing proportion completed high school. The number of public school teachers (in thousands) rose from 1,014 in 1950 to 1,408 in 1960 and 2,059 in 1970 [1]. There was little further increase till the 1990s; the number rose to 2,979 thousand by 2001, in response to smaller average class size and a slight increase in enrollments. As a result the median years of teacher experience declined from 11 in 1960 to 8 in 1970, but has been increasing since, to 12 in 1980, 15 in the 1990s, down to 14 in 2001 as retirements increased. The average age of public school teachers is increasing, from a low of 33 in the mid-1970s to 46 in 2001 [2].

Teachers are retiring rapidly. But the proportion of new teachers in their first year of teaching has been falling from 9.1 percent in 1971 to 2.1 in 1996 and 3.1 in 2001 [3]. These rates if maintained are far below long term replacement needs, given the age distribution of the teaching staff and the high attrition rate of young teachers, which is over 50% in the first five years. Chemistry and physics teachers have the shortest average stay; they are most likely to have alternative opportunities [4]. Teacher retirement rates are slightly in excess of new teachers in their first year, both around 3% of total faculty. But annual turnover is in the 12-13% range, not all of it away from teaching. The Department of Education estimates that 2.2 million new teachers will be needed in this decade. It also estimates that among new hires, 240,000 should be middle school and high school math and science teachers. The enormity of this impending need is indicated by the fact that the total number of public school teachers in 2004-05 was just over three million. Increasing the number of starters is not the only option; reducing the number of leavers is another. Both are needed.

These estimates may be too low. If teachers become better qualified in their subject, they also become more competitive in the wider labor market; their attrition rate may rise. Possible changes in curriculum in the future would further increase the need for teachers in particular fields. If more students take courses in science and math, and take more courses in these subjects, then more teachers qualified to teach in these fields will be needed. The potential scale of this problem is enormous. It is not enough to have all science teachers major in their field unless we settle for the current inadequate average curriculum. If all high school students are to take physics, now taken by only 28%, we would need nearly four times as many physics teachers. What if all students were to take second year algebra as well as geometry, and from qualified teachers?

A major part of the supply problem is the fact that only 10% of women college graduates, who account for nearly three-quarters of public school teachers, now go into teaching. In 1960, almost 50% of them did [5]. These percentages overstate the absolute decline because a larger proportion of college-age women graduate and the labor force participation rate of women ages 21-65 has increased. But these increases are far from enough to compensate for this shift in occupational choice.

The explanation that educated women had few choices and now can enter any occupation is exaggerated. Another explanation is demographic. According to Thomas Sowell [6] the rise in women's share of college degrees and professional employment in many occupations is largely explained by, or associated with, increases in age of marriage and declines in birth rates. Women enter teaching in large numbers during baby boom periods because teaching schedules are more family-friendly than most jobs; the daily schedule and summer vacation is more compatible with child care than a 9 to 5 job plus overtime 12 months a year. Leaves of absence are easily arranged without penalty to pay or careers. Teaching is a dead-end occupation; few see it as a stepping stone to administration. Thus reentry is not a problem. According to this explanation, occupational preference depends on family structure. Some teachers who drop out may return to teaching later, as many as one in four do.

Recruitment needs are not just for replacement of teachers retiring or leaving their jobs. To the extent that smaller classes are desired, then there must be a corresponding additional increase in the total number of teachers. If enrollments increase,. more teachers would be needed to maintain a constant ratio of teachers to students. They could increase as a result of net in-migration, a slight rise in the share of the age group completing high school, and perhaps in the increased need for teachers of remedial education in response to new national and state minimum standards for high school graduation. In addition to the school-age population, there is preschool and kindergarten enrollment of 3-5 year olds, which rose from 37.5 to 64.3% of the age group between 1970 and 2005; full day enrollment rose from 25.5 to 70.7 % over the same period [7].

Needs for more teachers go beyond mere numbers. Teachers are specialized: by subject, teaching methods, the kind of student they are trained or suited to teach. Elementary and high school teachers are not interchangeable. Recruitment efforts must consider the diverse needs of public schools. They might include retraining older teachers whose specialties are in oversupply.

What is described above as a problem is also a rare opportunity to reform the public school teaching profession.

Here I seek to understand the problem of teacher supply and quality. In Chapters 6 and 7 I will look at some of the numerous proposed 'solutions'. The most frequently mentioned is money, a catchall which can be used on one hand for higher pay, on the other to reduce class size (which assumes recruitment of additional teachers). A related approach is recruitment of teachers who are not the product of our schools of education. This is partly money, but not by increasing pay for all the teachers we already have, good and bad alike. This in turn implies circumventing the stranglehold on teacher training and recruitment and certification by schools of education and teachers unions. Each 'solution' implies a particular cause and results in unintended consequences.

First, a look at the occupational status of teachers, why it has fallen. Chapter 8 will consider what may be done to raise that status, facilitating recruitment and retention of high quality teachers. Second, what about the quality of the teachers we have? Is it satisfactory? If not, why not?

OCCUPATIONAL PRESTIGE OF TEACHERS

When Teachers College first applied to Columbia University for affiliation, it was rebuffed: "... there is no such subject as education and, moreover, it would bring into the university women who are not wanted" [8]. Nevertheless it was eventually admitted, in 1898. This derogatory attitude toward schools of education and toward the students who major in them persists, and hampers attraction of able students.

The present and future career teaching faculty in public schools reflects the ability of public education to attract and retain college graduates. But primary and secondary school teaching has not been a very attractive occupation for college graduates. It ranks fairly low in the hierarchy of occupational prestige from the perspective of college students choosing majors and careers, as implied by the large decline in the proportion of college students choosing to major in education, and the large proportion of majors who choose not to teach. Some potential teachers are concerned with pay, others with working conditions, yet others with status or prestige.

The ranking of secondary school teachers in terms of occupational prestige has changed little in the past century, hardly at all between the first extensive survey of occupational prestige in 1947 and the last, in 1989 [9]. This ranking is that by the general population, not college students. Judging from the occupations of similar rank, it is higher than that implicit in decisions by college students. But the major reason given by teachers who leave teaching is the lack of community support. If popular attitudes toward teaching remain as they were in 1989, they may not translate into community support.

The absolute status of high school teachers, as distinguished from its standing compared to other occupations, has tended to decline. First, the status of a bachelors degree has declined as a result of the large increase in the share of the population who have college degrees. In 1950, a high school diploma was an exception; college degrees were rare. Now, high school graduation is the rule, most graduates go on to college, and nearly a third finish. In March 2006, 28% the population 25-29 had college diplomas; the percentage of employed persons in 2005 ages 25-64 with a bachelors degree was 21.3%; an additional 11.6% had some postgraduate education [10]. The educational requirement of most high school teachers, a bachelors degree in education, has changed little for two generations. A college degree has become too commonplace to serve as a major determinant of status without qualification. Is it a Harvard degree, or Dogpatch U? What major? Teachers are no longer part of a small educated and knowledgeable elite, making teaching less attractive as an occupation.

Table 2-1. Educational Attainment of Population 25 years of Age and Older

Year	High School		College	
	Age 25+	Age 25-9	Age 25+	Age 25-9
1940	24.5%	38.1%	4.6%	5.9%
1950	34.3%	52.8%	6.2%	7.7%
1960	41.1%	60.7%	7.7%	11.0%
1970	55.2%	75.4%	11.0%	16.4%
1980	68.6%	85.4%	17.0%	22.5%
1990	77.6%	85.7%	21.3%	23.2%
2000	84.1%	88.1%	25.6%	29.1%
2006	85.5%	86.4%	28.0%	28.4%

Source: National Center for Education Statistics. (2007). *Digest of Education Statistics* 2006, Washington, DC: U.S. Government Printing Office, Table 8.

It is true that now a majority of public school teachers have done some graduate work, but this is not a factor in hiring, not a requirement. The job comes first, graduate work may come later. The proportion of teachers with more than a bachelors degree has increased from 23.5 % in 1961 to 56.8 % in 2001 [11]. Since 1995 more masters than bachelors of education have been awarded every year. This increase in proportion of teachers with postgraduate degrees correlates with increasing average age and years of experience of teachers.

Unfortunately, teachers who go on to a masters degree almost invariably opt for education, not for the subject areas in which they teach. There is no evidence that this explosion of postgraduate degrees in education is associated with improved student achievement [12]. Masters degrees in education consist mainly of courses in educational administration, management, philosophy, teaching methods and the like. Very little graduate course work is in the subject taught; teaching methods are not a substitute for mastery of subject matter. The additional degree does not offer the increased respect accruing to masters degree holders in other fields, especially the sciences. Most teachers earning masters degrees have no reasonable expectation of jobs as principals or higher-level educational administrators. The main motivation is increased pay. In some districts teachers are required to obtain a masters degree in due course.

The downgrading of a college degree has been magnified by a slower increase in jobs which in the past required a college education than in college graduates. Whereas professional specialty jobs grew from 11.5% to 16.1% of employment between 1975 and 2002, the percentage of the population 25 and over with a college degree jumped from 13.9 to 26.7%. The occupational distribution of college graduates has been downgraded, a higher proportion are in jobs that a generation ago were held by high school graduates. This topic will be elaborated in chapters 4 and 5.

Second, from the beginning of current standardized tests, education majors have ranked near the bottom, in SATs, in GREs. Many college graduates know this. It is one reason that education majors should not be teaching math or science in high school. (Every rule has its exceptions.) Teacher status will reflect college major and subject taught to some extent. I would expect the status of college graduates by major to be ordered in a hierarchy somewhat correlated with the occupational hierarchy. Thus pre-med or physics would rank high, most humanities would rank low to middling, and education would be close to the bottom. An additional reason a degree in education is held in lower esteem than degrees in chemistry or math or history or English may be that the education major has few alternative professional job and career opportunities, in particular opportunities that make use of a major in education.

Third, with the dominance of schools of education, high school teachers are not viewed primarily as experts in a particular subject, secondarily as teachers. Forty or fifty years ago, many full time public high school teachers had majored in the subject areas in which they taught; now most in the public schools have majored in education. It is widely held that those who did not major in the fields in which they teach are not particularly well qualified to teach at the high school level. Although publicity has focused on teachers of science and math without degrees in their fields, the same reasoning applies to other fields. American students are notoriously ignorant of American history. How many of their history teachers majored in history? - a smaller proportion than in any other subject. So both the choice of major and the lack of academic preparation for the subjects taught tend to lower the status of teachers as compared with their status in the past.

Fourth, the proportion of workers in occupations with higher prestige has increased, and in occupations with lower prestige has decreased. The proportion of the labor force in 'professional specialty' occupations, such as MDs, lawyers, college professors, scientists, most engineers, has increased sharply as noted above. (It replaced a broader category, professional and technical occupations, whose share of employment rose from 8% in 1950 to 15% in 1975.) It is the only occupational category which has had an average educational attainment of 16 or more years of education for the past half century. Executive, administrative and managerial workers, many of whom are also higher on the prestige scale than public school teachers, grew from 9.4% in 1975 to 15.1% in 2002. At the same time, the proportion of workers in occupations with lower prestige than teachers: service occupations and blue collar occupations: operatives, fabricators and laborers; precision production, craft and repair workers, plus farming, declined as a share of employment from 49.5% in 1975 to 39.2% in 2002 [13]. Even with no change in status ranking on occupational status scales, the relative status of teachers in the labor force has declined.

Fifth, public school teaching in the past had higher prestige than today, at least among women, because most educated women had few alternatives. Now that women can even join the Marines, the lack of alternative opportunities is no longer a factor. Many able and educated women who would once have gone into teaching have chosen other occupations, reducing the average quality of teachers. This is more important for elementary schools, whose teachers were and remain predominantly women, than for high schools. The steep decline in the proportion of female college graduates entering teaching since 1960, from 50% to 10%, has been noted. It may be no coincidence that as alternative opportunities for women multiplied, student test scores declined.

Sixth, the students - the clientele of high school teachers - are no longer a select group. Sixty years ago no more than a third completed high school. Teaching a select third is more prestigious than teaching every Tom, Dick, and Jane. One consequence of the near-universal enrollment and high rate of graduation from high schools, and the huge increase in college enrollment and graduation, is that status as a high school teacher, or even as a college professor, has to be qualified: where do you teach, whom, and what?

Employers matter; a computer programmer for IBM has higher status than one for a local bank. The status of the school itself is reflected in that of the teacher. The decline in respect for public schools and the debasement of the high school degree have negative effects on teacher prestige. But public high schools range from highly selective magnet schools to schools that are little more than inferior child care centers or dropout stations. Colleges range from two-year community colleges and trade schools to research universities. Teachers at magnet public schools or elite private schools are more respected than teachers in the run of the mill public school. They can retain highly qualified teachers that other schools cannot attract.

Seventh, occupations are not homogenous - students and subjects matter. Teaching in high school has higher prestige than teaching in elementary school or preschool. Teachers of advanced placement courses are more highly regarded than teachers of standard courses. The institution, the students, the subject all have some influence on the status of the teacher. This is another way of saying that jobs matter, not just occupations.

Educational attainment and earnings are known ex ante and typify the entire profession. On the other hand, the status of the employer and the quality of students is only established ex post and will vary widely. Only some teachers can benefit from the necessarily exclusive status of particular schools or school systems, or subjects taught.

The occupational status hierarchy refers to collective ascriptive status. There is also individual achievement status, whatever the occupation. Achievement refers to jobs rather than to occupations. Public school systems are reluctant to recognize or reward for merit, one reason so many good teachers leave.

For all occupations combined there is substantial correlation between prestige and education and earnings, but not for particular occupations [14]. Doctors or judges are not respected because they earned postgraduate degrees, nor for their income. It is the activity that lends prestige. Raising teacher pay is unlikely to affect occupational prestige. (This issue will be considered in Chapter 8). The problem of mediocre prestige is more fundamental, a characteristic of a society. that respects doers, achievers, practical pursuits, and does not view teaching in these terms. Teachers are talkers, not doers. Many people view education as an obstacle that must be surmounted in order to succeed in the job market rather than as a valuable activity in itself. The pursuit of knowledge is for the nerd.

RELATIVE INCOME

What about income, the other major factor associated with occupational prestige? The decline of public school teacher status in terms of educational attainment has also occurred relative to economic factors, primarily relative earnings. The most relevant comparison is with earnings of other college graduates working full time full year. You will not find it in the *Digest of Education Statistics*. Since most teachers are female, and earnings of female college graduates have risen more than those of males, the most appropriate comparison in terms of school ability to compete is the trend in earnings of female graduates.

Public school teacher pay has declined relative to pay of college graduates in the past 30 plus years. Since real pay fluctuates up and down over this long period, the precise difference depends on selection of terminal years. Starting with 1970, average teacher pay has increased 11%, whereas earnings of male college graduates have risen 23% and those of female graduates, 102%. This is not the place to discuss the reasons for the large difference in earnings between male and female college graduates. But Table 2-2 makes clear that the relative and even the absolute difference between male and female graduates has been narrowing. Teaching pay, once nearly twice that of female college graduates, has been roughly the same for the past ten years. That may help explain the large decline in the proportion of female college graduates entering teaching. But private schools can hire teachers for less money than public schools.

These results are surprising. Female public school- teachers in 2005 earned the average of all female college graduates working full time full year, whereas male teachers earned much less., only two thirds as much. (I am assuming that male and female teachers earned the same; male teachers are concentrated in secondary school, which pays slightly more than elementary school, but pay depends on years of experience.) The average teacher is older, has more years of work experience than college graduate workers 25 years of age and over. Accounting for this difference would reduce slightly the ratio of teacher pay to that of other college graduates.. On the other hand, teachers are paid to work not more than ten months; if one reduces the pay of other college graduates by one sixth, teachers are paid significantly more than female college graduates. They also have greater job security than most workers, a non-wage benefit.

Teachers' lobbies will always claim that teachers are underpaid relative to alternative occupations; this is their job. One can pick a comparison to prove their case, or to refute it. What matters is the motivation of teachers and prospective teachers, what is the importance of earnings, and how do they visualize their earnings compared to relevant alternatives. All we know for sure is that not enough able students are entering teaching, and that attrition rates of young teachers are very high.

Table 2-2 reveals that teacher pay has been declining relative to pay of other college graduates. Has it also declined relative to average pay? The differential between teaching and average pay since 1959-60 has never been less than 5%, never more than 22%. The modest fluctuations, partially explained by changes in the age distribution of teachers, show no clear trend. Any comparison of ratios over time is approximate because of major changes in occupational distribution as well as in educational attainment. But as suggested above, this is not the relevant comparison.

In comparing pay one needs to keep in mind that salary scales of public school teachers are compressed whereas those of most other college graduates are much more dispersed. The average age of teachers is higher and has risen faster than that of workers as a whole. Since older workers with more years of experience typically earn more, teacher pay should have risen slightly over time relative to that of all workers, or all college graduates, merely to stand still. It hasn't.

Teachers' compressed salary scale is more than just the difference between a civil service and a market salary structure. State or federal civil service has many rungs in its occupational ladder, our decentralized public school system has three at most: teacher, principal, district superintendent, with little prospect that any one teacher will ever move up. Teachers and prospective teachers are unlikely to conceive their economic status in relation to the mean of college graduates; they are aware of the low ceilings they face compared to open-ended possibilities in many other occupations. Female teachers are unlikely to compare their earnings only to earnings of other female college graduates, ignoring the higher earnings of male graduates.

Table 2-2. Estimated average annual Salary of public school Teachers:
1959-60 to 2004-05

	Current dollars			Constant 2005-06 dollars		
School year	All teachers	Earnings per full-time employee	Ratio teachers salary to full time employee earnings	Earnings, full time college graduates age 25 and over		
				All teachers	Male	Female
1959-60	$4,995	$4,749	1.05	33,828		
1969-70	8,626	7,486	1.15	45,440	62,257	24,930
1979-80	15,970	15,088	1.06	40,935	59,993	23,547
1984-85	23,600	20,819	1.13	44,401	58,980	27,858
1989-90	31,367	25,647	1.22	49,158	65,534	33,072
1994-95	36,675	30,606	1.20	48,522	67,353	43,725
1995-96	37,642	31,561	1.19	48,482	65,782	46,211
1996-97	38,443	32,789	1.17	48,140	68,688	46,111
1997-98	39,350	34,346	1.15	48,413	73,363	48,552
1998-99	40,544	35,978	1.13	49,033	74,273	48,106
1999-2000	41,807	37,800	1.11	49,141	79,058	50,555
2000-01	43,395	39,257	1.11	49,318	78,696	50,484
2001-02	44,666	40,031	1.12	49,873	77,124	53,166
2002-03.	45,776	41,004	1.12	50,020	75,495	52,254
2003-04	46,752	42,547	1.10	49,993	74,927	50,964
2004-05	47,750	---	---	49,568	76,452	50,453

Source: National Center for Education Statistics.(2007). *Digest of Education Statistics* 2006 Washington, DC: U.S. Government Printing Office Table 75; U. S. Census Bureau, *Current Population Survey*, Annual Social and Economic Supplements.

Undergraduate and graduate diplomas in education open few doors outside the school system. The lack of good professional alternatives for public school teachers may affect adversely their earnings and inferentially their status. Although educational preparation for a variety of jobs and occupations does not per se improve status or earnings (the MD is the counterexample of a highly paid and narrowly specialized occupation), it cannot but contribute in the case of an occupation such as teaching whose status and earnings are low compared to many others with the same educational attainment.

Pay may be adequate in comparison with other college graduates, and prestige higher than pay would indicate. But this is for teachers drawn predominantly from the bottom quarter of college graduates. If new teachers were to come largely from the top quarter, then pay must increase, and somehow so must the prestige of public school teaching. And that cannot be bought, it must be earned.

TEACHER QUALITY

Who were the teachers when student achievement was higher, namely before the 1960s? The evidence (see chapter 3) on reading textbooks indicates that students in elementary school learned much more in the late 19th and early 20th centuries than in recent decades.

Amazingly, many of the teachers had no college education at all; they were mere high school graduates. Although by 1900 all states had public normal schools, typically of two years duration, students admitted usually had only two years of high school, few were denied admission, and most never completed the course. But most teachers had never attended a normal school. By 1921, 18 states required high school graduation for teacher certification, 4 required some additional education, and the remaining states had no definite academic requirements [15]. The standard of normal school - two years beyond high school - was replaced by a bachelors degree in education after WWII. Teachers without these qualifications have been largely excluded from public schools. More recently, an increasing proportion of teachers, now well over half, have earned a masters degree, predominantly in education. But there has been no corresponding improvement in student achievement. There must be something wrong with the training and/or the selection of teachers.

Over the same time period there have been important non-school alleged contributions to learning resources, both for students and for the general population. The first was libraries, the Carnegie libraries in particular. Then came radio, followed by TV, and now computers. Again, there is no evidence that the proliferation of sources of information over the past century has led to improved student achievement. The human brain has not improved in speed or capacity, and for long there has been more information readily available than anyone can master.

How is it that students learned more of the basics (reading, writing, arithmetic) as well as history, when their teachers had never gone to college, or only for two years, than now, when most of their teachers hold a bachelors in education, but also a masters degree? The evidence of superior learning long ago includes the elementary school textbooks used, years more advanced than those in use in the same grades today, and a decline in literacy, noted among draftees since World War I. The great majority of public school teachers are hard-working and dedicated; many work under trying conditions; many are underpaid; some are great teachers. But their job isn't getting done. How is it that we have many high school seniors who are semiliterate and have trouble with simple arithmetic after 13 or 14 years of school? Why so many dropouts? There is something rotten in the realm.

The beginning of the abrupt decline on standardized test scores taken by high school seniors was in 1964, when the vanguard of the baby boom generation began completing high school. Few claim that this generation was much dumber than its predecessors. Starting in the early 1950s there was a huge increase in the number of elementary school teachers. Were all these new teachers responsible for the subsequent decline in learning and test scores? Or was the culprit the curriculum, or the pedagogy? Here I consider the quality of teachers, leaving pedagogy and curriculum to the next chapter. However, there is no separating them; the relation could be additive, or multiplicative.

There is no single simple cause of the poor performance of public schools, but poor teacher quality is one factor without whose correction quality of education cannot improve. It is also a problem we can do something about. Dysfunctional families, negative pressures of peer groups and of egalitarian ideology that dumbs everything and everyone down are not so easily subject to public policies.

In the first three decades of the twentieth century, the ratio of elementary and high school students to college graduates was very high, declining sharply starting shortly after the end of WWII as college enrollments zoomed. This meant that in the earlier period, demand for teachers in elementary and high schools was large relative to the supply of college graduates, large relative to other demands for college-trained workers. Schools were better able to recruit from high achievers in college than they have been in recent decades. And perhaps a high school diploma and a college degree assured a higher minimum level of quality and core of common knowledge that it has in recent years.

In the 1930s, during more than a decade of double-digit unemployment rates, teaching positions were attractive to some of the best college graduates, some of whom remained in teaching for the remainder of their working lives. The 1950s and 1960s was a period of extraordinary growth in public school enrollment. A large number of new teachers had to be hired, sharply reducing the average years of teaching experience. Pay improved, teachers found it easy to get jobs, they had job security and job mobility [16]. Given the large demand, it is reasonable to assume that hiring needs required a lowering of standards and that the quality of new teachers in this period was lower than average. It was necessary to hire more teachers who had not majored in the subject they were to teach. This may account in part for large declines in average SAT and ACT test scores starting in the 1960s The decline leveled off in the 1980s but was only partially reversed despite the increasing average number of years of teacher experience.

Many states require or are in the process of requiring that high school seniors pass an achievement test in math and English to graduate, and as many as 12 % of seniors are failing in some states, even though the tests are in most cases fairly elementary and are multiple choice. Students are allowed to take the test as many as 5 or 6 times, and despite availability of remedial help some are still failing [17]. In most cases it may not be their fault, but to continue awarding diplomas without some quality control devalues the diploma for all graduates. It also results in very high dropout rates in the first year or two of college, as well as excessive remedial course work, much of it non-credit. Other subjects suffer from the same problem.

The most publicized failure is in math. The complaint in some school districts is that the math test for seniors included multiple choice questions in algebra and geometry, whereas students in these districts have never taken either. Math is more than just another subject; it is the language of the natural sciences, and to some extent of the social sciences. Without it many doors are closed, and so are minds. Schools complain about the difficulty in hiring teachers who can teach math. It's a vicious circle: either teachers who don't know math teach it, or the requirement is dropped from the curriculum. In either case, most high school graduates are poorly prepared in math, so very few major or even minor in it in college, therefore high schools cannot hire competent math teachers. Math teachers stay much longer than physics and chemistry teachers, because so many of them do not know enough math to work in this field in the private sector. Imagine what would happen were the high school graduation tests to include chemistry, physics, and biology?

It is difficult to quantify the shortage of teachers who majored in the subjects they teach. Many degrees awarded by schools of education are not bachelors of education but bachelors of arts or sciences. Many who claim to have majored in math or science in fact received degrees in math or science education from schools of education, with limited course work in the subjects they teach. The same is true of other subjects, with most of the course work not in the subjects to be taught but in "education" theory and method.

Ingersoll [18] examined the incidence of underqualified teachers, defined as out of field teachers in secondary schools for the academic years 1987-'78, 1990-'91, and 1993-'94. His findings for public schools were:

English	24.1%
Math	31.4%
Life science	32.9%
Physical science	56.9%
Social studies	19.3%
History	53.1%

His in-field definition was very generous: a minor. For math, a minor in math education rather than in math was enough. If a minor in math proper were the minimum qualification, then only 33% of math teachers were qualified. One reservation is that the percentages of underqualified teachers as defined by college preparation is slightly higher in private schools than in public schools in most fields, yet student achievement is considerably higher. But private schools need not renew contracts of underperforming teachers, and their pay can reflect both market and merit. In sum, beware of single causes and simple solutions. The significance of subject matter qualification may be inadequately studied.

The acute shortage of teachers who have majored in the subject matter they teach has multiple causes, but it is at the heart of poor student performance in high school. We suspect that a large proportion of those currently teaching in secondary schools are not good teachers of their subject matter, not for lack of method but for lack of mastery. The decline in student performance on standardized tests, and their mediocre ratings in international comparisons, imply as much. More direct evidence is the performance of education majors on SATS and GREs, which has fallen in recent decades, and remained always at or near the bottom in comparison with majors in other fields. These are the college graduates who have become the teachers of our children today, and perhaps were our teachers some time ago. Standardized test scores do not measure teaching ability, but they can indicate command over subject matter. Low scores on computational skills are a drawback for teachers of math and some sciences. And it is difficult to argue that GRE verbal scores - education majors score just below engineers - are not important for effective teaching. Teachers have to communicate, whatever the subject.

In some subjects the supply and quality depends on alternative opportunities. It is not just pay, but openings. The end of the cold war and subsequent fall in defense spending should have improved prospects of hiring in the sciences and math during the 1990s. But the information technology boom of the 1990s had the opposite effect. However, it was the expansion of job opportunities for educated women outside the traditional occupations of teaching and nursing - (and decline in birth rates) that sharply reduced the proportion of women graduates going into teaching. It was not just greater opportunities, but the narrowing of earnings differences between men and women in other occupations that reduced teaching pay relative to alternative jobs for women, even if not for men.

There is little doubt that the sharp decline in women entering teaching has lowered the average quality of teachers. Corcoran, Evans and Schwab [19] compared female college graduates between 1964 and 2000 who went into teaching with those who did not. They found a substantial decline in relative ability using standardized test scores. The probability of entering teaching fell by half for most ability deciles, dramatically for the top decile. In 1964, 20% of females in the top decile of high school graduates went into teaching; in 1992 it was under 4%. The data above refer to decline of quality of beginning female teachers relative to other high school and college graduates. Since the quality of high school and college graduates has also declined, as suggested by standardized test scores, there has been a substantial decline in ability of new female teachers.

It is not just the supply of capable starting teachers that matters, but what is their turnover, and how many who leave return later on. Since the teachers who score highest in standardized tests are the ones with the shortest teaching career, turnover is not just about numbers but a factor influencing the quality of teachers [20]. Cutting turnover may improve quality, but it also raises costs, since salaries are based on years of experience. I am not aware of any data comparing leavers and stayers in recent years vs. several decades ago, either in terms of percentage or relative ability.

Unionization, which started as an influence in the 1960s and soon became prevalent in public schools, is another factor contributing to the reduced average ability of teachers. All unions, not just teacher unions, seek to raise pay, limit effort, and increase job security. Smaller class size is one way to reduce effort, and pay based on experience, not performance, contributes to security. The typical union pay scale does not discriminate by ability in hiring, or by performance in pay increases. It is also, like all civil service pay structures, compressed relative to market wage structures. Thus a starting teacher may be well paid compared to alternatives, but experience a gradual decline in relative pay over the years, contributing to high turnover. Hoxby and Leigh [21] propose that in addition to the pull from other occupational opportunities, there is a push resulting from pay compression. They find that pay compression accounts for most of the decline in the share of teachers in the highest aptitude category, and some of the increased share in the lowest aptitude category. Hoxby [22] attributes to unionization the fact that early on, increased school inputs raised student achievement, but have not done so for decades since. She concludes "I find that teachers unions are primarily rent-seeking, raising school budgets and school inputs but lowering student achievement by decreasing productivity of inputs."

Peltzman [23] conducted a statistical analysis of numerous possible correlates or causes of student test score declines, including school inputs, organizational changes, and unionization. The one variable highly significant, and with a large coefficient, was the increase in unionization of teachers, which was minimal until 1960, then grew very rapidly, leveling off by 1980. Assuming that unionization was a major factor in the persistence of lower test scores, the question is why? The most plausible explanation is the influence of unions on teacher hiring, retention, and tenure, and on seniority as the determinant of pay and teaching assignments

What is remarkable about the decline in student achievement, as measured by scores on SAT and ACT, is the suddenness and steepness of the decline, starting around 1964, continuing until around 1980, then leveling off, with minor ups and downs since. The decline in test scores of high school seniors must have been the outcome of reduced achievement in earlier grades; well before unionization became a significant factor. The vanguard of the baby boom generation entered first grade in 1952. Unions may have helped keep test scores low later, but could not have initiated the decline. The huge increase in the number of public school teachers needed to accommodate the baby boom generation - 48% between 1950 and 1960, and another 33% by 1970 - meant large numbers of new inexperienced teachers. This must have been a factor. Yet the large increase in average teacher experience in recent decades has not resulted in much gain in student achievement.

In the past, curriculum was dominated by the humanities: English, foreign languages, history, geography, literature, plus basic math, fields whose content change very slowly. In recent decades the sciences, to some extent the social sciences, have gained importance. Their subject matter has grown and changed rapidly, and in many cases has become more abstract and complex, more mathematical, particularly in the physical sciences. But teaching staffs and curricula have not adapted, one reason American students do poorly in international comparisons. Students should receive more instruction in math and the sciences than they did in the past, but if anything they receive less. Physics and chemistry teachers are the ones with the highest rate of turnover.

An adequate supply of capable teachers in these expanding fields of knowledge requires more majors in scientific and technical fields in college; which in turn requires that more college freshmen enter prepared in math and science. To accomplish this, public schools must be able to hire teachers who have majored in math and science. How to break the circle? It cannot be done in the short run. The supply is not there; higher salaries largely rob one school district to staff another. Importing qualified teachers from India and elsewhere would be a start. More use might be made of graduate students as part time high school teachers. In ten years there would be an increase in the number of college graduates majoring in these fields, allowing more to be hired. In some fields, even majors need to keep learning, for much can happen in their field during a career of forty years. Preparation for jobs is not the only reason for updating the curriculum. This is a technological civilization; adults should have some idea of the world in which they live.

Colleges are not graduating enough scientists and mathematicians to meet the needs of the economy and also of public schools. The economy relies heavily on immigrant workers in these fields. In 2004 only 2.2 % of bachelors degrees awarded were in math and the physical sciences. This is a dramatic decline from the 6.9% in 1960 (see table 4-1 in Chapter 4). Many advanced degrees in these fields are awarded to foreigners (see chapter 5). So few college students major in math and science in large part because so many learned little of these subjects in high school. A diminished share of high school graduates have the interest or the preparation to major in these fields in college. Meanwhile, job openings in business, industry and government for science and math majors have increased, offering earnings that far exceed those of teachers.

Degrees in math, physics, history do not qualify a college graduate to teach high school in most states, but a degree in education may permit the recipient to teach anything. This might be plausible if teachers were drawn from the top quartile of college graduates. But if they are drawn from the bottom quartile, and have no subject matter major, or often even minor, what can they teach at the secondary school level? Today's teacher is also expected to be social worker and to mold children's attitudes, values, and beliefs, but lacks a major in psychology or philosophy.

Which is the chicken or the egg is ancient history; I would blame the schools and departments of education for decades during which they have had a near-monopoly in supplying public school teachers in all subjects. Monopoly isn't necessarily bad; what is done with it is what counts. Educator stress on methodology to the relative if not absolute disregard of subject has been a disaster. Fads pretending to be new and improved theory succeed one another. Forget facts, rote learning, just learn how to think; think about what? Don't learn, just learn how to learn; how to learn what? what is knowledge for and for whom? So a clerk with a high school diploma can't figure out a 10% or a 50% discount on a sales item. Yes, there are computers, but who is to design them, and who will be able to take advantage of their capabilities? In a search for first causes we turn to Chapter 3.

Chapter 3

QUALITY OF EDUCATION AND EGALITARIAN VALUES

Chapter 2 considered the problem of teacher supply and quality. This chapter is concerned with the content of instruction and the methods of instruction as determinants of student achievement. It focuses on public elementary and secondary schools.

Public and private schools are radically different institutions. No one has to go to private schools; they are not free, nor an entitlement. They do not have to accept every student who applies. Even if nonprofit, private schools compete in the marketplace, ruled by the performance principle. They must compete for students on the basis of quality, curriculum, cost and other considerations. And they compete for support other than tuition revenue from alumni and other benefactors. Far from striving for uniformity, private schools try to distinguish themselves from other schools, resulting in greater diversity than among public schools. Those that stress student achievement are elitist in enrollment, grading and promotion policies. They have wide discretion in choice of teachers and in teacher pay.

Public schools are agencies of governments, shaped by democratic processes and values. Education is compulsory, in democracies and dictatorships alike. In the United States, it is compulsory to age 16 in some states, 18 or high school graduation in others. Consequently public education is available free in every state through high school. Education is an entitlement, and high school graduation is approximating entitlement status. Even libertarians rarely propose that school attendance be voluntary [1]. Most students in public schools have no choice of schools; assignment is based on residence. Some concerned parents make residential choices on the basis of the quality of public schools in the area.

Public schools do not stand alone; they are members of school districts, dependent on local and state funding over which they have little control, and subject to regulation on teacher certification, pay, curricula, teaching materials and techniques. A combination of compulsory school attendance and a growing sense of entitlement to a high school education are conducive to grade inflation, social promotion, and watering down of learning requirements. They amount to egalitarianism, a natural bias of any democratic institution; but egalitarianism is compatible with leveling up as well as with leveling down.

Can we blame the students? It is only plausible to conclude that the average ability of high school seniors today when 72% of the age group graduate is lower than it was in 1940 when only 51% graduated. But there has been little trend in graduation rates since 1960; rates peaked at 77% in 1969, bottomed out at 67.5% in 1998 [2]. One should not expect high school seniors to do as well today as their predecessors two generations ago. However, elementary school education was already universal then, so there is no demographic reason to expect a decline in student ability. Curriculum at the elementary level changes or should change less than at higher levels. Therefore, decline in achievement of elementary school students over recent decades is more measurable than for higher levels of schooling.

Why have educational policies and practices in public schools led to so much neglect of learning in recent decades, and why did these policies gain acceptance when they did? I suggest that there are three belief systems underlying our discontent with public schools. First is the downgrading of scholastic achievement as the primary goal of schooling and the stress on social engineering of behavior and indoctrination of belief. Second is the prevalence of downward egalitarianism in the educational establishment. Third is the desire for novelty as a surrogate for progress in the process of teaching. This adoption of a pretension of progress even in areas where there is no progress is typical of the arts and humanities in the past century, perhaps harmless in the arts, but not in pedagogy.

ACTION AND REACTION

Poor performance may be the result of poor teachers, or of poor teaching. The two are not the same, nor are they the only causes of poor performance. Although the first implies the second, the reverse is not true. School policies have become ideologically egalitarian. It is much easier to level down the educational content, the curriculum, and expectations of student achievement than to level up. Thus schools for many years have embraced grade and recommendation inflation, "social" promotion and a dumbing down of curricula to safeguard the self-esteem of the slow learners, or educationally-challenged (and of poorly prepared teachers). Many schools have abandoned the former practice of tracking or 'ability' grouping - this would be 'profiling' - although magnet schools and advanced placement courses are a compromise. They leave tracking to prospective employers, to select applicants and to discharge hires who are not up to the job, or to college admissions officers.

However, such efforts are limited by negative reactions to the consequences of leveling down. We now see nationwide concern about the poor performance of students in international comparisons, of high school graduates in college and in the job market. There is a trend toward leveling up, what with more homework, longer school years, weekend and summer study for laggards. But leveling up means an end to social promotion, many more failing grades. Some twelfth graders would not receive a high school diploma, which generates its own counter-reaction, not only from those (and their parents) who fall by the wayside but from egalitarians appalled by the consequences.

Conflicting reactions are partially attributable to different perceptions of school performance. According to one survey, 77% of students, 73% of teachers, and 62% of parents believed that high school graduates had learned the basics, but only 35% of employers and 22% of college faculty agreed. Most high school teachers are deceiving themselves, or their concepts of the basics are sharply at odds with those of college and work.

Every force generates a counter-force. The egalitarian ideology in public schools in the United States leads to enrollment in private schools, not all of which are bitten by the same bug; to home schooling, which is counter-egalitarian, strongly opposed by teachers' organizations; to use of tutors out of school. Public schools themselves have had to defend themselves, not by expanding tracking, Darwin forbid!, but by establishing magnet schools which are the same thing under another name, and by offering advanced placement courses. Perhaps tracking by schools is better for tender egos than tracking within schools. But only large cities can manage.

DEGRADATION OF CURRICULUM

In 1918 the National Education Association (NEA) was a professional organization; it did not become a labor union until much later. That year its Committee on Reorganization of Secondary Education issued a report spelling out 7 goals of public school education. Amazingly, only one (command of fundamental processes) referred to academic learning.(The others: health, worthy home membership, vocation, civic education, worthy use of leisure time, ethical character) appropriated for schools the role formerly associated with family and community. The NEA assumed that curriculum content was not important, that "life adjustment" rather than academic or vocational learning was the principal function of schools [3]. It was presumptuous then, and now. Most of these goals had little in common with parental or with public expectations of schools. Nevertheless, the educators eventually had their way, and the past forty years chronicle the complaints of parents and the public about the consequences [4].

The sharp decline in high school seniors' SAT and other standardized test scores starting in the early 1960s reflected a decline in learning which started much earlier. Machlup, writing in 1960, compared school curricula of the United States with those of Canada and 8 European nations, and concluded that "..the educational objectives now attained in 12 years could be attained in 9 or 10 years of school" [5]. There would be some loss of play time.

The decline in the academic curriculum started many years ago, before the second world war. Its share of course enrollments dropped from 67% in 1928 to 57% in 1961. Since then there have been periodic reform movements; but changes in the course distribution of the academic curriculum and in its share of the total curriculum, as measured by enrollments and credits, have been small and short-lived, except for the decline in foreign languages [6]. In the nonacademic curriculum, health and physical education, also known as sports, has grown spectacularly over the same time period, from 5 to 16% of enrollments, whereas business has fallen.

Enrollments are poor indicators of trends because there has been a large increase in the proportion of courses that are only one semester or shorter. On the basis of credits earned, the academic share dropped to 60% for the period 1976-81, rising slightly since, but still well short of the 73.5 in 1958. In math and science, there appears to be an increased bifurcation: more students taking advanced courses, and more students taking only very basic courses. The proportion of students enrolled has declined in algebra, geometry, chemistry, and physics [7]. Angus and Mirel [8] describe secondary school curriculum as an amalgam of conflicting interest groups rather than a policy choice. The curriculum, especially in secondary schools, has lost focus. Surveys of course enrollments reported 175 distinct courses in 1922, over 2,100 in 1973. This explosion of courses reflects lack of agreement on what students should learn or teachers should know [9].

Most nations have national educational systems which at least establish content standards for all schools. A few have regional systems. The United States stands alone as a local and state system, which in many cases is little more than advisory to individual schools and teachers. Thus there are many standards for curricula, as well as for teacher certification. Curricula and textbooks are closely related. It is curricula that determine the choice of textbook adoptions, and eventually guide the work of textbook writers and publishers. It is easier to compare leading textbooks over decades and generations than to attempt to compare curricula in our highly decentralized educational "system". In some subjects: math, the sciences, reading, writing, grammar, composition, foreign languages, to a lesser extent social sciences, learning is so sequential and cumulative that it is possible to arrange texts in order of difficulty and complexity.

At the elementary level the textbooks used for reading and math are simplistic compared with those used a century ago. Illiterate and innumerate high school graduates are one outcome. But causation is complex: dumbed down textbooks are written because there is a demand; they are adopted in part because students are ill-prepared. Many textbooks and teachers manuals are also riddled with ideology, not just in social studies or history but even in math and English.

Enrollments and course credits do not tell us what is being taught, how much is being learned. They are not consistent with the decline in college entrance test scores. In a large country one can always find examples of anything. But examples do not lead to conclusions. What we want to know is representative behavior and performance. Averages themselves obscure much information. On performance we have test results at many levels, and in several subjects, which are representative of the school system as a whole. On behavior, we do know what subjects are taught, and for how many students and how long: the curriculum. But we cannot know what goes on in every classroom or perhaps even in a "representative" classroom. What we do know is the texts assigned to students, and the teaching manuals for teachers. We can measure the content of the textbooks and teachers manuals of the leading publishers. Much of this information can be quantified. Changes in textbooks and in teacher manuals provide more specific information on course content. They tell us that there has been simplification of key courses in elementary and middle school, that at the very least, students entering high school today have been less well prepared than they were in the past.

From the reading materials used in schools we can infer much of what is taught in schools of education, whose faculty play a leading role in writing, designing, and approving these books. We know intentions, as filtered through publishers, although not how faithfully they are carried out by teachers, nor how effective their influence on students. But most teachers are graduates of the schools of education, and all are subject to guidance from boards of education.

Curriculum content sets a ceiling on average educational achievement. What the degradation of academic requirements and multiplication of mindless courses do is restrict the future learning and occupational opportunities of the majority. In college they are not capable of majoring in the fields with high cognitive content, with rigorous scientific or mathematical or logical requirements. They crowd into the soft majors, the new made-up majors, with little job prospects utilizing their college education. This did not matter in the days when higher education was for a gifted or wealthy elite, but today it means lost years, lost public investment. Mare [10] attributes the decline in aptitude and achievement test scores for high school students after the mid-1960s in part to changes in the curriculum.

Reading

Stotsky [11] has compared elementary school reading textbooks published in the 1990s with those in use a century ago. The ones in current use are markedly inferior in vocabulary, both in the number of new words and in the difficulty of new words presented. They are also inferior in complexity of sentence structure, of expression and thought. They lag years, according to some estimates, as much as 4 or 5 years, behind those used a century ago. Furthermore, their content is larded with bad English, dialects so-called, and with foreign words that will be of no further use in educational progress. These characteristics reflect an ideology that all ways of speaking and writing are equally good, and implicitly so are all languages. Standard English is just another dialect. But they are not equally useful in this place at this time. And they are very unequal in literary quality. This intrusion of ideology into the process of mastering language guarantees the poor reading and writing performance that is abundantly evident. Whether one looks at 9, 13, or 17 year olds, there has been essentially no change in their reading ability since the 1970s, nor in SAT verbal scores, still well below their levels in 1960.

If students do not learn to speak, read and write standard English, schools should be held accountable for the consequences. Perhaps it is no better than any other English dialect, but there must be one common dialect. Those who do not know it will have great difficulty in using a dictionary. They will not succeed in searching the web. If they use idiosyncratic spelling, their e-mails will not be delivered. Those who do not know "correct" spelling or understand standard punctuation will misunderstand text and will have their writing misunderstood. Those who use standard English are not going to become multi-dialectic for the sake of linguistic equality.

The literary classics which were part of the curriculum in the nineteenth and early twentieth century have been replaced by more up to date writings, some of them deserving literature, some drivel, on the pretext that the classics are passé, written by dead white males and females, reflecting politically incorrect views of society and interpersonal relations. The real reason is that the older literature employed a large vocabulary and complex structure, beyond the reading capabilities of most students today.

The most extreme claims of degradation in reading are made by John Gatto, award-winning English teacher in Manhattan. He states that fifth grade readers before 1850 are comparable to college freshman literature readers today [12]. I would suggest that one reason for the difference is that the most important book read in those days was the Bible, with rich vocabulary and diverse and complex structure and expression. Compare it to its equivalent today, the sports pages and soap operas. Students who lag in ability to read and write are handicapped in every subject once they enter middle and high school. Perhaps that is one reason less history and almost no geography is taught in high school any more: too much reading and of course, too much rote memory, which is a no no.

Bilingual education, often taught by teachers who don't speak English very well, amounts to a subsidy for such teachers, who have little incentive to expedite proficiency in English. It is also a means of enforcing ethnic segregation even on English-speaking students [13]. Governments at every level, by publishing forms and instructions in other languages, do what they can to preclude the need for ever learning English. That is the outcome, whatever the intent. Good deeds sometimes have bad consequences. Fortunately immigrants know that it is in their interest to learn; their native-born children will speak English as their first language, avoiding the handicaps burdening their parents.

Math and Science

We cannot compare science curricula or texts in current use with those prevalent a century or even half a century ago; much has changed in some subjects, new subjects have arisen, and their role in society and economy has grown. Students should have more exposure to science and math today than ever before. But we can compare curricula in this country with those elsewhere. Schmidt et al. [14] have examined math and science curricula for 29 countries responding to TIMSS surveys. Their findings provide some clues to the poor performance of American students in these subjects. They examine the seventh and eighth grades, and the earlier grades in less detail. American schools are first in the number of math topics included in content standards, in textbooks, in teacher instructional time, and in topics tested in the eighth grade. By contrast, the nations which have been doing best, such as South Korea, Japan, Hong Kong, cover a much smaller number of topics. The same is true of science in the eighth grade. America is not number one in number of topics for grades 1-5, 6 and 7, but it is at the high end, whereas the top-performing countries, except South Korea, are much lower. From the number of topics covered one can draw only one conclusion: that the teaching and learning of many if not most of the topics must be superficial, lacking focus [15]. This conclusion does not consider the preparation of teachers in math and science, but the average American teacher is not as well prepared as teachers in the countries that score high. The superficiality of math and science teaching in this country may be one result. It is a combination of numerous and diffuse topics, fewer courses, less time spent on teaching and studying than in other advanced nations, and poorly prepared teachers.

Schmidt et al also look at the gains in math and science knowledge between the seventh and eighth grades and the factors subject to influence by the educational system contributing to gains in learning [16]. Textbooks are important in the United States both directly and through their influence on teacher time allocation. But instructional time is less significant than instructional quality and expectations of performance. Drill and practice in eighth grade math and science in the United States do not appear adequate for the level of attainment sought by most students in most countries; neither is concentration on absorbing knowledge and learning to perform routine processes. Curriculum is also a factor; learning is interconnected: learning of particular topics influences ability to learn some other topics. Thus a structured, coherent curriculum enhances gains in learning from one grade to the next. " ...the logic of subject matter disciplines plays an important role in school learning" [17]. The American curriculum lacks focus, coherence. A comparison of the United States with Japan, France, Spain, Norway and Switzerland also found mathematics and science for 9 and for 13 year olds taught in America low in curriculum and in cognitive complexity [18].

Flanders [19] examined three mathematics textbook series and found that 35-60 percent of the material was review. New material was a declining share from the third to the eighth grade, where it was only 30 percent. With so much repetition one would expect all high school seniors to be comfortable with basic arithmetic, percentages, and simple graphs.

The lack of structure and coherence is one outcome of state and local control of public schools. It is also a consequence of the high mobility of students in this country, many of whom are often repeating what they learned in past years, or caught short because they missed some topics in moving between schools. Some claim that even within a single school a change of teachers in moving up a grade may have the same result. Local autonomy has its costs.

Unfortunately the textbooks of different publishers vary widely in content and quality. Given the sequential nature of math learning, a coherent program through successive grades is best approached by sticking with the texts of a single publisher. With a mobile student body, this is often impossible. There is much unnecessary repetition, omission of important topics, and great variation in quality. *Mathematically Correct*, an organization devoted to improving mathematics education, reviewed textbooks for the 2nd, 5th, and 7th grades, in terms of adequacy as preparation for algebra in the 8th grade [20]. Only one publisher merited an "A" for all three grades. Four earned "B", not quite up to expectations for algebra-readiness. Four more earned "C".

Two publishers flunked, receiving an "F" grade. They were the two in the group whose math programs were supported by the National Science Foundation and based on guidelines of the National Council of Teachers of Mathematics in 1989. Apart from inadequate content, they incorporate unproven or discredited instructional methods that diminish achievement. Students guide their own learning, work in groups, invent their own math language, facts and computations, are not expected to memorize facts or formulas, and are told that correct solutions are not important. They let calculators do their computation. Such texts have been derided by some as "fuzzy math".

These textbooks set ceilings on student achievement which in all but one case fail to prepare them adequately for algebra in the eighth grade. They almost guarantee an inadequate mathematical preparation in high school and bar those who go to college from majoring in any fields requiring mathematics, crowding them into humanities, soft social sciences, and the new single-issue majors. The results? an enormous gap in math proficiency within each grade, 8 years between top and bottom quartiles of 17 year olds. Thirty four percent of students in post-secondary math in 2000 were in remedial courses, up from 28% in 1980 [21]. So much for the net effect of reform movements as of that date.

Chapter 2 mentioned the high proportion of secondary school teachers under-qualified in the sense that they lacked even a minor in the subject taught. I suspect this is one reason for the huge inequality in student achievement in math and science (also in other subjects) and it may be a partial explanation for the undemanding character of the curriculum and of the textbooks used.

In secondary school, students are introduced sequentially to different sciences. Given the poor math competence and lack of coordination of math teaching and science courses in the U.S., most students are exposed to only some of the sciences. Few ever take physics, which typically is the last science course offered, and the one demanding some math. This lack of exposure, and of coordination, has been blamed by some for the poor performance of American high school students in international competitions in science. It is the practice in Europe and Asia to expose students simultaneously to all the sciences, in every grade in high school, presented with regard to the mathematical competence of students in that grade [22]. Math and science teaching are complementary; if students are weak in math, they will not go far in most sciences. An analysis of seven high school chemistry textbooks in use in 1991 found that a textbook first published in the Sputnik reform era had the most disciplinary content (91.3%) while a textbook first published in the 1980s had the least: 25.7% [23].

The decline in proportion of students taking algebra, geometry, trigonometry in high school was the inevitable outcome of their poor preparation in elementary school. The same is true of science; as students advance in grade, the science they should learn becomes more abstract, theoretical, mathematical. Lack of numeracy and conceptual thinking is a handicap in chemistry and disqualification for physics, one reason why most students never take physics. Of course, the shortage of teachers who majored in these subjects, and in math, is a contributory factor.

Since the late 1980s there has been a large increase in the proportion of high school graduates who took geometry, algebra II and pre-calculus. What this means in terms of course content we do not know. There has been a slight gain in achievement for 9 and 13 year olds, but not for 17 year olds. Quantitative SAT scores did move up slightly in the late 1990s, before trending down since 2004. The proportion taking science courses has also jumped, notably for chemistry and physics, which have doubled since 1982 [24]. More students are taking honors and advanced placement courses in science and math. Somehow these increases in math and science course work are not reflected in the Program for International Student Assessment (PISA) achievement scores in 2003, but these are for 15 year olds. However, the National Assessment of Educational Progress provides data on 17 year olds as well as 9 and 13 year olds [25]. Between 1973 and 2004 there was essentially no change among 17 year olds despite all the additional math courses they have taken in recent years and despite significant improvement in math achievement of 9 year olds. In science, the achievement of 17 year olds in 1999 was below 1970, but 9 year olds showed slight improvement. Math SAT scores have edged back to their level in the 1960s, but critical reading scores remain well below the 1960s [26]. SAT scores have been "re-centered" upward in 1995, raising questions about comparability over time.

As we learned in international comparisons, American students consistently do better in early grades, but their performance deteriorates as they move up to higher grades. All the additional science courses high school students have been taking in recent years may have lifted their performance slightly above the level of the late 1970s and early 1980s, but they still fare poorly compared to students a generation earlier. None of these comparisons go back to the 1950s and early 1960s, when scores were higher than in 1970. One wonders about the content of all this additional course work. And where are the additional teachers coming from? When advanced placement statistics was initiated in 1995, almost none of the teachers had ever taken a single course in statistics.

History and Social Studies

If elementary school readers are loaded with ideology (see below), it is not surprising that texts in history and social studies present a distorted if not outright false vision of reality. The Texas Public Policy Foundation team of 16 academic reviewers examined 26 social studies textbooks offered by major publishers for adoption in 2002-2003 [27]. They include 6th grade social studies texts, 7th and 8th grade history texts, and high school history, government, and economics texts. Sixteen academic reviewers found a total of 533 errors of fact or interpretation. The results were not all bad; reviewers found no errors in 3 of the texts, but the report indicates that two of them were reviewed by a single individual. But they found 121 errors in one text, 95 in another. As expected, most texts exhibit an anti-Western, anti-

American, anti-white, anti-capitalist perspective. The discovery of the Western Hemisphere is discussed without mentioning 1492 or Christopher Columbus. Prejudice in the United States is equated with government-sponsored genocide and holocaust in other nations. Discussion of technological progress fails to mention Edison and other notable inventors. Much more surprising to me is how many of the errors are simple ignorance or stupidity of authors who are assumed to know their subjects. There are numerous false statements, some intentional, others just ignorant, and numerous omissions, again some deliberate, some attributable to neglect or ignorance. Readers may disagree on the balance between deliberate distortion and ignorance, but both are abundantly represented. It should be stressed that the findings are not vague generalizations but highly specific; that they refer not to isolated cases but to the textbooks of the leading publishers of textbooks.

The same foundation reviewed 23 social studies textbooks introduced in the 2003-2004 school year and found 491 errors of fact and interpretation. Some publishers corrected most of the errors; others did not. Much in these texts is not error but distortion through omission of important information and through overstatement and understatement to produce a politically and socially correct version of reality. Some of these texts are best described as tracts. History textbooks are written to fit state book adoption regulations. They aim to bolster ethnic self-esteem more than to teach history [28].

It is not just textbooks. History standards were released by the Center for History in the Schools in 1994, endorsed by leading educational associations and funded by the Department of Education and the National Endowment for the Humanities. They were so extreme in condemnation of Western and American civilization, so unbalanced in their coverage that they were condemned by a Senate resolution in 1995 by 99-1 [29].

The case for curriculum coherence is less obvious for the humanities than for math and the physical and social sciences. But focus: limitation of topics in a school grade and greater concentration, should improve learning gain in any subject. Ravitch recommends that teachers should select their own reading materials and original sources, getting rid of state adoption laws. But Mel Gabler, textbook reviewer for 40 years, fears that with local autonomy, teachers unions and publishers would block out parental interests, whereas the later can be organized statewide and have some influence. McCullough favors abandoning textbooks altogether, they are no longer needed [30]. (Maybe some teachers need them).

Chapter 2 discussed the problem of teacher quality, of adequate preparation for the subject matter they are to teach. But if in addition to teaching a particular subject they are to promote and lead discussions of a myriad social, political, economic and scientific issues, then the vast majority are hopelessly incompetent. The worse the textbooks, the better the teachers need to be. If the issue is relevant to the subject, discussion is fine, but not the pretense of knowledge, not the dictation of conclusions. Unfortunately the introduction of such issues is not limited to courses where they are appropriate, whose teacher should have some knowledge, such as history and social sciences, but intrudes into the humanities: English, even sciences and math.

Time Allocation in the Academic Schedule

Even with excellent teachers and texts, how much students learn depend on how much time and effort they devote to learning. Compared to other advanced nations, the American school year is the shortest; the school day is very short; time devoted to study out of school is less than in most countries. Compared to a generation ago, curricula from elementary school through high school, and now in college, devote less time to traditional academic courses that demand effort and rigor on part of the student (and of the teacher). A study of 15 comprehensive high schools in Detroit found that most of the decline in the academic share of the curriculum occurred in the 1930s. It was concentrated in math and foreign languages [31].

In high school there are more electives than in elementary and middle school, so curriculum and texts are not the only consideration. What proportion of students take courses in particular math and science subjects, and how many courses do they take? Part of the problem with enriching the science curriculum in high schools is that it would require a huge increase in the number of teachers qualified to teach some sciences, physics in particular. But part is that it would require reallocation of time from other activities, or longer school days.

The indicator available is not hours but the number of credits earned by high school graduates. Academic credits declined from 73.5% of the total in 1958 to 65.5 in 1990; they bottomed out at 59.9% in 1976-'81 [32]. The largest decline was in English. As to math and science, inequality of curriculum and credits has increased. High school enrollments in elementary and practical math courses and in college-level courses has increased, but fallen in standard math courses in between. Most graduates have credits in biology, more than half in chemistry, but even after recent increases, only 28% in physics. The decline in academic study is understated because it fails to account for the introduction of nonacademic issues and concerns in academic course time which have little to do with preparation for either college or work: therapeutic education, viewpoint indoctrination, social engineering.

The number and variety of courses and more informal activities that may interest students but do little to add to useful knowledge or development of cognitive skills has multiplied [33]. Many schools stress sports and entertainment; others stress compulsory community service: much of it follower-ship lacking initiative or leadership, just saluting communitarianism. Most make time for indoctrination; it may be about current ideological fads, or the evils of religion, or the equal value of all views and practices other than those prevalent in America. If this seems an exaggeration, the reader should examine teachers guidebooks as well as textbooks. It is demeaning that our children's' teachers need these guidebooks. Many interest groups seek to advance their cause in the classroom. One of the most successful is the promotion of gay and lesbian life styles under the pretense of tolerance, starting as early as possible, in kindergarten at the Estabrook elementary school in Lexington, Massachusetts. The school sought to deny parental legal rights to opt out or even to be informed [34]. Teaching of sexual techniques in elementary school is commonplace. But there are many schools whose priority is learning. Of course, public schools cannot avoid influencing values and attitudes, but they should be those endorsed by the community they serve, not those promoted by the NEA, teachers colleges, and diverse pressure groups. They have no right to exempt themselves from the democratic process.

This reallocation of student time is a factor in poor academic performance. Parents do not appear to object to the stress on extracurricular activities; they overestimate the performance of their children's schools [35]. I suspect that one reason the nonacademic curriculum has become so prevalent is that it that it minimizes the need for or opportunity for grading students and ranking them in terms of performance and permits some students to do well who lag in reading, writing and arithmetic. Claims for their contribution to cognitive or other attainments fall flat in the face of decline in achievement.

Drill is not fun, but it is OK in sports, the one component of school curriculum where outcome still matters more than process, where meritocracy still rules. I suspect this is also true of piano practice, although few students ever learn to read the notes. Study, learning is work; not all work can be fun. But life is not an amusement park - satisfaction comes from accomplishment for those who put out the effort, not from ruling out failure by lowering standards.

Reduced time alone can account for some of the degradation in texts, in classroom exposition and learning. But the watering down of learning has gone beyond that, to reflect the well-intentioned desire that no student be left behind. This implies reducing the pace to that of the slow if not the slowest. The result is little stimulus or incentive for many of the rest.

The downgrading of the academic component of school time and effort is justified in several ways. First is the assertion that information is increasing at a rapid, possibly accelerating rate; current information will shortly become obsolete and therefore is not worth learning. This view is expressed as opposition to rote memory and to facts. Pedagogy based on this mentality is applied to reading and mathematics, as though English and arithmetic will soon enter the trashbin of history. Another issue is what kind of information is increasing rapidly, and is it unrelated to, or is it constructed on, the foundation of what we already know? The implicit assumption of the new pedagogy is that it is unrelated - there is no need to build upon the foundation of the past. Henry Ford would agree: "history is bunk". There is also a confusion between information of transient value and constant change, with knowledge of lasting interest. One does not teach the time of day or the current temperature or the price of eggs, but the astronomy, physics, and economics that determine them.

Second, given the explosion of new information and the obsolescence of the old, what schools should do is teach students to think, not burden them with facts. The naive version of this view is that thinking is independent of subject matter, of memory itself, just a general purpose skill that can be taught. There is a misunderstanding of the memory process whereby we are able to accumulate and to recall and use vast amounts of information; rote it isn't.

Third, some argue that with modern technology there is no need for students to learn arithmetic, much less algebra or geometry. Let them use calculators. I would like to see such students solve simple algebraic or geometric problems with computers! And who needs literacy? So much is available to those with ears to listen and tongues to speak: cell phones appear to be a substitute for literacy.

The case for increasing, rather than decreasing, the amount of time devoted to academic subjects is simple. In the natural sciences there has been much progress, and progress is continuing. More is known, more is being discovered, more needs to be taught and learned. Physics, chemistry, biology and various applied sciences are more comprehensive and complex than they were even a generation ago. To a lesser degree the same is true of the social sciences: more is known, more should be taught and learned. All of these subjects employ mathematics to a greater or lesser degree. The need for mathematical competence has increased, and can only increase in the future.

In addition to the case for academic education of the citizen, there is the case for increased teaching and learning for the future worker. The share of jobs requiring little knowledge continues to shrink, the share demanding a minimum competence in one of the sciences and mathematics is increasing, and expected to continue increasing. We cannot continue relying on immigrants for these jobs to the extent we have in the past (see chapter 5).

The reduction in academic time has been accompanied by a reduction in vocational preparation for those who will enter the labor market instead of going to college upon high school graduation. This has been cut back, eliminated in many schools under the pretext that everyone is college material and college-bound [36]. Because of the high labor market mobility in this country, schools are the logical site for vocational education that is occupation-specific. Job-specific training must remain the responsibility of employers. Too many who are not interested in a college education are compelled to attend community colleges anyway to receive the training formerly available in high schools.

IDEOLOGY

Why this debasement of academic learning while simultaneously advocating college for all? Why the promotion of a social and political agenda? One must consider the values that drive this educational revolution. How have they come to diverge from the demands of parents, colleges, and employers? Beyond values lurk the pretensions of unelected educationists which extend far beyond the limited social agenda of a John Dewey. Public schools cannot avoid influencing values and attitudes, but they should be those acceptable by the community they serve, not necessarily those endorsed by the National Education Association or inculcated in teachers colleges.

Self-Esteem and Group Identity

If there are simple answers, they would include the concern with the self-esteem of minorities, slow learners and free riders, and the self-esteem not of students but of the educational establishment. Such concerns entail hostility toward the selective outcomes of democratic processes and competitive economies.

Some insight is provided by the subject content of school readers. Stotsky's analysis of elementary school readers of all major publishers was not limited to vocabulary and sentence structure. She also examined their cultural content: readings are selected to shape children's' thinking, to induce "right" attitudes on social issues in particular political directions. They share an anti-civic, anti-western, anti-American orientation [37]. Readings have become multicultural, not in the original sense of promoting tolerance and understanding, but as a means of enhancing self-esteem of some groups, preaching individual identification with ethnic groups, encouraging separatism, as key to achievement. It has been described as "victim lit", "white guilt lit". These aims are made explicit in teacher guides [38]. They also promote adult causes often of little interest to children and beyond their comprehension, and outside the expertise of the teacher. Stotsky accuses current texts of cultural, intellectual, and demographic dishonesty. For instance, in an American history textbook, among presidents only Lincoln is mentioned. None of the great inventors is included in a discussion of technological progress. After all, they were the wrong race, and the wrong sex to boot. If they cannot be disparaged, at least they can be ignored. This is the content of texts designed to teach reading and writing; texts in history and social studies, already discussed, are worse.

Not even math and science are immune from ideological infection, although it is not as widespread in textbooks as it is in other subjects. Ethnomathematics [39] is a school of thought that downgrades standard mathematics. It stresses two points: one, that Europeans did not invent all mathematics, and two, that mathematics is culture-bound, there are other mathematics to be found even in primitive cultures. By analogy with multiple intelligences, one culture's math is as good as another's. The same points are made with respect to science. The tiresome jihad against Eurocentrism in mathematics is directed at a straw person; I have never met anyone who believed that Europeans invented mathematics. The argument that third world countries and members of some minorities are unfairly handicapped if taught "European" math implies that they can get along just fine in today's world with some alternative math. It is an argument for apartheid.

Powell and Frankenstein redefine mathematics as activity-specific practical knowledge of relations and quantities [40]. But mathematics is about generalizable principles, not about specifics. Long ago archers in Asia or Africa learned that to hit a distant target they should aim above it. The ethnomathematician might believe that archers discovered the law of gravity long before Newton and worked out the complex math of ballistic trajectories, and that makers of bows had a deep understanding of physics. Knowledge of the history of mathematics and its cultural origins is of interest to college math majors and cultural anthropologists. In elementary school, even in high school, it is a distraction at the expense of mastering standard math. Different approaches to arithmetic calculations or geometric proofs should be taught if justified by performance, not for the sake of cultural correctness.

Why should Americans who have benefited so much from "European" math and science be so hostile to their benefactors and dedicated to limiting their students' opportunity to benefit as well? Is the alternative proposed returning to alchemy, witch doctors and crude empirical engineering? Is it a retrogression in the interests of egalitarianism? This view seems implicit in S. E. Anderson: "Our duty is to lay the seeds for a more egalitarian educational system based on the assumption that anyone can learn anything" [41]. It is also an excess of multiculturalism in the interests of self-esteem of some, not others, that seems to deny progress in human history, and to advocate retrogression. Unfortunately students don't learn about other societies and cultures either. What they get is heavily expurgated and imaginatively sugar-coated versions, from teachers who often don't know their subjects and textbooks that prefer fiction to facts. There is a shortage of Shakespeares, Newtons, Mozarts, Edisons, Einsteins in most other cultures, as Charles Murray [42] has documented, but they can be invented.

This concern with self-esteem is based on the assertion that it leads to improved performance. There is no evidence to this effect, and performance in recent decades of obsession with self-esteem would lead us to the opposite conclusion [43]. It does lead to unrealistic expectations. What has increased is anxiety. Twenge [44] found that teenagers and adults in their twenties born since 1970 experienced a great increase in the rate of clinical depression and suicide. The eventual collision with reality was a factor.

The very proposition that self-esteem is more easily achievable on communitarian than on individualistic terms has yet to be demonstrated. The drive to define identity in ethnic terms, to undermine individualism, to tribalize America, is based on an implicit assumption that members of minorities are inferior and can't make the grade. They should not have a self-image associated with individual performance. For the same reason, grades, anything that rank orders individuals on the basis of performance, are to be regretted, abolished if possible. Unfortunately the disjunction between values in primary and secondary schools on one hand,

and colleges and the world of work on the other, fail to prepare under-performing students for frustration and failure, while curriculum debasement increases the risks of both.

School efforts at identity formation are not just in service of self-esteem for some, but as a pretext for ideological identity construction. They are riddled with contradictions. Identity defined by ethnic, sexual, socioeconomic or other shared characteristics involves exclusion of all who do not share them. But schools also preach common humanity, identification with the species. Whether a sense of identity is possible without exclusion I leave to psychiatrists. Global identification, given some of our fellow humans, requires a superhuman suspension of judgment. But the individual is also assured of his or her narcissistic uniqueness. It must be rather confusing to a young child.

Judging by the textbooks, public schools are contributing to the fragmentation of society, to cultural balkanization. One wonders about the aims of the interest groups that have so shaped school inputs (including the mental biases inculcated by schools of education on future teachers). Self-esteem seems to be too frail a lever for so much baggage. Muddled thinking is a more plausible hypothesis. Perhaps they have never heard of the Law of Unintended Consequences. Who is responsible for the textbooks? Although many interest groups seek to influence textbook and classroom content, the primary decision maker is the school system. Large states, such as California, through their decisions on textbook adoption, have a dominant influence on textbook publishers. They in turn are subject to multiple pressures, but it is the professional educators who have the most clout.

In fact what many schools preach is utter confusion. On one hand each student should be a self-regarding narcissist, on the other a minion of society. Different isms conflict. Relativism is nihilism; there is no fulcrum. It conflicts with multiculturalism: the effort to tribalize a nation which never was tribal. Each tribe regards itself as better than others, vive la difference! Multiculturalism rejects the process and the ideal of the melting pot, that most egalitarian of American ideals, whereas egalitarianism is a commandment. There is no coherent agenda or ideology, just a sort of teenage rebellion rendered chronic for lack of a sense of direction or destination, sometimes no more than a loser's lament. This is education?

Secular Religions

The teacher as social worker may have to be involved in crisis management, which is situational. But psycho-engineering - psychotherapist pretensions at molding beliefs, values, personalities, are outside teacher jurisdiction. Apart from the question of teacher qualification, they raise ethical and ideological issues for which our society provides no blueprint. There is no 'democratic' man as counterpart to Lenin's Soviet man; no Lysenko school of pedagogy, although there are pretensions. Yet schools proselytize and indoctrinate a variety of secular ethical and religious beliefs which have no academic role, some of which have little if any objective validity [45]. They may not be violating the separation of church and state, because these secular religions have few churches, but they are certainly providing religious education just as much as the anti-evolutionists would if they could. They promote feeling over fact, faith over reason. By secular religion I mean faith, belief in absolutes beyond question by facts or logic, intolerance of dissent. Current secular faiths are almost the exact counterpart of traditional religions. They have their angels and devils, Eden and Armageddon and Paradise and false gods, such as the worship of Wall Street by soulless billionaires.

The most widespread secularist faith, with its many sects, is a communitarianism infused with hatred of wealth, business, profit, capitalism. Marxism was the great secular religion of the 20th century. One would expect that Communist parties would have disappeared in the face of the dismal experience of all national experiments in communism. Past secular Utopias ended in disaster; the few model societies remaining are despotic and desperate. But believers are still around, going strong in several nations that experienced the worst excesses of Communist rule. Crypto-Marxism remains embedded in some of the ideological fashions of the time, such as egalitarianism and anti-globalization. I suspect that the failure of Marxism has contributed to the current goulash of overlapping sects and the frequent sprouting of new single-issue crusades. All this does not imply that *Das Kapital* does not merit serious discussion. It is the fundamentalist belief, not the rational debate, that is a problem.

The leading faith of the 21st century, which shares the same hatreds, is a primitive environmentalism, that resents the human race, 7 billion creatures exhaling carbon dioxide, converting the wilderness to habitat, granary, economic resource. Genuine concern for the environment has been converted into revivalist sectarianism seeming to focus on an apocalyptic vision of global warming. This popular secular faith is not to be confused with rational concern about combustion of hydrocarbons or the unintended consequences of modern processes of production and consumption. Geography, ecology, climatology, oceanography, economics are respectable areas of inquiry. True believers exhibit every characteristic of American sects: revivalism, missionary zeal, and above all, faith beyond facts, beyond reason. Like sects of the old World and the Middle Ages, environmentalists envision catastrophe, but they also offer salvation. The modern Eden is much the same as the old, Mother Nature in ignorance and bliss; but what is missing is a roadmap to Paradise. The worship of nature was the first primitive religion, Nature is God, and there is a panoply of saints: ozone, snail darters, spotted owls, swamps, the forest primeval. There is also a host of Demons: loggers, hunters, hydrocarbon fuels, population growth, and by implication, wealth and its uses.

Some sects are anti-technology as well, modern Luddists. who would abolish most large organizations except their own and the government and return o an imagined simpler life in harmony with Nature, whatever that is other than human nature. Much of the recent railing against big business, capitalism, has nothing to do with Marxism. Rather it is a cultural nostalgia, a rearguard defense against the Industrial Revolution. It seems in keeping with the neglect of math and science in curricula. The special hostility of both faiths is focused on the United States the great infidel that denies them power. The secular religious seem more fundamentalist and devout than the church-goers.

Another quasi-secular religion frequently pounding on school doors but usually denied entry is currently known as Intelligent Design. I do not know whether its advocates are unaware of the limited scope of Darwin's theory and its compatibility with their own, or confuse biology with cosmology, or whether posing as anti-Darwinians legitimizes their demand for equal time. Some school systems present theological or metaphysical theories of the origin and evolution, fate and function of the universe and the place of everything in it. It reduces the time available for modern science, but the important matter is that it is not college-preparatory, nor job-preparatory, with the remote possible exception of theological seminaries.

Credo ergo sum; credo quia absurdum. Schools and colleges have become pulpits and pews for the preachers of secular religions. They are accused of propagating Groupthink, but that is a mistake, for thinking presumes rationality. What they propagate is Groupfeel. There are one-worlders who demonstrate against globalization; cultural relativists who equate cannibalism with the British Parliament; biological relativists who would accord the cockroach equal citizenship if not the vote; moral relativists who deny evil and free will: we are only victims, but there can be no victims without evildoers. Relativism is just a cover term for nihilism, the anarchy of terminal narcissism that rejects external objective reality, shared values and personal responsibility. Multiculturalism, offspring of tolerance of differences, becomes an Age of Apartheid. E unum pluribus!. All this takes time away from academic learning and cognitive development, at taxpayer expense. These cults are propagated in schools by teachers and textbook writers most of whom don't know what they are talking about.

Whatever other functions high school education may have, preparation for college and/or for jobs must come first (and most other aims are embedded in these two goals). That is not the way some educators view their role. ".. the underlying question throughout all this work is how the cultural action involved in teaching and learning ethnomathematics can play a role in the economic and political action needed to create a liberatory society....a pedagogy of the oppressed can bring about a subtle shift in ideological climate that will encourage action for a just socialist economic and political restructuring" [46].

The preaching of secular religions is a puzzling revolution difficult to understand. The shaping of children into adults who are socially concerned and interactive, ethically aware, politically involved, seems to be a legitimate role for teachers, supposing they are competent for the task. The involved citizen is part of the national ideology - a secular religion of sorts. But policy-driven, conclusion-based indoctrination is another matter altogether, beyond the jurisdiction and competence of the teaching establishment. That teachers put up with preaching speaks ill of them. How particular secular religions came to convert the professorate and subvert the schools of education is a separate issue, beyond our concern. The proselytization that passes for teaching can only be described as hubris. Its products are adults who are terminally opinionated and therefore invincibly ignorant.

People may disagree on where to draw the line between secular religions and plain political propaganda. Neither has any place in public schools. Both dominate more than the textbooks and teachers guides. The 2003 convention of the NEA (National Education Association) passed resolutions on such educational issues as abortion rights, gun control, affirmative action, homosexuality, national health care, immigration and multiculturalism. It objected to English as the official language because it would allegedly deprive non-English speakers of education, social services and employment, and disregards the God of Multiculturalism. NEA's advice to teachers on the first anniversary of the September 11, 2001 attack on the World Trade Twin Towers was to avoid mentioning Arabs or Muslims and to focus on past abuses of native Americans, African-Americans, and others in this country. This is an educational organization? This is a labor union?

Public schools are secular and should be secular. The government, and public schools are government, has no role in adopting or preaching any religion, secular or sacred, in particular not to captive audiences whose attendance is compulsory. That means resisting efforts to teach cosmology, evolution, anthropology in literal Biblical terms. But it emphatically does not mean insistent and persistent attacks on religion, in particular the religions of the vast majority of Americans. Yet this is exactly what a small minority of government employees and some employees of government-subsidized private universities do - as self-appointed guardians of true belief who see it as their missionary task.

Private schools, which are subject to parental choice, are free to promote whatever faiths they wish, sacred or secular. Whether they forgo eligibility for public funds is a debatable issue. What government schools can do, and did in the past, is teach the core values and beliefs implied by citizenship. This is not a nation defined by ethnicity or geography, but by the core ideology embodied in the Declaration of Independence, the Constitution and Bill of Rights. It is these, and the history of progress in their implementation, that binds us together and sets us apart from all other nations. They are taught much less frequently or intensively than in the past, for they serve as antidotes to efforts to proselytize ethnic-cultural divisiveness and other secular faiths.

In respectable colleges, only a few faculty members in appropriate departments are considered competent to teach subjects such as climatology, ecology, industrial organization, sexuality, comparative anthropology, ethics, political theory. In secondary schools, and even in primary schools, some teachers pontificate on all these subjects about which they are almost universally ignorant.

Equality in Education

Why have school curricula undergone so much degradation? One reason is to promote increased educational attainment, and equalization of attainment. An annual survey of college freshmen found that the proportion with an A average in high school keeps rising, to a record 47.5% in 2004, compared to 17.6 in 1968; the proportion with C's was 5.1%, compared with 23.1% in 1968 [47]. Meanwhile, high school achievement scores declined. Some students learn because they wish; others because they must. Egalitarianism: grade inflation, social promotion, automatic graduation, whittles away the carrot and eliminates the stick. Egalitarianism is not just a policy imposed from above; it is widely accepted among the rank and file of faculty, and student body as well. It is lowest common denominator egalitarianism, easy on teachers and on most students. As one result, much talent remains untapped. But it hasn't worked. While grades have risen and achievement declined, the proportion of the age group completing high school dropped from its peak in the late 1960s. and early 1970s and has yet to return to that early high.

Another justification is the preservation of self-esteem among low-performing students, and among members of some minority groups. This concern for self-esteem is individualistic, not ethnic. Educators tell us that a high opinion of one's own abilities and achievement contribute to good performance, but offer no evidence. Circumstantial evidence points in the opposite direction: students in nations that outperform American students by a wide margin in math and science have a much lower perception of their own competence in these fields. Perhaps that is why they study harder and learn more. Students who regard themselves as very able and knowledgeable often lack the drive to study. Certainly the increased stress on self-esteem is not reflected in improved performance. Perhaps it is an end in itself regardless of consequences.

Teachers enforcing high standards are often intimidated or reproved and their classes avoided. High-performing students are disparaged as teachers' pets or nerds. Egalitarianism permeates the culture; no single agent bears responsibility for its prevalence. But those in authority must assume responsibility for its consequences.

Another aspect of the desire for equality of education is the pretense that all students are college-bound. This pretense is implemented by a reduction or elimination of vocational education preparing for jobs those students who are not college-bound. School counselors offer little help to those who are work-bound, devoting their time to advising on college applications. Almost every student in elementary school and in high school is told that opportunity is unlimited, that he or she can become anything he or she wants. This egalitarian doctrine is nonsense of course, but provides the theme for many graduation orators. It also generates expectations, even feelings of entitlement, that are bound to be frustrated in the vast majority of cases. No one talks about the fallacy of composition. Not everyone can be a doctor or a lawyer; the demand does not exist. Besides, who would provide food and shelter?

Standardized tests are the Maginot Line of quality education. They provide information to students, parents, teachers, and school administrators, whether or not they have other consequences. They are under attack because they reveal differences in achievement between individuals and groups of individuals not randomly selected. Tests with the same distribution of scores for all groups would have no possible use, since they would not discriminate between individuals (or groups) in the qualities relevant for the tester. Standardized tests also highlight shortcomings of schools and teachers, and that is why teachers and their unions oppose them.

Social promotion to protect tender egos is a common practice. But the egos are not just those of the students. It contributes to increasing inequality of achievement as students advance in lockstep grade by grade. Such inequality encourages teaching to the lowest common denominator, watering down the curriculum to the neglect of better students. Any egalitarian system runs into the free rider problem. Group study, group work exacerbates this problem. He (more rarely, she) does not participate, does not work, study, learn. The free rider may receive more attention and reward than top students, but lacks incentive to pay his way in the absence of consequences. It is not egalitarian to flunk, to expel, to fail to promote. Then why work? And study is work. In fact, why should others work, if there is no reward for excellence? From the viewpoint of incentives and rewards, egalitarianism is devaluation. But tender egos are badly bruised in the end when they are denied diplomas or do badly on standardized tests for college admission. Somehow more than a quarter of the age group do not graduate on schedule; most of these never graduate, although many get some certificate of equivalency. There has been no improvement in graduation rates in thirty years; it was higher in the 1960s.

The high school diploma has come to be regarded as an entitlement, not an achievement. This is one result of "social" or lockstep promotion and grade inflation. A high school senior class in many if not most schools includes some who are well-prepared for college, others who barely pass muster, and quite a few who never mastered material taught years earlier. After years of automatic promotion it is extremely difficult to enforce minimum standards for high school graduation. To be realistic, quite a few students will never meet such standards. Should they be allowed to debase the diploma for everyone else? Should college become a necessity because the high school diploma carries little weight with prospective employers?

Schooling should be fun we are told. The process of learning should be made as interesting and enjoyable as possible, fine. Relate the x's and y's, the adjectives and adverbs, the dates and the names to everyday life as much as possible. But if entertainment takes priority, students become averse to effort, deficient in knowledge and cognitive ability, ill prepared for college and unprepared for life. Adults must work hard from time to time, they must do things they do not want to do. It is better that they should enjoy hard work, that they should willingly accept responsibility, rather than be trained for perpetual adolescence, incompetence and frustration. School is not entertainment. Life is not an amusement park.

Discrimination against High Achievers

The junior high school I attended long ago had eight sections in each grade. Sections with low numbers were predominantly girls; sections with high numbers were predominantly boys. I'll leave it to the reader to figure out which were the fast or smart sections, which the slow or dumb ones. That was tracking. Now it is a dirty word unless referring to manmade satellites circling the globe. Tracking is discrimination, a word which has lost its previous positive meaning; it is profiling, which is no longer a neutral term. It is not extinct, but it is less prevalent than in the past, although at the high school level the diversity among students in learning has increased, justifying more, not less, tracking.

The availability of advanced placement and honors courses in many high schools could be interpreted as upgrading rather than dumbing down of curricula. It is a form of tracking. But much of this is what once was the standard fare for most students. The proportion of high school students taking honors and advanced placement courses has zoomed, but in any field it is a small proportion of high school graduates. Standardized test scores do not reflect this. Either these courses are misnamed, or college-level standards have dropped.

Are honors and advanced placement courses an effort to accommodate the brighter and/or more motivated students, or just a device to keep them out of private schools and home study? The answer will vary from place to place. They contribute to grade inflation because it is common practice to award bonus grade points to students who take these courses. The result is that there are numerous college applicants with grade point averages higher than 4.0. But across the country, funds for teaching gifted children are being cut, altogether eliminated in 17 states.

In 1999, the proportion of college freshman class taking remedial courses in math and languages reached an all-time high; the proportion in science a 20-year high, and the proportion in English, reading, and social studies a 9-year high [48]. Surveys of college freshmen taking remedial courses were conducted for 1995 and 2000. In both years, 28% of freshmen took one or more remedial courses. In 2000, 22% took courses in math, 14% in writing, and 11% in reading. The average time taken to complete remedial course work increased slightly from 1995 to 2000 [49].

Grade inflation was initially correlated to the watering down of the academic curriculum. In spite of all the negative publicity, inflation continues. The grade point average of high school graduates rose from 2.68 in 1990 to 2.98 in 2005 [50]. The average rose in every subject and in every successive year studied. In fact the extent of grade inflation has been understated to the extent that it was associated with the dumbing down of course work. Grade inflation is a form of discrimination against high achievers: if there must be grades, then almost everyone gets good grades, a large proportion are awarded honors, thus devaluing grades and honors.` It is a grand deception.

Many high schools no longer provide information on the class ranking of seniors, allegedly in behalf of good students who rank high but not at the top of very good high school senior classes [51]. Nearly 40% of high schools have either stopped ranking or ceased giving rankings to colleges. Nashville, and Tennessee, are attempting the impossible: to make all students equal, or to appear equal [52]. Honor rolls are abolished, or kept in security safes. No one who fails to make the honor roll can be shamed. Student work will no longer be posted on bulletin boards. Rather than neglect the effort of the worst of students, the school will neglect all effort and accomplishment. Spelling bees are being considered for elimination or at best to be conducted in secrecy. Grades are meritocratic and cannot be tolerated. I would like to get a job in a Nashville school: not much pay, but almost nothing to do. This is an extreme example of nationwide efforts to diminish accomplishment, destroy incentives, in the idiotic belief that the result is high and universal self-esteem (and some believe further, that this in turn will lead to greater effort and accomplishment, in the absence of any incentive or recognition). The Lewis-Palmer high school in Monument, Colorado has taken a different tack. Its 2006 graduation featured 15 valedictorians, each allotted 30 seconds to speak. Some schools have as many as 30 or 40.

If it is almost impossible to flunk and easy to get an A, there is not much student incentive to do well. What about the teachers themselves? What incentive do they have to teach their students well if they are saddled with dumbed-down books, compelled to grade over-generously for fear of career consequences of demanding more of their students? Can egalitarianism be confined to the student body or must it apply to faculty as well?

To parents, grades mean just one thing: an index of achievement. That is why parents are much more satisfied with their children's schools than with public schools in general. After all, their children are getting A's and honors. But to the teacher and the school, grades have other meanings [53]. They may reflect achievement; they may simply recognize effort, hard work, with little learning. High grades are dispensed to keep the students happy, to avoid hassles with disappointed parents, to pretend that the teacher and the school are doing well, to keep school system administrators and local community leaders off their backs. The large number of high school seniors with good records who fail simple multiple choice standardized tests and are denied diplomas is one indication of the scale of the deception. The anger of the students and their parents is fully justified. Taxpayers should be outraged. Unfortunately there is a tendency to direct anger at the standards and not at the schools and teachers who are at fault. Shoot the messenger.

There remains one escape: much school time and energy is devoted to sports and to other activities that have nothing to do with academic subjects, depriving students of learning time at school, and energy for homework later. Sports are over-stressed in school, yet sports are meritocratic. Somehow in sports it is impossible to hide who is the fastest runner or best batter, passer, pitcher, player. In sports, one team wins, another loses, one player is first, someone else is last. Competition is war, and victory goes to the best team, with the best players. This is meritocracy run amuck in a swamp of egalitarianism. Guess which activity elicits the most interest, provides the greater incentive to perform? If they motivate students who are otherwise bored or indolent, that is fine, but there is no spillover of enthusiasm from sports to the classroom. Perhaps some who do poorly in math or English can shine in sports, but there is no inverse correlation between classroom performance and distinction in sports. Sports have minimal cognitive content. Much bilge is spilled over how much sports and other recreational activities contribute to character, but college performance and employability depend on reading and quantitative ability, not on batting performance. Nor is it clear that sports contribute more to character than learning math does. Perhaps time and energy are better spent on egalitarian pursuit of knowledge.

Local newspapers often publish articles on local high school students who have won regional and national awards in science, math, sometimes in musical performance. Go back a generation or two, and a disproportionate number of the award or fellowship winners were Jewish. This is no longer true; most now are first or second generation Asians: Chinese, Indians, Koreans. But take heart; in another generation or two they also will become Americanized.

Anti-Individualism

The anti-meritocracy bias in education today: anti-testing, anti-grades, anti-standards, is anti-individualistic. Individualism is a term applied to a number of conflicting concepts. One meaning is that all individuals are of equal value, and should receive equal treatment, perhaps including equal grades. This definition is about equality, not about individuals. The equal value of all individuals is the core of dumbing down of curricula and the goal of college for all. A second meaning of individualism is simply uniqueness; everyone is different, and should be treated accordingly. A third meaning is autonomy: the individual makes his/her own decisions. Child-centered teaching, to be discussed under pedagogy below, sees each individual as different, unique; it also confers some autonomy on the student. It implies differences in treatment and in outcome. Although non-meritocratic, it is not anti-individualistic.

The egalitarian bias is reinforced by the widespread process of collective studying and learning: joint activities, projects, products, so that the abler or more diligent students do most of the learning and work, the others share the credit. It is all done under the pretense that it is a process of socialization, preparing students for life in the adult world, team work. Unfortunately, in the world of work, employees are hired, rewarded, promoted, fired as individuals, not as teams. It is also a means of minimizing work for the teacher. It conflicts with the allegedly child-centered approach, with the teacher as mere facilitator, the child self-educated. Scratch the polysyllabic mumbo jumbo and you have avoidance of individual grades or comparisons as one motive, minimizing teacher assessment burdens as a secondary motive, and majority free riding as the result. Individualism in education requires meritocracy. (In large classes, some group work can be useful as a substitute for one-to-one contact between teacher and each student. No one is lost or overlooked, and students can help each other learn. This procedure works better in a culture such as Japan's, but can be useful here in proper context, with safeguards against free riding. It also covers up the large differences in ability within a single class.)

The social agenda promoted by schools of education and embedded in textbooks and teacher's manuals is radically anti-individualistic. In the name of identity politics and search for self-esteem, the student is defined as merely another member of a large group, deriving identity there from, having none of his or her own. This group is primarily ethnic and racial, secondarily socioeconomic. A second characterization of group identity is a Marxist dichotomy of oppressors and oppressed. Both are meant to fragment and divide society, to ululate a litany of losers, to export responsibility. How self-identification as a victim can boost self-esteem is beyond my comprehension. But it is a handy excuse for failure. It reflects an "animus against what are perceived to be western values, particularly the value placed on acquiring knowledge, on analytical thinking, and on academic achievement itself. Its educational goals are now almost completely social and political, not civic and intellectual" [54].

THE EGALITARIAN ETHIC

"The year was 2081, and everyone was finally equal. They weren't only equal before god and the law. They were equal every which way. Nobody was smarter than anybody else. Nobody was better looking than anybody else. Nobody was stronger or quicker than anybody else. All this equality was due to the 211th, 212th, and 213th amendments to the constitution, and to the increasing vigilance of agents of the United States Handicapper General" [55]. But the Handicapper General and his vast bureaucracy were more equal than others.

The basic problem of school quality is egalitarianism, not pay, class size, spending. It is a social, not just a school issue. Issue, not problem, because it is a choice, not an exogenous imposition. But the consequences of social choices should be pointed out; the choices should be transparent, not muddled or hidden.

Egalitarianism does not require low standards, discouraging achievement. The nations that score highest in math and science are precisely the nations where the gap between low and high achievers is small; they would not score so high otherwise. American egalitarianism by contrast results both in low performance and in the second largest gap between low and high achievers among OECD nations. We do have greater ethnic diversity than the Asian tigers or Finland, who score at the top, but we also have a greater capacity to accommodate diversity and assure mobility.

Changing Meaning

Egalitarianism is a polysyllabic word of many meanings. Politically it may simply mean one vote for every adult. In terms of values, it means that each of us is worth as much as anyone else, has equal rights. Economically and educationally it may be taken to mean equal opportunity, which inevitably results in very unequal outcomes. This was its meaning in the 18th and 19th centuries, according to Fogel [56]. Egalitarianism in America was a legacy of the endless frontier, in sharp contrast to egalitarianism in Europe, where it has been a revolt against class and privilege.

Egalitarianism of outcomes was promoted by the age of the "robber barons". The evidence of great wealth of traders, bankers and industrialists, and its abuse, temporarily generated resentment of differences. The Great Depression led to a combination of income redistribution, constraints on the rich and powerful, and entitlements for the poor and weak. The resulting increase in security combined with a large rise in incomes following WWII reduced risk aversion. Change in the structure of the economy from dominance of resources and capital to rise of talent and skill accompanied a return of equality of opportunity, with greater stress on advanced education.

Egalitarian Agendas in Schools

In education egalitarianism initially meant equal opportunity at the elementary school level. This required availability of free public elementary schools. As the goals of egalitarianism advanced to include secondary school education, the number of free public secondary schools had to expand accordingly. But mere availability of free schooling through the twelfth grade was not sufficient to create equality of opportunity. Lower- income children had to be denied the alternative opportunity of working. Hence laws were passed establishing a minimum working age (education was not the only justification for such laws). School attendance was made compulsory, as the goal of opportunity was revised to include outcomes. The maximum age for compulsory attendance was raised over time, more or less in keeping with the minimum working age, now 16. Now many states require school attendance to age 18 or high school graduation, whichever comes first. (But enforcement is weak.)

The egalitarian ideal prevailing in schools of education and among public school teachers and school systems for the past half century is equal outcome: everyone passes, grade distributions narrow, everyone graduates from high school, everyone is admitted to college, and in some future egalitarian Utopia, everyone will have a college degree and presumably a professional or managerial job. Public school teachers practice what they preach: new teachers all receive the same pay and advance in lockstep on the basis of seniority. Merit pay is strongly opposed. Public school egalitarianism seems out of step with the society, perhaps reflecting the social perspective of the early twentieth century. It is anti-meritocracy.

Equality of outcome requires inequality of opportunity. Numerous tactics have been devised toward this end. One is grade inflation and social promotion, so that differences between students are covered up. Another is admission of any graduate of a public high school in a state to some public college or university in that state. A third is affirmative action. Fourth is a new escalation, college for all. A fifth is the practice of grouping students and grading them as groups rather than as individuals. According to S.E. Anderson, one of the six pedagogical disasters in mathematics education is precisely testing students as individuals rather than as members of study groups [57]. The last tactic is a redefinition of intelligence: there are Gardner's seven intelligences [58], now eight, perhaps more, and many different abilities. Everyone is intelligent and able according to some concept of ability. Some relativists might go further, and make the pathetic claim that all 'intelligences' are equal, all 'abilities' are equal, whether they refer to higher math, language fluency, baseball hitting, singing, introspection. Still, not all high school diplomas are equal, nor are all high school graduates. This line of reasoning carried too far would conclude that some animals are smarter than humans in spatial and kinesthetic intelligence, and probably in social intelligence as well. Gottfredson concludes that "..multiple intelligence theories may do little more than squander scarce learning time and significant opportunities for improvements in the quality of American schooling" [59].

How can one reconcile egalitarianism conceived as equality of outcome, of achievement, with the facts that some students do much better than others? One divorces achievement from attainment, and incidentally redefines meritocracy. One adopts "luck" egalitarianism [60]. Attainment is largely a matter of the luck of the draw, be it genetic endowment or environmental support or cultural milieu. What an individual becomes, accomplishes, lies outside the individual's control, it is the accidental product of external conditions. The attainments of the gifted and blest are discounted. Likewise, those disfavored by genes or environment are not accountable for lack of attainment. This line of thought carried too far eliminates all individual responsibility, all achievement. Egalitarianism at the limit rejects individual freedom, free will.

To the extreme egalitarian there is no merit whatever in meritocracy. Granted, individual achievements and rewards under a "meritocratic" system such as competitive capitalism are not all merited; they are in part a function of the rules of a game that dictates that some will gain and some will lose. Individual outcomes are influenced by chance and luck, but they are not randomly allocated, as they would be in an egalitarian system. Individual choices and abilities matter most.

There is an American tradition of admiration for those who overcome great handicaps, whose attainment is truly an achievement. But it does not disparage the achievements of the gifted. It is under attack. But half a century of effort to equalize outcomes has failed. In fact it has proven counterproductive. The unfortunate consequence of downward egalitarianism is an increase in inequality of attainment, more unequal in the United States than in other advanced nations. Higher educational attainment for almost everyone increases differences in knowledge. Some students will achieve regardless, most don't have to. Upward egalitarianism, as practiced by Asian nations that score at the top in math and science competitions, does result in reduced inequality of attainment.

Every characteristic of public schools mentioned so far, with the possible exception of some secular religions and political propaganda, can be understood as part of an egalitarian agenda. There is a compression of grade distributions; anything else is elitist, which is a derogatory term. Teachers oppose standards and standardized tests which permit ranking schools and students, as well as teachers. Many oppose tests and grades altogether. There is opposition to surrogate standards implicit in charter schools and voucher schemes as well. All this in face of the fact every teacher learns that there are large differences among students in their ability to learn, as well as in their willingness to study.

Differences in achievement must be reconciled with egalitarianism. How to do this? Academic intelligence has been over-stressed, it is a bias of the dominant elite; it must be discouraged. Academic subjects, standard English, math, science, should be downgraded as well as dumbed down,. They reflect only mathematical-logical and linguistic intelligences, perhaps spatial. The classics should be neglected, replaced with modern scribbles. Schools should reward interpersonal, intrapersonal, and kinesthetic intelligences. Unfortunately, these intelligences are useless in mastering traditional academic subjects. So what? Superior performance must be explained by circumstances beyond individual control. Then it is possible to accept differences in performance, but they should not merit differences in reward.

Egalitarianism ultimately adopts a subjective attitude toward knowledge rather than recognize that some are superior to others. Evasion of rules of grammar and of spelling are the most common examples. In the classroom, the teacher hesitates or refuses to correct error. Personal feeling is allowed to overrule the dictatorship of facts and logic. Everyone is entitled to an opinion regardless of knowledge; one's uninformed opinion is as good as another's.

Identity must be redefined in collective terms. Multiculturalism, initially a plea for tolerance and for knowledge of other cultures, has mutated into tribal self-segregation stressing differences instead of bridging them. The psychological horizon, the subjective territorial boundaries of the student are deliberately constricted. Multiculturalism comes in two versions. One is empty relativism: the equal value of all cultures and beliefs. Egalitarianism on a collective scale seeks to inflate the self-image of under-performing minorities and destroy the 'arrogance' and self-esteem of the majority by rewriting history and distorting current events, as reflected in curricula and texts in English, history and social studies, to some extent even science and math. The moral, aesthetic, intellectual equivalence of all cultures equates diverse opportunities for self-realization. This is the pretension. Lives there a human being who regards himself or herself no better and no worse than anyone else? And if such a being exists, would we really like a society consisting of such beings?

The second version of multiculturalism is hostility to the cultures and values and ethnic groups dominant in the United States. It attacks the pursuit of knowledge, the primacy of cognitive ability, the objectivity of truth and reality. It values subjective belief over factual evidence or logic, cares little for scholastic achievement. Its impact is felt throughout the curriculum [61]. This is the dark side of the benevolent and hopefully beneficent version of egalitarianism discussed above.

The efforts of educators over a generation to tribalize America have failed, with the partial exception of some African American self-anointed political leaders who collude with educators to stress divisiveness and victimhood instead of opportunity and achievement. The dividers have succeeded in one respect: promoting ignorance about the origins of the shared core values of America, how they have evolved and their role as the cement of our multiethnic society.

Another feature of the egalitarian ethic as reflected in public schools is the propaganda (or philosophy if you wish) of college for all. The contradictory combination of a dumbing down of education and the pretense that all high school graduates should go to college have resulted in frustrated expectations and wasted years in the lives of many students. Vocational education in high school is criticized as an impediment to social mobility, as anti-egalitarian. High school teachers and counselors fail to serve the numerous students who are not college-bound but work-bound, or those who are college-bound but should not be.

School vs. Society

It is not that those who defend current school practices and those who would change them have different values. It is that they order and weight the same values differently. All favor equality of opportunity. But it results in inequality of outcomes. Everyone would prefer some constraints on inequality, at the limit the complete equality reflected in the one man one vote ideal. If the value of opportunity outweighs that of equality, the outcome is meritocracy. If the value of equality outweighs all other values, the outcome is egalitarianism. The conflict is camouflaged by differences in beliefs about reality. Thus no test of ability is believed to measure ability, and disbelievers reject any results that reveal differences between groups; some approximate rejecting innate differences in ability between individuals. Believers in tests on the other hand are convinced that adequate provision can be made to account for differences in circumstances resulting in differences in performance. The debate under these conditions cannot be resolved by data or tests, and results in ad hominem attacks on credible proponents of unpopular views, such as the attacks on the Bell Curve. Ad hominem attacks do not mean that the attackers have no leg to stand on, but standing on just one leg is precarious and tiresome.

Resentment of great inequality is a widespread attitude. It is economic in content: at the extreme, overthrow the 'malefactors of great wealth'. The majority favor taxing the rich, some to use the revenues to benefit the poor, others simply to level the distribution of income. But personally they all wish to do better, and want their children to excel in school, that is, to do better than other children. I have known exactly one liberal egalitarian who was willing to sacrifice his children's education on the altar of equality, and I suspect he regretted his decision.

What people want is outcome; opportunity is just a way station. But few want equal outcomes. Equality of opportunity might have meant once that everyone could have 40 acres and a mule. But with the end of an agrarian society opportunities lay elsewhere. In the towns and cities opportunities were diverse and limited. Not everyone could be a blacksmith or a banker. With the growth of large organizations, both private and public, opportunities became more hierarchical. There is little room at the top. Equal educational attainment does little to change the hierarchical structure of outcomes. Even equal incomes would have limited effect on the structure of occupations. The allocation of individuals to outcomes, once feudal inheritance, then socioeconomic and demographic, has become meritocratic, based largely on individual ability to perform. Equal opportunity now means mainly access to education, just one determinant of the ability to perform.

Employers want basic skills and disciplined work habits. They care nothing about multiculturalism, student narcissism or fashionable ideologies. If they don't get what they want from high school seniors, they can up the ante and recruit from college seniors, or from immigrants, and that is exactly what they have done. Parental concerns are much more like those of employers than of educators.

The one feature of public schools that does not appear to fit within the egalitarian ethic is the widespread promotion of assorted secular religions and political agendas. They do exemplify the primacy of belief over reason, of subjectivity over objectivity. Their promotion is part of the one-sided power struggle of teachers against parents. Teachers propose to teach how to think, but also what to believe. But why? Secular religions and political agendas are promoted by schools of education and their publications for teachers, certainly in teachers textbook guides, and by the National Education Association. But that only pushes explanation one step back. Does it simply fill the vacuum resulting from the downgrading of academic subjects, and the poor preparation of many teachers in their subject matter? Does belief in some secular creed, and the ability to propagate it in the classroom, give a sense of self-esteem to teachers who are not highly respected in the community? Or is it School of Education imperium? It is their job to shape the future by promoting Groupthink and Groupfeel?

Sowell [62] sees a common motivation: a one-sided power struggle, for only one side is aware of the struggle to shape and control the minds of students. Determined effort is made to undermine the authority of parents, family, but also of social institutions, particularly religious institutions prevalent in America. The push for multiculturalism as relativism is but one means of undermining authority. Educators have moved far beyond Dewey's concept of their role in socialization, civic preparation of students for life in a democratic society.

Why this effort by public schools to undermine all outside influence on students, to dominate? What for? These are two separate questions. We are not talking about an elite eager to impose its superior wisdom on the unwashed masses. We have instead faculties of education, second-class citizens in colleges and universities, and public school teachers, whose performance on standardized test is not higher than that the average for high school seniors. It is a professional and intellectual underclass that proposes to dominate the thinking of the next generation through their monopoly on education. The only word for it is hubris.

If this sounds like a conspiracy theory, it is not for lack of resemblance. It is characterized by self-righteousness, salvationism, intolerance of divergent views [63]. It seeks to impose conformity under the cloak of diversity. It dissimulates its activities and objectives so parents will not know what is being done to their children. It suffers from logorrhea - incomprehensible and meaningless jargon to "épater les bourgeois" and the self-delusion of superior knowledge. According to Jacques Barzun [64], "At present, our 'liberal' teachers college products show but the bare markings of a totalitarian force - the zeal for inducing the 'right attitude'; a thick-skinned intolerance toward all who doubt or criticize so much goodness; and a special language, a flatulent Newspeak, which combines self-righteousness with permanent fog.....it is a manipulation by sentiment and dubious authority, exercised by the least educated and the most vapid minds of the nation." Barzun [65] sees egalitarianism as a disease of democracy. He attributes the unsatisfactory state of schooling and learning to democracy. In the school system, "Amiable stupidity is protected... the characteristics of Intellect - its scarcity, its eccentricity and intangibility - prevent the democratic public from entertaining about it a just view or a straightforward emotion." ... "...the starting point of conversation is contradiction, and this democratic manners do not tolerate...full democracy has extended the no-politics or-religion rule to any strong opinion." The cause of distress is the democratic rule of everything for all, a rule that sees distinction and discrimination as invidious. Barzun assumes that egalitarianism under democracy implies leveling-down. In other countries, and here in the past, it meant leveling up. American democracy is individualistic, a democracy of opportunity.

It is easy to point out democratic nations that maintain high standards for their schools and students. The American people had higher standards for education and expectations from students a century ago than have prevailed in the last half of the twentieth century. It is not democracy, but egalitarianism, whose meaning has changed during our democratic history.

There is another more sinister 'explanation', bordering on conspiracy, not of teachers, but of the individuals and institutions that have shaped teacher education, pedagogy, ideology and curricula over much of the past century. It is the egalitarianism which equates all cultures, all values; seeks to undermine nationalism, which condemns Western culture and values and individuals for their claim to superiority and their constraint on behavior; which decries religion and its discrimination between right and wrong. It is concerned with groups, not individuals. This 'conspiracy' is the collective effort of individuals who would destroy western society as a necessary condition to prepare the way for implementation of their vision of a just and egalitarian world communitarian society. Hence the attacks on family, religion, individualism, Western culture. What others see as child-centered education they see as rejection of all authority: parental, governmental, religious, expert (teachers excepted).

This thesis is expounded in great detail by Eakman [66]. He attributes most of the deficiencies in curriculum and pedagogy, as well as ideological and political indoctrination in schools, to thinkers who seek to undermine Western institutions. He tags the Frankfurt School (Institute of Social Research) founded by Georg Lukacs in 1923 as the fountainhead of this 'philosophy'. Some of the more prominent exponents studied there. Many of the leading 'thinkers' were Europeans, some of whom migrated to America. Eakman exculpates Dewey and the Progressives. Kilpatrick, considered by others as the leading prophet of the current educational culture, is not mentioned.

Eakman's *Cloning of the American Mind* is an adversarial, confrontational book, but whether or not one accepts Eakman's diagnosis or agenda, there is much evidence in 570 pages of individuals and groups whose promotion of these ideas is cynical, not from conviction, intended for disruption rather than conversion. Eakman attributes it to devotees of world revolution, mostly Communist, but some who flit between Nazism and Bolshevism, who would make St. Marx feel bourgeois guilt and John Dewey consider dropping out.

They share the belief of Wilhelm Wundt and Robert Owen in the dominance of environment as determinant of behavior and achievement. They are millenarians, not simple-minded Utopians. Millenarialism involves struggle against Satanic forces, evil conspiracies such as Western culture, capitalism, big business, traditional religion, and, soto voce - democracy, that tyranny of the majority that obstructs the tyrannies of unelected minorities.

If schools and teachers are to shape the environment under which children develop and learn, they must minimize other influences. Hence the attack on parental authority and, among the ideologues, on the institution of the family, the most important source of inequality in environmental influences. At the extreme are advocates of removing children from their families, making school the dominant environment. If these deep thinkers were logical, they would ban the teaching of Darwinism in schools since it is based on genetic differentiation. I would hope that all teachers believe that environment, schooling in particular, makes a big difference. But the belief that genetic differences are unimportant can lead to the egalitarianism of Victor Lysenko.

Eakman's numerous quotations are damning, there is little doubt about the intentions of many individuals cited. It is another matter to attribute to largely European ideologues a dominant influence over schools of education, school boards, and the evolution of public schools for generations. Teachers are not marching in step, they move more like a mob with a poor sense of direction. However, it is the only 'explanation' which seems consistent with the virulent anti-western and anti-American dimension of public school education and left wing ideology propagated in the name of learning. But other aspects of the curriculum: dumbing down, grade inflation, growth of the nonacademic component, pedagogic techniques, are more plausibly attributed to Columbia Teachers College than to the Frankfurt School.

Ideology and indoctrination masquerading as public school education is an old story, often told, widely known. The National Education Association continues issuing commandments on policy and ideology irrelevant for learning or cognitive development. This agenda is best described as counter-Darwinism, a secular version of Intelligent Design, by human hands. Given the failure of communist experiments elsewhere, here its public policy agenda is largely in remission. Instead the stress is on creating the new human being, and on counter-culture or deconstruction of everything in the dominant society. But dreams of Utopia compete with memories of Eden. As Marxism declines, Luddism is on the rise.

Why do so many educators believe there is no objective reality or truth or morality, that nevertheless (logic is not their forte) the West, and the United States in particular, are evil and oppressive? How can I explain the passion against majority preferences, this hatred of the foundations of American society and civilization that infects some who are its beneficiaries? Above all, why is there so much intolerance among educators? Some of it is frustrated Marxism, the opium of the 'intellectuals'. Perhaps it is because in America socialism of the Marxist persuasion has never achieved political power. Here communitarian influence has been driven by values and guilt and pragmatism in the tradition of a Bismarckian welfare state rather than millenarian revolutionary ideology. Furthermore, it is the leading capitalist nation. But much of the railing against capitalism owes nothing to Marx, more to Thoreau. Whatever the answer, it would only lead to further questions.

Communitarian or socialist ideology is compatible with a variety of educational policies and curricula. It does not imply what Eakman ascribes to the Frankfurt School, nor the practices common if not prevalent among American public schools. Donald Weiss [67], former Marxist, neo-Hegelian, presents a reasoned and plausible alternative. He revises Marxism in the light of history since *Das Kapital*, including the failure of communism and the collapse of the USSR. His core value, which he regards as the essential irreducible goal of socialism and Marxism, is a classless society. He believes it to be attainable through education within a competitive market system. He admits that central planning is inferior to competitive markets in efficient allocation of resources, and likely to remain so indefinitely. His approach to a classless society is not by destruction of the old but by reform of education to afford parity of educational opportunity to all.

Like others, Weiss accepts diversity, but to him it means parental freedom to choose among many educational alternatives that which they regard as most appropriate for their children. Weiss recommends much greater reliance on private schools because they can offer the diversity of educational options that public schools will not. This is very different from diversity training in many schools, which indoctrinates class and ethnic warfare against dominant groups, and imposes common views and values: anti-business, anti-religion, anti-Western, pro-alternative life styles.

Why Egalitarianism?

Why the egalitarian religion? Why now, why here? Why downward-biased? Why prevalent in schools of education and in the humanities, much less so in the sciences? There may be an element of resentment in condemning elitism or meritocracy. This is a technological society, an engineering culture; not everyone fits in. Those who can, do; those who can't, teach. But the egalitarian religion is in the American tradition. Aspiration, optimism, belief in progress are characteristics of the society. Why else promote universal college education without a corresponding growth in the positions toward which college graduates have been conditioned to expect?

Society

The egalitarian urge was always there, but contained by status societies, hierarchical societies, monopolies of power and wealth that could enforce their will. Here there was no hereditary aristocracy to monopolize opportunity, social mobility provided insurance against instability. Only the scarcity of opportunity permitted the continuance of an elitist system of high school and college education. With the post-WWII explosion in high school graduation and college attendance, higher education itself became a universal goal within the reach of most. Too many graduates reduced the probability of success. Rather than lower expectations, defining success downward, schools have widened the gap between opportunity and outcome. Everyone can try, but not all succeed. Egalitarianism comes into conflict with competition and meritocracy.

Christopher Boehm [68] claims that an egalitarian ethic is a legacy from prehistoric hunter-gatherers, who cooperate in hunting, share their kill with other members of their social group, and practice sexual division of labor: men are hunters, women care for children and the hearth. It must deal with three threats: the urge to dominate, envy, and the temptation to free ride, all individualist behaviors. Equality-based social traditions of foragers suppress status rivalry and individual competition, enforce consensual decision-making and police free riders. The invention of human moral community is a prerequisite: sharing, cooperation, altruism extend beyond the limits of the nuclear family.

The United States perhaps more than any advanced nation resembles the nomadic hunter-gatherer societies. When most lived off the land in North America, the cultivation of empty lands, the ever-moving agricultural frontier, encouraged mobility. But economies of scale are absent in the hunter-gatherer society. By contrast, modern societies, polities, and economies require scale to function. Scale means hierarchy; equality is replaced by opportunity. This means free rein within limits to the urge to dominate (we call it competition in both economy and polity), but constraints on the accumulation of power and its uses. Today, geographic mobility underlines a weak attachment to others as well as to place. Job mobility, another aspect of nomadism, could also be interpreted as weak attachment to the tribe. In recent decades American society has experienced a decline in attachment to the family and large scale avoidance of the family commitment we call marriage. It has undergone a breakdown in specialization by sex in work, and growth of two-worker families.

American egalitarianism is a powerful and widespread ethic, but it is not a legacy from hunter-gatherers. Sharing beyond the basal social unit, the family, is the exception. Many communities exhibit little civic virtue. Democracy in earlier centuries was limited to an elite, to free persons in a slave or serf society, to property owners, to men only. Egalitarianism is rather associated with democracy as it has evolved in the last two centuries. It is a dream found in most underclasses around the world, and throughout history. But in the United States it permeates the overclasses (with the individualistic qualification that equality is for others). But it coexists with great income inequality, the result of competition for jobs and occupations, much like the feast and famine life of hunter gatherers. The desire for equal outcomes butts heads with the hierarchical structure of occupations and individualism in this country, with elitist traditions and structures in others.

Fogel [69] traces the evolution of egalitarian concepts during the history of this nation, all of them in the name of democracy. He points out that in the 18th century it was not even an individual but a social concept: equal treatment of the American colonies and the home country. During the 19th century, equality of opportunity was the prevailing meaning. It is only in the 20th century that egalitarianism came to mean equalization of outcomes for many, with the resulting debasement of education and decline of learning.

All of Fogel's concepts of egalitarianism are compatible with democracy. But democracy has evolved. In the 19th century, suffrage was limited, hence more compatible with meritocracy than in the 20th, when suffrage was extended to the most risk-averse and least-advantaged elements of the population. Equality of opportunity entails significant risks for all, and high risks for many. Women and disadvantaged minorities tend to be the most risk-averse components of society. Their growing empowerment contributed toward shifting public sentiment toward greater risk aversion, reinforcing the drive for equal outcome. The growth of entitlements, of affirmative action seem to reflect this shift from equality of opportunity to equality of outcome. This evolution seems inevitable. When opportunity was quite limited for most, equality of opportunity was the primary desideratum. As ample opportunity became widely available, aspirations shifted to equality of outcome. Risk-aversion particularly favors downward egalitarianism. A shift from individualism to communitarianism also favors downward egalitarianism over meritocracy or upward egalitarianism. Schools preach the democracy of the underdog.

Today it is obvious that equalization of outcomes is impossible in an advanced society. The quest for identity and self-esteem is diverted from the hierarchy of education/occupation/income to diverse individual objectives not subject to ranking or invidious comparison. The meaning of egalitarianism is up for reconsideration

Fogel [70] speculates about a fourth Great Awakening, a fourth stage in evolution of egalitarianism in America, characterized by the goal of equality of opportunity, but no longer defined in economic terms but in terms of what he calls spiritual or immaterial assets: self-realization. The major change bringing about a rethinking of egalitarian goals is the large increase in longevity and resulting leisure. Adults may live a year in retirement for every two years worked. Even during working years, there is much more leisure than before. Working hours are shorter, labor is less exhausting, housekeeping chores are much reduced by technology and low birth rates. What one does with one's life is no longer defined just in terms of occupation and career; what is one to do with all that leisure?

Fogel's Awakening can also be seen as an individualistic circumvention of hierarchy. Leisure can be more equally distributed than income. Equality of immaterial condition is subjective. Concern for self-esteem, once regarded as a means toward achievement, becomes an end in itself. Self-esteem is redefined as self-realization within myopic limits exemplified by multiculturalism. It defies comparisons, invidious or not, and eludes measurement.

I would add another major change: demographic. The family is no longer a central concern for many people. Many are childless, few have more than two children. This also means that older people will have few siblings, few close relatives. A much higher proportion than before already live alone; marriage is in disarray. One third of households are nonfamily, and 27% are single-person, both rising. Under these conditions self-realization is no longer a family affair.

Whether in economic terms or in years of educational attainment, most of us are much better off than past generations. It is not clear that improvements in material welfare will continue indefinitely. With mass consumption approaching saturation and low birth rates, economic growth loses much of its urgency in the public mind and so does equality of incomes. Perhaps it is time for other priorities. What next in the itinerary of egalitarianism? What are these spiritual or immaterial assets which Fogel says are now the objects of equal opportunity? Millions have always written poetry; this requires no space or equipment. Now we have millions of dedicated potters, painters, musicians, gardeners, collectors of all sorts of things, millions of would-be book authors. Travel and tourism is a growth industry. Every June the papers picture sexagenarians, even octogenarians, who returned to school and are now donning cap and gown. The quest for knowledge in infinite directions may be the most common intangible asset. This is the positive side.

Lee Harris [71] sees a global rather than American historical evolution from hierarchy to egalitarianism. He describes it as evolution from a family model of organization to a team model. It bears substantial similarities to the agenda as described by Eakman, absent the conspiracy undertone and the anti-Americanism. Harris is speaking of society, Eakman of education. Harris views the United States as the paramount example of the team model of society. But it is a development, not an agenda. Team spirit implies downgrading of the family and loyalty to the family, and ridding the world of pursuit of a superior status. "No one is special, and you are condemned for thinking that you are." The team is communitarian, not individualistic. But Harris recognizes that "The struggle for superiority is not simply...narcissism, but an unalterable aspect of the human condition." Teams can be highly competitive, but they are short-lived, transient without attachment to some permanent object of loyalty, a sense of identity.

Schools

The difference between the analyses of Harris and of Eakman is that Eakman sees an attempt by schools to destroy the sense of national identity without providing an alternative object of common loyalty or mission. The effort of schools to tribalize America can be viewed as an attempt to form multiple "teams", to create multiple identities, to undo, wittingly or not, much of a century of progress toward an egalitarian opportunity society. The evolution of democracy from "tribal" societies is a historical fact, but primarily when they share a common identity. It is rare indeed in societies which are truly multicultural, India being the major exception. The difference between Harris and Boehm on one hand and Fogel on the other is that Fogel's fourth awakening may presage the phasing out of common goals, common indicators of attainment, the dissolution of the team, the end of meritocracy as a social value.

Boehm, Barzun, Fogel, Harris all shed some light on egalitarianism as it has evolved in the twentieth century America. But they do not tell us whether egalitarianism can remain compatible with meritocracy; whether downward egalitarianism can be converted into upward egalitarianism, whether reform of school curriculum and pedagogy is in the cards.

What can we conclude? Schools should be responsive to the society in which they function. Egalitarianism practiced by public schools is not a reflection of the values of society but in conflict with them. Schools have gone much too far beyond the 20th century society shift from a selective meritocracy to a bland equality. Skills that should be acquired in schools are now central to economic survival for the individual and for the nation. This was not true in the 19th century. Higher standards are imperative, egalitarian or not.

The job of schools is to train for the future, not the present. Perhaps they are ahead of time. The curriculum is revised to downgrade its academic largely labor-market oriented component and to expand sports, entertainment, knowledge for consumption rather than production. Students prepare for a life containing as much leisure as labor. But preparation for a life full of leisure is not what the public has in mind for tax-supported government schools. It is doubtful whether many would approve such use of their tax payments.

Affluent mass leisure has no historical precedent. Whether it can long persist in a highly competitive global economy is an open question. Schools should not forget that the quality of leisure, the opportunities it offers for self-realization, depend heavily on attainments in the labor market. They pay for leisure and its uses. The unemployed have much leisure but little self-realization. Western Europe is ahead of us: a short work day, very long vacations, early retirement, and chronic high unemployment which many idle citizens regard as state-subsidized leisure. Their economic growth rates have lagged behind America's. With an aging population, absent change in policies and behavior, there is a good chance that growth will come to a halt. The price of affluent leisure in a society of the elderly is high taxation of the labor income of the young.

PEDAGOGY

The discussion so far has focused on what is taught. Here I focus on how, the methods of teaching. A century of progress in theories of education and learning has failed to improve knowledge or learning at all on average, despite undoubted improvements in special education. What is the point of compulsory schooling if after thirteen years many high school seniors remain semi-literate and troubled by simple arithmetic?

A characteristic of elementary school teaching, which it shares to some extent with high schools, is the dominance of method over material, with achievement lost in the shuffle. This is an exaggeration, but it is the preference of schools of education and often the only resort of their graduates, given their lack of command of the subjects they teach. It is a preference that can be justified in early years of school - I would hope that college graduates in education would have mastered subjects taught at the elementary school level. But it cannot be justified at the middle and high school level. Dominance of method over material ill prepares high school graduates for shock therapy in universities where the priorities are reversed, and faculty are selected on the basis of mastery over the subjects they will teach.

Apart from over-emphasis on method, schools of education have a propensity to discard methods which have prevailed for centuries, whose results have been tested and proven for generations, in favor of some current fad or novelty with no evidence for its superiority or even for its adequacy. They are infected with the American ideology of progress, that the old must give way to the new, that new is better. This may be true usually in science and technology, but it does not follow that it applies to the mental process of teaching and learning any subject. Furthermore, progress in science and technology is subject to the test of peer review and competitive markets. This is not true of innovation in a monopoly of supply with compulsory attendance, whose customers are children with parents who are poorly informed or misinformed. What has improved is our knowledge of various types of learning disabilities and how to help students with special needs, largely thanks to new technology, to neurologists and psychologists, not to schools of education. But for the vast majority, cognitive processes have changed little if at all for centuries; there are no new ways of learning, no ways better than existed in the past.

Over the course of centuries we have accumulated much experience on how to learn and how to teach. It is presumptuous to believe that we can reject past experience and greatly improve upon it. I doubt that there are any new teaching methods, all have been tried in many places over millennia. There are new media. Radio and TV are alternatives to reading, for those who have mastered language. Computers and the internet are alternatives to listening, for those who have mastered reading. They are new sources of information, not teaching methods. They may supplement but not supplant the teacher.

According to the new orthodoxy, teachers should not teach; children should learn on their own, with the teacher as "facilitator", whatever that means. If one were to carry this philosophy to its logical conclusion, students should reinvent writing, arithmetic, the wheel. Living in a civilized society should mean that we take some past achievements for granted and do not require children to challenge them or rediscover them. That is a waste of time and energy, besides being a recipe for failure. It is also a pretense; no child will rediscover much of human knowledge, but most children could learn if so directed.

Another element of prevailing pedagogical doctrine is the dislike for facts, the rejection of rote learning, drill, memorization. It is only logical that knowledge of geography and history among high school graduates has declined and is shamefully poor. It is a partial explanation of limited knowledge of the sciences and of foreign languages, all of which require knowledge of numerous facts, which can only be acquired by memorization.

Students are to learn to think, to reason, not to amass facts. It is not evident what they are to reason about, or with what fact-free resources, or how they are to solve what problems, lacking know what or knowhow. It is not clear how students can be tested about these fact-free accomplishments, perhaps one reason for the overwhelming opposition of the educational establishment to standardized tests, and of many to any tests.

Reasoning requires facts, data, sorry about that. How knowledge of facts leads to findings depends on the subject. It may require statistical analysis in some cases: are prices rising or falling? Often the facts are not known, only the problem is known, and the thinker must collect data. What facts to look for? The thinker must have some hypothesis, some assumption, on the basis of which to collect them. But hypotheses do not float in a vacuum; assumptions are not arbitrary. Their selection, and the facts to which they point, must be based on some understanding of the phenomena in question. Suppose we want to know if it is going to rain. We can analyze data from many days, some sunny, some rainy; what do rainy days have in common which sunny days do not? Or if we have no data, we must start with a different question: what are the conditions under which rain is highly probable? What data shall we collect? Temperature, humidity, wind velocity and direction, cloudiness, days of the week, phases of the moon? The choice of a hypothesis or assumption must be based on relevant knowledge. Facts and their interrelations differ from subject to subject. Reasoning is domain-specific. There is no evidence of all-purpose reasoning ability irrespective of subject, nor that recent graduates are better than or even as good in reasoning as their predecessors. Logic, the course devoted to reasoning, is rarely taught. Other courses in which reasoning is essential, such as math and some sciences, are a diminished part of curricula.

Reading

Much attention has been drawn to the poor performance of American students in math and science compared to that of students in many other countries. What has been less noted is their poor performance in reading as well. That alone would handicap students in every other field; its improvement is fundamental. Reading is the key to the whole of human knowledge. It is almost a prerequisite to effective writing, the main means of displaying and applying knowledge in many fields.

The evidence is overwhelming that for alphabetic and syllabic writing systems, phonics is the best method of instruction [72]. Experience for the past three thousand years may not have had the benefit of scientific knowledge of neurological function, but it would be surprising indeed had it not arrived at a superior method. Gatto asserts that basic reading, writing and arithmetic can be taught to motivated students in a hundred hours [73]. According to G. Reid Lyon, chief of the Child Development and Behavior branch of the National Institutes of Health, "...the development of phoneme awareness, the development of an understanding of the alphabetic principle, and the translation of these skills to the application of phonics in reading words are non-negotiable beginning reading skills that all children must master in order to understand what they read and to learn from their reading" [74]. Yet for generations students have been taught by the look-say or whole word approaches as though they were a superior, or even adequate, substitute, in spite of evidence to the contrary.

The phonetic alphabet also provides the simplest and most useful means of classifying knowledge for the purpose of easy retrieval. Without alphabetical ordering there is no single simple way of organizing knowledge, no single way of retrieving it. Some knowledge is lost, or difficult to retrieve from archives or libraries or books.

Widespread look-say approaches to reading at best result in limited literacy. The student can only read words whose shape is familiar, as though reading Chinese ideographs; he cannot read new or unknown words. And he makes many mistakes. It is a tremendous burden on visual memory for a student to advance beyond a puny reading repertoire. The average fourth grade student taught this way can only read some 1,600 words, whereas fourth graders taught phonics read 24,000 words [75]. Learning to read a foreign language this way simply multiplies the burden on memory. For educators who decry rote learning, it is amazing that they endorse a "system" that imposes a heavy burden on visual memory and never leads to full literacy: the ability to read words one has never seen before, and words that one does not know.

Why is it used? Support for them is based on theories, not on scientific evidence. Nevertheless in most public schools phonics is either absent or takes second place despite evidence for its superiority not only for the average student but especially for students with learning difficulties. Some educators feel that it is a new approach. These methods are not new of course; that is how learning to read started in Mesopotamia and other early civilizations long before alphabets were invented. They disguise differences in reading skills: no one is fully literate, there is no simple way of ranking students in reading ability; everyone knows, remembers some words, not others. Whether the egalitarian imperative bears some responsibility for student illiteracy I do not know, but the suspicion is there. It is certainly present in the concept of "reading readiness".

Non-phonic methods are not alternatives, but should be supplements to phonics, to provide interest and motivation for some students, to deal with the fact that written English is not fully phonetic. But the exceptions to phonetic English are themselves phonetic rules. Phonics, whether taught explicitly or absorbed surreptitiously, inadvertently, is the only guarantee against illiterate high school valedictorians. Part of the problem is that generations of teachers still working were taught to downgrade phonics in schools of education, not taught to teach it. It is plausible that preferences of adults are influenced by their learning experiences: Could it be that the limited role of reading as a preferred source of information reflects pedagogy in elementary school?

Literacy

The National Center for Education Statistics conducted national surveys of adult literacy in 1992 and 2003 [76]. It tested for ability to read prose, documents, and quantitative materials, such as graphs, charts, tables. The average score was unchanged for documents and for prose, increased slightly for quantitative, from 275 to 283. However, there was some increase in educational attainment, which should have raised scores. Looking at changes for given levels of educational attainment, prose and document scores were lower in 2003 for every level, and significant for most. For quantitative there were no statistically significant differences. The proportion reading at a proficient level dropped from 15 to 13% for both prose and documents, but was unchanged for quantitative. The proportion below basic, i.e., functionally illiterate, was unchanged at 14% for prose, fell for documents (14 to 12%), and for quantitative (from 26 to 22%). Amazingly, 13% of high school graduates were illiterate in 2003, up from 11% in 1992, and another 39 % (up from 37%) were reading only at the basic level. Most declines in literacy by educational level were not statistically significant, but the sharp decline in the proportion of college graduates (40 to 31) and adults with postgraduate training (51 to 41) who were proficient in reading was statistically significant. These numbers lend credibility to claims, hard to prove, that literacy was higher half a century earlier, and that so was the quality of high school and college graduates.

The vocabulary acquired through normal everyday interaction is limited. The much greater vocabulary of educated adults is learned mainly through reading. The decline in reading by adults is bad news. It can be explained only in part by the popularity of radio, TV and now the internet as alternative means of obtaining the same information and experience. Those who remain semi-literate, the look-say readers, are permanently handicapped by a small vocabulary, not just a reading vocabulary, but as a speaking and thinking resource as well.

If vocabulary is limited, publications adapt. That is one reason why textbooks on all subjects have become simplified, as have student reading assignments. More demanding textbooks, higher standards require an ability to read only attainable via phonics. Newspapers, magazines and many books will have a much more restricted vocabulary than if there is full literacy. The process is self-reinforcing: readers acquire less vocabulary because publications use fewer and simpler words.

Test scores of draftees in the two world wars, Korea and Vietnam show a decline in literacy over time. There are assertions, hard to verify, of higher literacy in 1850 Boston than in late 20th century. Early claims are also based on the high ratio of some book sales to population. The decline in the 20th century coincided with the de-emphasize of phonics. Correlation is not causation, but how else to explain the decline? Stotsky [77] stresses the decline in vocabulary in elementary school readers over the past century as well as in complexity of sentence structure and paragraph development. Change in reader content and teaching methods have complemented one another.

Students in many school systems spend a great deal of time in their high school junior and senior years memorizing long lists of vocabulary words, the better to confront the SAT. It is an attempt to deceive college admissions officers into thinking that they can read and write. Schools have been doing this for decades, in an asinine effort to compensate for lack of literacy and/or reading or both in elementary and middle school. It does neither, as continued decline in SAT verbal scores suggest. But it does divert time and effort from learning. Teaching to the test is nothing new, just an accusation once aimed at the SAT, now also at the No Child Left Behind legislation. There is little teaching involved in committing students to memorizing vocabulary lists.

Literacy defined as understanding of text is a matter of degree. Outright illiteracy declined during the twentieth century. But the level of literacy among the 'literate' also declined. Nearly half of the adult population reads at the elementary school level and most of the rest at the middle school level. But high performance in reading depends not only on technique employed in learning to read in elementary school but especially on knowledge of the subject involved [78]. Literacy, like thinking, is domain-specific. High level literacy across a broad spectrum of subject matter presumes wide knowledge, not what the average student acquires in primary and secondary public schools. In fact knowledge influences reading technique. Thus the decline in knowledge resulting from the smaller role of academic studies in school and their reduced complexity must bear some responsibility as well. This process is also self-reinforcing: bad teaching methods early on result in a smaller vocabulary, less reading, and greater difficulty in reading. Less reading in turn limits the growth of vocabulary, knowledge, and the attainment of high level reading ability over a wide range of subjects.

The decline in reading of books, especially nonfiction books, equates to a decline in learning and knowledge. There has also been a decline in magazine and newspaper reading and I suspect - I have little evidence - that the greatest decline is precisely in the magazines that have the most to offer in terms of knowledge and thoughtful analysis. My evidence is the frequent invitations I receive to accept a free copy and a discounted subscription to renowned magazines, even two subscriptions for the price of one. The suggestion that people are simply reading all these useful books and magazines on the web instead is preposterous - that is not what people do on the web. Besides, much of the decline in reading took place before there was a web.

Individual knowledge has declined, in history, geography, math and sciences, language, even most social 'sciences'. How do we know? The decline in adult literacy and reading; in SAT and other tests for high school graduates, the decline in GREs taken by college seniors thinking of graduate studies; the pauperization of the textbooks from which students learn.

Meanwhile our needs for learning have increased, especially in the sciences, whose knowledge base keeps growing. The basic tools of learning: literacy and numeracy, have not changed in the past century. Perhaps achievement of numeracy has increased, since now most receive at least 12 years of instruction, whereas a century ago many never made it to the grades which typically study algebra and geometry. But those who did, learned more than they would today. Over the long term, knowledge in some fields may have increased for the same reason: they are studied in high school, which nearly everyone attends, whereas school-leaving in the 8th or ninth grade was typical early in the 20th century. But for a given level of schooling, knowledge has declined.

Reading and Cognition

Literacy is more than the open door to the cumulated knowledge of mankind. It also enhances our ability to learn and to use what we know. Reading and writing represent an evolutionary leap in cognitive ability [79]. To a considerable extent thinking is subvocal speech; those who lack the words are cognitively impaired as well as limited in ability to learn and communicate. Einstein laughed when he was told that, but try to conceive or explain $E=MC^2$ without a large vocabulary of abstract concepts and their corresponding words.

Phonics tutoring of problem readers actually changes how their brains operate, according to a new imaging study from Yale [80]. The researchers imaged the brains of 49 poor readers, aged 6 to 9, while they performed simple letter-recognition tasks. Instructors then gave 37 of the subjects daily phonics tutoring for 8 months, while most of the other 12 got ordinary remedial reading. The phonics students made sustained improvements; brain imaging showed "substantial normalization" of the brain's 'reading pathways' in particular, more activity in an area that recognizes words instantly without first having to decipher them. In many poor readers, "the system is there but has not been activated properly," says coauthor Sally Shaywitz.

There are cognitive differences between readers and nonreaders, as well as between good readers and poor readers. Reading, and writing, are more abstract, objective, analytical, logical, precise, than oral communication [81]. Readers display larger vocabularies and greater range and complexity of expressions. There is some dispute over the extent and nature of cognitive gains associated with literacy, but little doubt that they are significant [82]. Among them are the ability to generalize instead of thinking only in particulars, to use analogy, and to classify according to common abstract properties [83]. Such abilities are not absent among illiterates, but found with much greater frequency among literates.

There are larger claims, that Greek alphabetic literacy was an essential enabling factor in democratic ordering of society and politics, in development of logic, of analytical and critical traditions in the study of nature and history, in the externalization and objectification of notions of time, space, self, and nature [84]. Such claims refer to societies rather than to individuals. Yet the advantages of literacy for individuals must translate into gains for the society at large.

Mathematics

Next to reading, quantitative ability is the most important foundation of learning. Its importance has expanded greatly in the last century, as field after field of knowledge advanced from mere accumulation of data to their systematic organization and the discovery of patterns and rules. This process of evolution, found early in astronomy and physics, more recently has been extended to all the natural sciences, and much of the social sciences. Schools should teach more math than in the past, not less. Elementary understanding of statistics and probability, not part of the traditional math curriculum, is very useful in daily living, not just in technical matters. Humans in their individual lives and in communities are much freer than ever before. They have numerous behavioral choices not open to them in backward societies. They need to know how to understand data and evaluate alternatives.

Math teaching in elementary schools is characterized by exposure to a large number of topics without adequate drill, or understanding, much repetition of the same material in successive grades [85]. Shallow exposure to many topics is also characteristic of secondary school math, but at that level the main problem is that most students take little math relative to their counterparts in other advanced nations, or to previous generations, not in terms of courses but in terms of content mastery. Mathematics is one subject where learning is sequential. Drill and memorization make a contribution to thinking, problem-solving.

In this area too there is resistance to time-proven methods of teaching in favor of new math, fuzzy math, ethnomath, rainforest math, allegedly more creative than routine learning of arithmetic procedures. In extreme cases of child-centered learning, math should be developed by students rather than via abstract principles and 'pseudo-problems' [86]. Each child is expected to reinvent not only arithmetic operations, but perhaps geometry, algebra. Error is tolerated, for whatever reason: in the interests of self-esteem or perhaps the relativity of truth. Under these conditions, who needs math teachers who know math? The National Council of Teachers of Mathematics K-12 curriculum minimizes drill and computation; instead, "do maths" [87]. Its curriculum, adopted in 1989, was endorsed by the Department of

Education in 1999 over the opposition of parents and 200 distinguished mathematicians and scholars. The National Council retreated somewhat in 2006, no doubt in response to poor math scores, but the damage has been done.

Calculators are valuable tools to perform calculations that are time-consuming and error-prone if done with pencil and paper. But would graduates know how to use their calculators and computers to run a regression, or even calculate a percentage? By analogy, one can master a foreign language without memorizing vocabulary or learning grammar; just carry a bilingual dictionary in your pocket and use your vivid imagination.

Stress on problem-solving in real world scenarios seems plausible, on the implicit assumption that students will reason from particular problems and solutions to general principles, thereby learning how to solve a wide variety of other problems. But this rarely happens. Transfer of learning from abstract examples and general principles to real world problems is also difficult, but more likely. This issue extends beyond mathematics: how best to teach and learn to think. One area of mathematics related to real life is statistics, a subject rarely taught

There is little new in any of the new ideas championed by the educational establishment. As to the "new math", whatever that is, my mother was taught that way in the first few years of the twentieth century and was never comfortable with arithmetic. Analytic and critical thinking that cannot prove a geometric theorem or solve a simple algebraic equation is just the high-pitched chirping of a cricket.

These criticisms of practices in teaching reading and mathematics should not be taken as criticism of all innovation in teaching, not even in these fields. I certainly think that old style history, dominated by kings and dynasties, wars and battles should be replaced, although some replacements have proven to be even more absurd. Geography is much more than proper names, boundaries, natural features and resources; it should provide some understanding of geology and climatology. More time, not less, should be devoted to the study of history and geography today than in the past. The world has shrunk, we are all neighbors, and this is the indispensable nation.

Why the continuing prevalence of doctrines not supported by evidence, rejected by research? For one, there is the dominance of the idea of progress, the worship of creativity and innovation, and by nonlogical implication, preference for the new over the old. But also there is educators' longing for professionalism, thus creation of a subject whose experts they can be, in which they seek pride. If physics and biology have much advanced in recent times, education must not be left behind. It too must invent or discover new theories and methods. But education is not a subject, as are physics, biology, history, other standard components of school curricula. It is only a set of processes, one which has not evolved much if at all in many thousands of years; long the proper study of psychologists and now, of neurologists. Change is difficult for high school teachers who did not major in the subject they teach, or even minor in it; for elementary school teachers who were biased in schools of education against traditional ways of teaching the building blocks of cognitive skills. Perhaps the resistance to change is analogous to Thomas Kuhn's discussion of the resistance of the scientific community to new ways of thinking. What educators once saw as new thinking is now old hat.

Critical Thinking

"…most secondary school students are not very proficient in the skills of good thinking. Most of them cannot solve problems, make decisions, or conceptualize very well. Nor are they very skilled at or even inclined to engage in critical thinking, such as detecting bias, identifying point of view, identifying unstated assumptions, or determining the logic of an argument." [88] Schools should teach thinking rather than concentrate on facts, many of transient relevance or dubious accuracy. Teaching to think is a noble goal, but who is to teach, what and how? Much is expected of the teacher in elementary and particularly in high school. Specialization may be a curse, but it is a fact of higher education and of working life justified by limitations of time and other resources.

It is a counsel of perfection. All teachers in middle and high school would have to major in the subject they teach, and perhaps so should teachers in the upper elementary school grades. But this is not enough preparation for teaching critical thinking in each subject. Keefe realizes that it will be necessary to develop appropriate subject curricula, not what is now available, and he suggests we must train cognitive specialists as resource teachers [89]. Today almost no one studies logic in college, certainly not in schools of education, nor is debate a part of one's formal training. Few teachers ever took a course in statistics. These are major tools of thinking, but to use them teachers also need an understanding of the thinking processes of students.

Humans feel, and humans think. It is too much to expect clear consensus definitions of so much of human behavior. The words on which most writers on the subject agree are themselves subject to a wide variety of interpretations: problem-solving, analysis, synthesis, deduction, induction, analogy, extrapolation. The experts, unlike the ideologues, agree on two things: thinking is largely subject or domain-specific, hence should be taught as part of each subject, not as a separate subject of its own; and by implication, it cannot be content-free (college philosophy and psychology majors excepted).

Most educators realize that critical thinking cannot be taught or learned in a vacuum; it must be embedded in a subject [90]. That means knowledge of facts, not just memorization, but understanding that leads to categorization, pattern identification, interrelation, ability to hypothesize. This understanding conflicts with the widespread disparagement of facts and memory as learning aim and method. Rote memory is a very limited tool. Most people can retain in immediate memory the magic number seven *minus* one or two items. It is complex cognitive processing - ordering, analysis, synthesis - which allows us to retain vast amounts of information and to make use of it. Different kinds of thinking are needed for different subjects, different problems. Whether diagnosing an illness or understanding ecological or economic developments, one deals with multiple causes, multiple effects. Some understanding of inductive reasoning is important to disentangle relations and predict outcomes. In some sciences, 'laws' and regularities prevail, and an understanding of deductive logic and traditional mathematics is needed. In other areas, much history, the humanities, quantification may be impossible, and critical thinking remains highly subjective, although causality, comparisons, analogies have a place.

Nisbet et al. [91] studied the effect of training college undergraduates and graduate students in several types of thinking The experimenters tested the generalizability of training in logic and in statistics across and within subject domains. Training in logical reasoning, various causal relations, proved ineffective; there was little transfer of learning. On the other hand, statistical training resulted in wide generalization. When graduate students were broken down by field, there were big gains among medicine and psychology students, fields which deal in probabilities and diverse causal patterns; no gains in chemistry a field which deals with necessary, deterministic causes, or law, another field not ruled by uncertainty. On the other hand. law students were able to transfer training in reasoning about conditional problems. The results confirm Thorndike's findings, that transfer of reasoning across domains occurs only when the domains share pragmatic inferential rules. The only reason to expect better results among high school students is the assumption that you can't teach an old dog new tricks; that students in their early twenties have already learned as much as they are likely to learn about rational behavior, that their response to problems is no longer adaptable.

Stress on thinking conflicts with the widespread stress on feeling, on equal valuation of informed and ignorant opinion, and with non-judgmental attitudes to bias and error. It also conflicts with child-centered education, with autonomy of each student to learn his and her own way, whichever. Unfortunately what passes for critical thinking in many classrooms is no more than the expression of unfounded opinions, of uninformed beliefs. With the intrusion of social issues in every subject, this parody of thinking, reasoning from conclusions to evidence, applies to teachers as well as students. It is odd that teaching to think is a major goal of the same educational ideology that stresses feeling, feeling, feeling.

With the increasing reliance on the internet for information and opinion, critical thinking becomes more important than ever. In the world of print there is much error and distortion, some falsehood, but also some process of review and refereeing before words are set to print. The publisher or editor bears some responsibility for the accuracy of what is printed. Radio and TV as sources of information are not as well monitored as books and magazines, but their public nature, and concerns for advertising revenue, set some bounds on misinformation. There are no such bounds on the internet. There is no procedure for assuring some reliability in the information and opinion provided on the web. It is all up to the reader to distinguish fact from falsehood, reason from ranting.

Another unintended consequence of reliance on the internet for information may be a decline in ability to remember. It may have been originally a limited consequence of print, but the web is worsening the problem. Once transmission of information and knowledge was oral, and human memories the only depositories. The Greeks and other ancient peoples trained their memories. If we are to believe Aristotle, better memories are associated with better thinking. The mind has more to work with. Our store of information and knowledge increases our potential to benefit from reading. Our capacity to mine the internet is enhanced by what we can bring to mind. Our ability to create more complex memories, more associations and longer-lived memories depends on the building blocks which we call rote memories. But the ready availability of information on the web reduces the need to remember, to reason, to know; one can always look up. The defamation of memorization in schools degrades our cognitive resources.

Child-Centered Education

Traditional teaching is libeled as following a factory assembly line or military model: children arrayed in rows and columns, a teacher lecturing and disciplining in front with no allowance for differences in ability, learning preferences, learning rates, school days and topics rudely interrupted by bells every 40 minutes. Students are all at attention, memorizing, calculating. given standardized tests. Child-centered education eliminates the teacher, who becomes a facilitator, an advisor, resource person, anything but an expert expounding a subject to all. The rows ands columns are reassembled into tables in random patterns, individual students are bundled into small groups or round the campfire circles facing each other. It is harder to get rid of the bell. Tests, grades are invidious comparisons to be avoided as much as possible. Nevertheless students learned more in the bad old days.

School is an unnatural environment, whether it follows the factory model, the military model, the campfire model, or the Stonehenge model, with students scrunching every which way on the floor facing each other. Planned, organized learning all day is 'unnatural'. So for that matter is most work, whether on an assembly line, behind a desk, or at a work table. I am not sure what is meant by 'natural': Hobbes, Rousseau or Thoreau, hunting and gathering, wielding a hoe, or just playing around. Natural learning is unplanned, largely accidental, by trial and error, by imitation, none of it systematic or coherent. What makes 'natural' so desirable, such a widespread standard, I have no idea. Always thought that civilization was a revolt against nature.

Students differ and schools should adapt teaching and learning to individual learning styles [92]. At the limit this approach becomes special education for everyone. It differs from the tutorial system of the traditional elites in that it is not primarily a one to one relation; children are clustered, and expected to learn from each other, not just from the teacher. It may also differ in that what is to be learned is shaped by individual student's interests and abilities, not by social desiderata. The only thing wrong with this approach is that it is Utopian. There are teachers who can meet the challenge, just as there have been teachers who succeeded in teaching six grades in a one-room school house, but they are few. Preparing and following a prescribed lesson course requires less knowledge on the part of the teacher, much less skill, than a child-centered, individualized approach. Nor is it clear that children in all communities would cooperate in such an unstructured environment.

There are different ways of learning. People have learning preferences, differential learning abilities. Teaching should take this in consideration. Neil Fleming [93] has developed a DARK (visual, auditory, reading/writing, kinesthetic) questionnaire to determine the learning preferences of students. Only 17 percent choose reading/writing as their dominant preferred method, 17.3% choose kinesthetic, despite the limited scope of material subject to kinesthetic learning. Visual-representative and kinesthetic are limited in the subject matter they can communicate. One does not learn languages that way, nor mathematics nor grammar. Visual-symbolic, or reading, has a very extensive range; so does aural symbolic learning: speech. Each can be supplemented in some subjects by visual-representative methods: illustrations. Reading/writing (visual-symbolic) is by far the most efficient method for most purposes; a decent reader should read faster than normal speech; he has control of the material: what to read carefully, what to skim, what to skip, whether to start at the conclusion. Quantifiable subject matter is often better presented in tables or graphs. A mortality table, or a weather map, contains much more and more precise information than a slew of sentences. But a high proportion of high school seniors cannot understand graphs or cope with arithmetic. Each approach must be evaluated in terms of the subject to be learned, not just student preferences. Fleming stresses that what he tests is preferences, not abilities

Some children learn best visually, others by ear. Teaching to the child should recognize this. Theoretically, literacy is irrelevant for learning by those who learn best by ear. But all, whatever their learning preferences or abilities, will live and work in a world that is vision-dominant. Numeracy also is important in life and work, whatever the abilities or interests of individuals. Numeracy too is vision-dominant. Homework, perhaps unintentionally, offers a learning mode different from that of the classroom. So do correspondence courses, which today can be both audio and visual. Apart from sensory differences in learning, there are cognitive differences. Some learn easily by deductive methods, others inductively. Some are better able to cope with ambiguity and uncertainty than others. Presentation of material in different ways enhances learning and retention. It is redundancy more than repetition.

Sensory differences in learning abilities are not all given at birth. In the early years they can be modified to some extent by suitable training. Sensory preferences are not the only differences in learning styles. Some learn faster than others, some learn better than others. We should do what we can for those who have learning problems, but dumbing down the curriculum is not to be confused with child-centered education. Nor does taking differences into account mean letting students run the class. What they imply is that there is no such thing as a or one best method of teaching. What all effective teaching has in common is motivation, not method.

The several 'intelligences' are not interchangeable. There is little transfer between some pairs. There are opportunities for any one single intelligence, or any one learning style, but they are limited. Learning methods to a considerable extent are subject or domain-dependent. Most worthwhile achievements require collaboration of more than one "intelligence", much learning requires more than one learning style to be efficient or even possible. One cannot learn to play a musical instrument visually, but one cannot learn to read music any other practical way. Both are needed, as well as kinesthetic skills. Math beyond the elementary level is abstract, extrasensory; visual expression is for communication and aid to memory.

Student-friendly teaching is not related to high achievement. The nations whose students do best in international math and science competitions, and which score high also in reading and thinking, are not noted for student-friendly teaching, quite the contrary. They do so well not because their top students are so good, but because their worst students do so well. Demands are high, and students are expected to meet them. The demands of child-centered education also appear to conflict with the teaching of critical thinking. Reasoning is not child-specific.

Scribner and Cole [94] examine the difference between formal and informal education. Formal education is the traditional highly structured classroom. Informal in this case refers to practical daily activities, toward which child-centered education has moved. Their findings shed some light on differences in outcome between subject-centered and child-centered schooling. The principal difference is generalizability: top down in formal teaching, bottom-up in child-centered learning. The first solves individual problems as examples of a class of problems. The second deals with them singly, in isolation; there is less structure in identification of problems, in organization of knowledge. Informal education is particularistic; it matters who a student is rather than what the student accomplishes. The value of information is related to its source, not to its content and consequences. Informal education fuses intellectual and emotional domains. "How do you feel? is the mantra of child-centered education.

Stebbins and others [95] studied 22 teaching methods for children from kindergarten through the third grade. They were classified in three groups: 1. direct instruction basic skills models, structured, formal; 2. cognitive conceptual skills models focusing on problem-solving skills, learning to learn; and 3. affective-cognitive models focusing on self-concept and attitudes toward learning, on student self-guidance. The traditional basic skills approach came out ahead not only in learning basic skills, but also on tests of self-concept. No approach proved notably superior in raising scores in cognitive-conceptual skills. But what is true of a group is not necessarily true of every member of that group.

If individuals have particular preferences and/or abilities, so do subjects and jobs. It is important to keep in mind that each individual will have to adapt to the world as it is; the world - the labor market in particular - is not going to adapt to the individual. Many teachers don't seem to understand the long run consequences to students of their educational practices. The conformity all students must eventually confront is not that preached at school. Taking stock of individual learning abilities and preferences should be used in advising on high school electives, in choosing college majors and electives, in job, occupation and career choices.

The stress on child-centered education may be related to the opposition to tracking, which is itself an attempt to respond to individual differences. The more heterogeneous the class, the stronger the argument for focusing on the child rather than exclusively on the subject. With homogenous classes, there is less need.

Special Education

Child-centered education usually implies considerable student autonomy on pace, content, method of learning, with limited supporting role for the teacher. Special education is a radically different sort of child-centered education, primarily for children with some learning disability. It is focused on eliminating or circumventing the disability, not on the student's preferences and interests, with special ed teachers very much in the foreground. Classes are small; instruction is by necessity child-centered, although the ultimate aim of special education is main streaming and subject mastery. Many special education students cannot learn in the average class, and some are disruptive, interfering with learning by others. Special education is a form of tracking, one which most teachers support.

There has been a large increase in proportion of students in special education since the passage of the Education for Handicapped Children Act of 1975, to 13.8% in 2005. This amounts to child-centered education for those who most need it. A partial reason for this large number is the failure of pedagogy in the first few years of elementary school. Some students who don't learn to read or to do simple arithmetic end up in special education who would not have, had effective means of instruction been used. The brains of many young children with 'learning disabilities' are malleable and might have adapted to standard methods had they been used effectively. Instead they are segregated and teaching is often adapted to their preferences and strengths instead of encouraging them to adapt. This is not to deny that most students in special education need and benefit from special trained help, whatever methods of instruction are used in the first grades. It is one means of promoting students regardless of attainment but not necessarily an example of social promotion. Special education students may progress at a rapid rate and fully deserve advancement to a higher grade. But their curricula and their standards differ by definition from those of mainstream students. Special education makes standard teaching easier by narrowing the teaching range, benefiting all students. It avoids failing grades or unacceptably low standards.

CONCLUSION

Public schools have defaulted on their responsibilities, pursuing other goals. Neither their curricula nor their standards have adjusted to the needs of students, the economy or the society. Most students will work, and the world of work is unavoidably competitive and meritocratic whereas the world of schools has become egalitarian and narcissistic. It is a conflict that cannot be resolved in favor of the egalitarian doctrines dominating public school systems; the price would be too high. Egalitarian markets don't work; even bureaucratic markets don't work very well. Schools must prepare students for living and working in an adult world. That world is not a Walden Pond or a Disney World and never will be. It is for most people, steel and concrete, glass and plastic. It values effort and results, not excuses and explanations, and cares little for self-esteem.

Ultimately the culture, the labor market, is not going to adapt to the individual; it is the individual who must adjust. This is not as insensitive as it sounds. There is great diversity out there. Engineers are not noted for their verbal fluency; many of them don't need it. But then they should let others write manuals for the general public. Historians are not noted for mathematical ability, but in most cases they don't use it. Yet in our age of over-information, a knowledge of statistics might be helpful. Lawyers need high verbal ability, but not calculus. But they need to be adept in the quasi-mathematical skill we call deductive logic, and for many, inductive reasoning as well. There are jobs and occupations for those who learn by ear and for those who learn visually, as well as for those with the kinesthetic abilities of a surgeon, musician, or athlete, even those whose major gift is taste or smell. But the distribution of jobs and occupations is determined by technology and market demand, not by learning preferences and abilities. There never will be a perfect match. Spoken language is oral by definition; written language, including mathematics, is visual. There is little special education in college, and almost none in the labor market.

The purpose of schools is to prepare the next generation to function successfully in the society in which they live. This means ensuring that they acquire the basic skills necessary to get a start and to continue learning after school as their particular needs require and as the needs of their society change. This involves also encouraging appropriate behavior patterns. It emphatically does not include an attempt to shape pliable children's' minds to the mold of whatever particular ideal society is fashionable in schools of education or seems ideal to particular teachers. Students will live and work in this evolving society, they are not to be trained as clandestine agents of change to suit their mentors. Schools should be the servants of society, not its makers.

Chapter 4

COLLEGE EDUCATION

"..here are college graduates, many of them cannot read accurately or write clearly, cannot do fractions or percentages without travail and doubt, cannot utter their thoughts with fluency or force...cannot trust themselves to use the foreign language they have studied for 8 years, and can no more range conversationally over a modest gamut of intellectual topics than they can address their peers consecutively on one of the subjects they have studied" [1]. This is the admittedly elitist verdict of Jacques Barzun nearly half a century ago, after the large increase in college enrollments following World War II, but before the even larger increase by the baby boom generation and the dramatic decline in standard test scores of high school graduates. Chapter 4 will examine the consequences for colleges of admitting high school graduates who are ill-prepared for college work, and how colleges have adjusted to a combination of decline in entering student achievement and increase in college enrollments.

EDUCATIONAL ATTAINMENT

Education is widely viewed as the open sesame to good jobs, desirable occupations and careers, as well as to income. One problem with this vision is the frequent failure to distinguish between individual and collective opportunities and gains: the Principle of Composition. More education and training may be of great benefit to specific individuals, but have little effect on the n's occupational structure and desirable job and career openings.

Trends

A large increase in educational attainment began immediately after WWII. It was a response to the subsidy provided by the GI Bill of Rights rather than demand for college graduates. The proportion of 25-29 year olds with college degrees nearly doubled from 5.9% in 1940 to 11% in 1960. The generation that benefitted from it is now past retirement age, but its example has been followed by the generations that came after. College completion doubled again to 22.5% of 25-29 year olds in 1980. The increase since 1980 has been slow, to 29.3% in 2002, down to 28.4% in 2006 [2]. The proportion of the population 25-29 years of age and older without a high school diploma sank from 61.9% in 1940 to 39.3% in 1960 to 13.6% in

2006. (Official figures on high school completion rates include GED and other high school equivalency tests.)

College entry has become a quasi-entitlement, a generation after high school graduation became the norm. The proliferation of community colleges offered local enrollment opportunities to many who would not have been accepted in traditional colleges and universities or who could not afford to go away to college. Some two thirds of high school graduates enroll in college; about half of them earn a four-year college degree.(Others finish two-year programs, most of which are job training programs, which in the not so distant past were taught in high school.)

Inequality in educational attainment has been greatly reduced. In 2005, the attainment of 76.7 percent of persons 25 years of age and over was concentrated in a four-year range, from high school graduation to a bachelors degree. In 1970, to reach an equivalent concentration, 78.3 percent, the range of educational attainment must be extended to eight years, from the 7th grade through the third year of college [3]. Inequality in educational achievement is another matter; learning disparities which widened throughout primary and secondary school continued to widen in college. It is not clear that reduced inequality in attainment has narrowed the gap in achievement; it may have increased it.

Increasing educational attainment of the employed labor force was a bottom-up process, greatly reducing differences in attainment. The difference in median educational attainment between the most educated occupation, professional, and the least educated, farming, shrank dramatically from 7 years in 1970 to 4.5 in 1991; for non-farm laborers, the gap narrowed from 5.8 to 4.4 years [4]. (Changes in occupational classification make it impossible to extend this time series.) In spite of large scale immigration of poorly educated workers in the past two decades, the median educational attainment of the two occupational groups with the lowest attainment: operators, fabricators and laborers, and farming, forestry and fishing, both averaging 12.4 years, slightly exceeds a high school diploma.

Attainment and Ability

From the 1920s to the 1960s there was an increase in the average ability of college students [5]. By then nearly all high school graduates in the top decile went to college, and most of those in the top quartile. What has happened since is, first, with a large increase in the proportion of the age group completing high school, some decline in the average ability of high school graduates. Second, the large increase in the proportion of high school graduates going to college had to reduce somewhat the average ability of college students, since most of the increase had to come from those in the bottom two quartiles. This helps explain the decline in SAT scores, and also in the GRE (Graduate Record Examination) scores.

As widely noted, high school education has been dumbed down, to accommodate the increase in share of the age group allowed to complete high school, as well as the egalitarianism that mandates grade inflation and curriculum debasement in elementary as well as in high school. Thus a decline in achievement was superimposed on a decline in average ability. Nevertheless, the proportion of high school graduates completing college has risen. It is implausible to claim that the average ability of college students is higher when 60 % of the age group enter college and 30% graduate than it was when 20% entered college and 10% graduated.

Open admission to state colleges and universities for graduates of high schools in the state is an old practice. Often the majority of freshmen would have to take noncredit math and English courses to bring them up to minimum speed. But once admitted, they were subjected to a Darwinian selection process. Now the Darwinian process has been watered down in admissions, in grading, in graduation. The right to admission has been constrained: admitted to some campus, but not necessarily to the flagship campus, which has become highly selective as a result of the huge increase in applicants. Once, college applicants were a small minority of their age group; now some 60% of the age group; but the attrition rate has fallen in four-year colleges and universities. Among 25-29 year olds, there was one college graduate for every 5.5 high school graduates in 1960, every 2.5 by 2006. The implication is a decline in quality of college graduates.

Most colleges and universities claim that they have become more selective, their students are better. For most colleges this claim borders on a Munchausen syndrome. It implies that students who did not go to college in the past were better than those who did, and thus increasing college enrollments raises ability. Socioeconomic status was a major factor in high school completion long ago, the main factor in college attendance and completion in the past, and still a factor today. But it is not plausible to argue that the socioeconomically gifted are less able than the socioeconomically deprived. Yet this is the implication of any claim that nearly tripling the share of an age group completing college sinc e 1960 is associated with an increase in ability of college students.

If standardized test scores taken by college seniors are down for most majors, either graduate enrollments in these fields are down or admission standards are lower and so is the quality of graduate students, and recipients of masters and PHD degrees. In fact, enrollments are up, and so are the number of graduate degrees awarded in most fields. In 1950, the number of masters degrees awarded was 13.4% of the number of bachelors degrees; the ratio doubled by 1960 and reached 40% in 2005. The ratio of doctorates awarded to bachelors degrees more than doubled from 1.5% in 1950 to 3.8% by 1970, changing little since. The large increase in graduate degrees was predominantly in the disciplines whose GRE scores have fallen; the number declined in most of the disciplines whose GREs have risen, math and science in particular. The professional schools whose graduates must pass licensing tests have remained relatively immune in curriculum content and admission standards.

Let us not pretend that changes over time in the quality of college students or in the contribution of colleges to student learning can be measured with any precision. Prevalent impressions are that both have declined; there is substantial circumstantial evidence that they have; and to my knowledge there is no evidence that they have not.

DIVERSITY OF POSTSECONDARY EDUCATION

What does college attendance, what does a college diploma mean? There is a wide variety of post-secondary institutions, great diversity in institutional objectives, in the programs offered, in students, and in outcomes for students. The community colleges, most of them two-year colleges offering associate degrees, are closely linked to the local economy and its needs. Local governments provide a significant share of their financial resources, and their students are predominantly local. Much of what they offer is training for specific occupations with local job openings. They are carrying on the task once performed by high schools, but much expanded, as more occupations shift training from job to school. They also teach remedial courses and the survey and introductory courses available in four-year colleges.

Community colleges serve a diverse clientele. Some students attend because their weak academic records deny them admission to universities.They hope to prove by performance that they are college material and gain admission later. Some attend for reasons of economy; they commute from home, pay low tuition, and perhaps transfer to a university offering a wider choice of courses in their major for their junior year. And for many, community colleges provides vocational training earning a certificate or an associate degree, leading to jobs. As the destination of many of the students who would not have applied or who would not have been accepted in college in the past, their main problem is the low level of ability/achievement of students. Attrition rate is high. Two-year college enrollments have increased from 19.6 % to 37.1% percent of total postsecondary enrollment between 1965 and 2005 [6].

At the opposite extreme are the universities with large graduate programs which are highly selective in admissions. Whereas community colleges are egalitarian, the universities are highly meritocratic, anti-egalitarian, rejecting many or most applicants. They also follow a policy of diversity, accepting students from selected minorities with lower qualifications than applicants from the majority. These two policies conflict to some extent, since the second is a hybrid: meritocratic within privileged groups, egalitarian between groups. Since both meritocracy and diversity require acceptance of students who cannot pay the full tuition, large subsidies in the form of fellowships, scholarships, loans are involved, leading to additional discrimination favoring students who can pay full cost to share the burden of accepting many who cannot. It's a complex tradeoff, whose balance will differ from one campus to another.

To be competitive in attracting the best students by whatever definition, universities invest in facilities and services that potential students find attractive. These are consumer benefits, most of them having nothing to do with education: luxurious accommodations, fancy sports facilities and entertainment opportunities, a beautiful campus: expenditures which drive up tuition costs, which have been rising much faster than the cost of living. An exclusive and gifted student body is a major contributor to university prestige, which in turn attracts donations from various sources and research funds mainly from government [7]. Many universities pay for student conspicuous consumption by skimping on teaching resources: overuse of graduate students for teaching, grading and assistance.

Much of this downgrading of teaching is the result of the huge increase in numbers of students applying to colleges and of college enrollments. Before this happened, elite universities were not so meritocratic; a large proportion of their students were the children of (wealthy) alumni. This had to change, first in order to compete for the promising students who in the past would not have gone to college at all, to protect their prestige as elite schools; second, because of changes in ideology toward college for all and egalitarianism and diversity defined in ethnic terms; and third, perhaps because alumni were having fewer children.

The problems then are the neglect of good teaching and the very high and rising costs of university study. Unfortunately they are not confined to a handful of brand-name universities. Too many less distinguished universities are more concerned with keeping up appearances or pretensions than providing a quality education. There is limited room at the top. Most of the universities with pretensions for elite status are bound to fail, and the student bears the consequences.

Another concern is research. Sponsored research is a source of revenue which can be used for multiple purposes. Research standing is also a matter of prestige which enhances ability to attract good students and research funding at the departmental level. There is much confusion between quality and quantity. The commandment of publish or perish for faculty tenure and promotion decisions is one byproduct. Time devoted to writing papers on narrow topics subtracts from time for teaching and students, leading to reduced teaching loads and the use of graduate teaching assistants. There is increasing reliance on nontenured and part time faculty for teaching. Research can also subtract from time available to keep up with the broader field, an important constituent of good teaching. Some departments with pretensions go so far as to discourage young faculty from wasting too much time on students or courses.

Prestige attracts top students, sponsored research, donations. These objectives are complementary. But what is the point, the ultimate goal? It appears to be prestige as an end in itself, since the top students in many cases are better entertained than educated.

In between the elite and wannabe universities and the community colleges are many other universities, and the four-year colleges. It is not possible to generalize. There are universities closely linked to state or community, which give priority to teaching and learning. There are numerous state universities with more than one campus, each with different admission policies, curriculum, objectives. Among the four-year colleges, there are elite institutions and others that strive for elite status; they too spend much of their revenue on consumer facilities and services for students. But they lack a cheap supply of graduate teaching assistants, thus faculty are more involved in teaching and advising students. Publishing papers may also be a priority, but the absence of graduate students as research assistants limits the possibilities for sponsored research.

The debasement of curriculum and degree requirements is commonplace in brand name and bargain basement colleges and universities alike.

DEBASEMENT OF COLLEGE EDUCATION

Admission Criteria and Enrollments

There is an abrupt change between the senior year of high school and the first year of college: from teachers whose major was in most cases education, to teachers with advanced training, often a PHD, in the specific subjects that they teach. They are not all good teachers, but they know their subject matter. This is one, not the only, reason why American colleges are highly regarded abroad, whereas primary and secondary schools are not. Unlike public primary and secondary schools, tenure and promotion are meritocratic, even if professional success is biased toward production of largely useless publications

Admission criteria for four-year colleges and universities have changed; in evaluating applicants they include a wide range of activities, such as sports, community service, hobbies, most of which have little to do with ability to meet college academic requirements. These additional considerations give admissions officers the opportunity if they so choose to downgrade objective tests of achievement/ ability and stress nonacademic considerations. At the high school level this means a redirection of time and energy from learning, fattening their resumes with sports, community service, and various activities other than on academic work because they are told that they must do this to be admitted to a college of their choice.

One reason for the change in admissions criteria is high school grade inflation, so that admissions officers find it ever more difficult to differentiate students by grades. One would expect greater stress on the SAT, especially SAT II, the best predictor of performance [8]. It tests for achievement in subject matter, not just ability. If this were the case, colleges would apply pressure in high schools to improve the subject content of their teaching. But there is strong objection to SAT or any standardized tests that can rank high school seniors by likelihood of doing well academically (and can also rank teachers and schools). The attack on the SAT comes both from the high school establishment which does not wish to see its shortcomings highlighted nor corrected ("teaching to the test" is a dirty phrase), and from colleges which do not wish to be constrained in acceptances or enrollments by any one test. A third, often the most important reason, is to allow colleges to circumvent standardized tests and meritocratic criteria in deciding whom to accept.

Colleges, both public and private, have an imperative to maintain enrollments, and a strong incentive to increase enrollments. A rising share of the age group entering college, multiplied by the huge baby boom generation resulted in a five fold increase in undergraduate enrollments between 1945 and 1975 and an even larger increase in graduate enrollments. Many colleges and universities overexpanded and over-hired, and faced the prospect of empty dorms and the burden of too large a tenured faculty [9]. The next generation was smaller, the 18-21 age group peaked in 1985 and remains below that level. The proportion completing high school is static. Colleges have high fixed costs: their infrastructure and its maintenance, and their tenured faculty, hence the pressure to maintain enrollments.

Colleges compete for better students; but many compete for students period. With most high school seniors applying to several colleges, all but the most prestigious colleges must accept far more than they can accommodate, guessing each year what proportion of acceptances will show up for classes. That means lower minimum standards. Expanded remedial college course work, much of it non-credit, is one consequence of the recruiting competition which raises costs but is necessary to avoid further lowering of standards.

Admissions officers must become acquainted with many high schools and their guidance counselors, spend more time reviewing applications and recruiting better students. They also have to be concerned with de facto ethnic and socioeconomic quotas. It is an added expense of college education.

The incentive to maintain or increase enrollments, to limit attrition, does not disappear after the freshman year. In fact, it persists even at the graduate school admission level. The incentives of top administrators to maintain or increase admissions convert into incentives to maintain enrollment at the departmental and individual faculty level. New faculty cannot hope for tenure if enrollments in their department and their specialty are dropping. Nor can they expect favorable student evaluations if they are too demanding. Tenured faculty can also feel threatened if they run short of students. Even if they have job security, they may face less desirable work assignments.

Despite the decline in quality of applicants and of admission standards, graduation rates have not fallen. The large increase in college applicants has permitted some elite institutions to increase the quality of their student body. The average net result across all higher education has been a decline in quality of both entering and of graduating students. College faculty has multiplied in numbers in step with enrollment while alternative employment opportunities for highly educated workers in the private sector have grown. It is only reasonable to assume that quality of faculty has also declined.

Apart from institutional incentives to maintain or increase enrollment, many public postsecondary educational institutions are required to accept students who graduated from high schools in the state. One response has been the differentiation of many state universities with two or more campuses, with open admission to some, not to others.

Grade Inflation

Grade inflation took off in the late 1960s and early 1970s as a means of avoiding the draft but has continued to this day for quite different reasons. Colleges cannot fully compensate for the achievement deficiencies of high school graduates either by remedial study or by Darwinian selection for advancement and graduation. They are not immune from the egalitarian values defining deficiency downward. The grade inflation prevalent in lower schools has infiltrated college halls, reducing the role of academic selection.

Grade inflation is a near-universal phenomenon among colleges and universities. In 1969, only 7% of college student grades were As, by 1993 this figure had risen to 26%; the percentage of Cs and lower dropped from 25 to 9 [10]. This can only mean inflation, certainly not improved achievement. GRE scores on average have declined for most majors. Large changes in the composition of the industry of higher education, in the students, and in curriculum preclude any precise indicator of overall grade inflation. Test contents may change over decades.

Elite universities are not exempt. In Harvard, 2000-1, 49% of undergraduate grades were As, double the 1966-7 share; only 6% were Cs or lower, compared with 28% in the earlier year; and 91% of seniors graduated with honors [11]. They will claim that they have become more selective, and more diverse (somehow this strikes me as a possible contradiction), and this is true of some elite universities. But graduation with honors is a relative achievement; for 91 % to achieve it is absurd.

Grade inflation has contributed to an equivalent of lockstep advancement from freshman to senior year and on to a diploma. It is economic pressure or disinterest more than academic failure that limits graduation rates. In many colleges and universities, grade inflation might be explained by the need to maintain enrollments, but not in the elite universities. Down the road, colleges are undergoing the same egalitarian leveling down experienced in elementary and high schools, lowering the quality of graduates, including candidates planning to teach in elementary and secondary schools. School failure has been promoted to college.

The value of grades as information for prospective employers, or for graduate school admissions, has been compromised. But there are other consequences. The incentive for students to do their best has been weakened. Grade inflation rewards mediocrity and discourages excellence, and student choice of majors and elective courses has been biased by expected grades to a much greater degree than in the past. For grade inflation has not been across the board; there has been much more in some disciplines than in others, and there are differences between instructors, even when teaching the same course.

The extent of grade inflation varies by discipline. A detailed study of undergraduate enrollments and grades in Duke University, 1998-'99, by Johnson found that majors in biology, chemistry, economics, math and physics received lower grades in courses in their major than they did in other courses. On the other hand, majors in the humanities and social sciences other than economics received higher grades in their major than in other courses.

[12] These differences in grading practices influence the choice of majors and the choice of elective courses. The study concludes that the grading disparity may reduce enrollment in natural science and math courses by as much as 50% [13] and reduce the number of majors as well. (It contributes to the shortage of potential high school math and science teachers and reduces the number of jobs for science and math teachers in college.) This pattern of grade inflation in Duke is believed to prevail throughout postsecondary education.

Why grade inflation and disparity across disciplines? Student evaluations of teachers play a significant role. They also contribute to watering down the cognitive component of a college education. Their evaluations are highly correlated with the grade they received or expected. Their choice of electives, and of instructors, is influenced by expected grades. Teachers on the other hand think, and rightly so, that their chances for tenure, pay increases and promotion are affected by student evaluations. The result is a built-in mechanism generating higher grades. Faculty compete for favorable evaluations by simple and amusing presentations. A faculty member who does justice to a complex subject, who has high expectations of his students, whose grades are not all As and Bs, risks receiving unfavorable evaluations and facing low enrollments. Faculty on short term contracts, adjuncts, and student assistants are particularly vulnerable [14]. At the limit, the asylum is run by the inmates: child-centered education promoted to college.

Student evaluations can make a positive contribution by informing administration if a professor is late or misses classes, whether he is available to students during office hours, whether he is responsive to student questions and concerns. But on the quality of a professor's class performance, the organization of subject matter, the clarity of explanations, the students best qualified to pass judgement should be teaching the course, not taking it. Evaluations from mature, well-prepared and motivated students would be helpful. But they are largely conducted by students most of whom are poorly prepared, many of whom are immature, and lacking in learning focus and motivation.

But why is grade inflation less prominent in science, math, and economics than in the humanities and some social sciences than ? Is it their content, facts and laws, or the scientific method of establishing them? In the humanities, standards are subjective; besides, there is no objective truth. Grading is much more of a burden in humanities courses than in math and science courses, and less easily defended. But these reasons were true a hundred years ago. It is in part the widespread prevalence of the ideology noted in lower schools. Grades rank students, and that is not an egalitarian thing to do; low grades are not good for student psyches. The role of ideology is new. I believe it explains the differences between the sciences and the humanities not only in grade inflation, but in changes in curriculum discussed below.

Curriculum Degradation

Unfortunately the changes in curriculum and the dominance of ideology in primary and secondary schools has been exported to colleges. First, college admission standards have been lowered to permit enrollment of a larger proportion of the age group than ever before. Absent a Darwinian selection process after admission, ie, a drop in college graduation rates, a decline in quality of college graduates was inevitable. Second, grade inflation has become the rule in most colleges, implying promotion regardless of achievement. Third, college curricula have followed the lead of primary and secondary schools, declining in academic content requirements and adopting a student-selected menu of courses as qualification for a degree.

College courses required of all students, starting with freshman English, were intended to provide a common core of competence and knowledge for all graduates. The college and university major was intended not just to produce a well-rounded and informed citizen, but to train in depth in some field, often but not always for an occupation, so that graduates could compete for jobs.

The former aims of education have not been rejected, but elbowed aside in terms of course requirements in a variety of spheres of knowledge. Specific curriculum requirements, the common core that once characterized college graduates, have been reduced or eliminated. The student is free to pick and choose from a large and diverse curriculum menu cafeteria-style. Faculty advising is forgotten by most students and most faculty.

Courses and majors with minimal cognitive content have multiplied, replicating the multiculturalism, group identity and secular religion ideology of lower schools. Facts, objectivity, reason, analysis are neglected in favor of values, subjectivity, relativity, ethical implications of knowledge [15]. The difference is that they lead not to higher levels of schooling but to graduation and a job market that has no openings for majors in multiculturalism, egalitarian ideology, ethnic identity, and few in secular religions. The students flocking to such courses often graduate with an interdisciplinary major in Intolerance. If any reader has any doubts, or has a child looking forward to college, I recommend looking up universities on the web and their undergraduate course offerings in the humanities and soft social sciences. It would be helpful to know what courses are taught by regular faculty, not by teaching assistants, but that information is not readily forthcoming.

In the past the main major lacking much intellectual content was physical education created for the primary purpose of allowing intellectually challenged school athletes to continue playing on college teams for four years. (This is not true of physical education training not intended for athletes.) Not any more. There is no simple way of assessing course content of history and social sciences, as there is for high school by examining the textbooks and teachers' guides. Departments still have the standard disciplinary courses. It is what goes on in the classrooms, in other departmental courses, and in readings other than standard texts that have changed.

The proportion of the freshman class taking remedial English and math has increased, given poor preparation in high school. But that has not preserved the integrity of these subjects. Math has suffered least, since students can avoid it in their schedules. But English has suffered from professorial attacks on grammar and logic, from emphasis on personal experience and expression rather than clear communication, from inroads of multiculturalism which views standard English as a language of oppression [16]. As in high school, reading lists tend to exclude the classics but feature pop culture fashions of the day. There is much deconstruction and ideological pandering in readings and in class.

In college, high school social studies are fragmented along departmental domains: sociology, political science, economics, psychology. As in the case of English, course content and professorial interests and perspectives go hand in hand. Pretend-social 'sciences' as taught in many colleges lack the scientific attitude, method, the interest in testing and refutation that 'science' implies [17]. A common idea of refutation is the ad hominem argument: the writer or speaker holds wrong views or values. This amounts to reasoning from instead of toward conclusions. Objectivity is a myth, truth and knowledge are social constructs. There is much ideology, and much victimology, in texts and in class. Sociology is the field which departs most from objective coherent analysis of social phenomena, economics is least affected, because it requires math and statistics for majors, subjects beyond the reach of ideology.

D'Souza [18] provides examples from some of the leading universities. Examples can be multiplied, but it is impossible to quantify their extent. Courses and majors in women's studies, black studies, peace studies, gay studies and deconstruction are now standard. Most of them are short on discipline and job prospects, long on opinion. They serve as a device for awarding degrees with little prospect of labor market payoff. The secular religion of victimhood has replaced the Christian tradition of sainthood and martyrdom, but it promises no heaven. In history there has been a multiplication of courses on extremely narrow and specialized topics, perhaps suitable for doctoral dissertations, but taught to students who lack a grasp of the broad sweep of history. Similar courses have multiplied in sociology, bordering on case studies of disadvantaged groups, with an ideological perspective that passes for deep thought. They serve well the interests of students who should not be in college: easy credits, high grades; of students who have not 'found themselves' and are looking for a cause as a substitute for identity in the culture of complaint, and for students lacking an understanding of the structure and functioning of society.

Young America's Foundation lists its choice of top 20 "bizarre and politically correct" courses offered in 2006. Thirteen of them are about sex.. Two of the 20 I find are worth a week or two of class time, but require lots of hot air to fill a semester. Judge for yourself on www.yaf.com. Why the proliferation of courses with minimal cognitive requirements, majors with little intellectual content? I can only speculate. Many, perhaps most colleges, with low academic standards of admission, need to maintain enrollment of tuition-paying students after the freshman year. They need courses and majors offering easy credits and high grades that many students will find interesting. But what of the elite colleges? And why should so many of the courses fulfilling this purpose be about sex, race, and anti-Americanism? Who devises and teaches such courses? Again I can only speculate. Many teenagers have always ranted and raved against the status quo and in behalf of causes fashionable at the time. Most of them grow up, but some remain oppositional adolescents to their dotage. A few of the latter end up on college faculties, sheltered by tenure in the Inanities. Their retention speaks ill of college administrators.

Some of the college admissions officers, administrators, faculty, the employees who make decisions on hiring faculty, on tenure and promotion, on curriculum content, on degree requirements - are dedicated to replicating public school teachings. After all, many college staff and faculty are products of the public schools since the latter downplayed academic studies, became pulpits of secular creeds, practitioners of egalitarianism, promoters of self-esteem.

The demoralization of college faculty is illustrated by the 87 professors at Duke University who publicly convicted their own lacrosse players of rape before the students were tried, and refused to retract or apologize after the players were exonerated and their prosecuter jailed and disbarred. In terms of affiliation, exactly 4 were in the natural sciences.There were no Economics or Psychology faculty among them, in fact 18 Economics faculty wrote in opposition to the prejudgment. The 83 were predominantly Women's Studies, Afro-American Studies, Writing and Literature, Cultural Anthroipology, and History, plus a few Public Policy, Sociology and Political Science.faculty.

Students have redistributed themselves from rigorous courses and majors (especially any which require some knowledge of or use of mathematics) toward less demanding 'disciplines'. Many departments have watered down their own requirements. Mickey and Minnie Mouse courses and recombinant interdisciplinary majors have proliferated to provide easy passage for students who are simply marking time in fun and games. College education has lost coherence as well as a common core. Like precollege education, it suffers from attention deficit disorder.

In primary and secondary schools, most students are passive converts or bystanders to the secular religions preached from the blackboard and textbook. In college, some students have ideas and knowledge of their own that lead to confrontations rarely found in lower schools. Freedom of speech and freedom of thought are under attack if not by particular professors then by the university administration itself, whose speech codes are a constraint on inquiry, on the very diversity colleges claim they seek.

One indicator of college performance is the Graduate Record Examination. The GRE subject matter component reflects the judgement of professionals in the fields as to what majors should know. So far it does not appear to have been corrupted. The dramatic decline in GRE subject matter scores of Sociology majors since 1965, who are now at the bottom of the heap, is evidence of the degradation of the curriculum; so is the incredibly low score of 425. (The GRE has now been discontinued for education and sociology.) The subjects which have experienced a large decline in GRE scores since 1965 also include English literature, French, History, and Political Science. There were large increases for Mathematics, the top scorer at 775, as well as Chemistry and Computer Science, substantial increases for Physics. The only science experiencing a (small) decline was Geology; the only humanities or social science discipline not experiencing a decline was Economics [19]. GRE verbal experienced a large decline, but GRE quantitative experienced a small increase. (Perhaps the inbcreasing share of foreign students taking these tests was a factor.) Education has reversed a long small decline, but remains close to the bottom. This is one GRE about whose content I have reservations.

There is an exception; the professional schools are largely immune, and so are the natural sciences and mathematics. But the humanities and most of the social sciences are terminally infected. It is the same division observed in grade inflation. Why are the sciences, business and math immune? In part because, unlike the humanities and to some extent the social sciences, and like the professional schools, they are occupation and job-related, and mastery of specific content is essential to maintain that relation. Would-be doctors and lawyers must pass exams related to their ability to perform. For another, the majors are smarter than other students, specifically in "g" and mathematical-logical intelligence. They are less easily conned, they question, analyze, demand evidence, proof. Last, a high proportion of faculty in math, natural sciences and engineering are foreign-born and received their early education in other countries. Mathematics is the moat that protects the castle of intellect from the tide of subjectivity. Economics is less infected than other social sciences because calculus and statistics are required for a major.

A word about affirmative action. Long ago it was intended to compensate for discrimination against blacks, native Americans, Asians and Hispanics. Now it is promoted in the interests of diversity. But diversity is defined implicitly as blacks, Hispanics, and native Americans; Asians no longer count; neither do women, except in sports and in a few fields in which they choose not to major. There are so many other possible kinds of diversity, why this single-minded focus on race and ethnicity? Diversity undefined is asserted to be good, but no evidence is proffered that it is desired nor by whom, and that it is good and for whom. It is egalitarian camouflage for the failures of our primary and secondary education systems especially in schools serving minority and low income populations. Unequal access to higher education is believed to correct for inadequate preparation pre-college, which it does not. Unequal opportunity is intended to result in equal outcomes. Why outcomes should be equal, and which outcomes should be equal, are not open to debate. In fact, outcomes are not made equal; graduation rates of blacks and Hispanics are much lower than the average. Sowell makes a case that the mantra of diversity has resulted in massive mismatch between minority students and colleges attended, with a resulting high rate of attrition [20]. It may have reduced rather than increased the number of graduates.

Affirmative action has been extended to faculty as well. Since some minorities are grossly under-represented in graduate schools and in PHDs, inevitably affirmative action leads to hiring many faculty low in competence and preparation, who are nevertheless tenured and promoted despite failing to meet the standards required of other faculty.

Devaluation of the College Degree

A college degree no longer implies any common core of knowledge or competence. The transformation of college education is only the last step in the debasement of elementary and high school education. This process has been accelerated by the redistribution of enrollments from private to public institutions of higher education. The latter are more subject to political pressures, to the influence of fashions. Learning expectations have declined.

The consequences for individual graduates are evident. One outcome is a growth in mismatch between college education and labor market needs. Many new graduates are unprepared to choose an appropriate form of work and manage their first job experience. They are unrealistic in their career expectations, don't believe in starting at the bottom. Still teenagers, superannuated, identifying with their peers and their fads, they are unable to delay gratification and think long term. Many lack initiative, are incapable of sustained attention or original thought but have a high opinion of their own gifts and performance [21].

The consequences for the economy receive less attention but deserve our concern. Today's graduates will be in the labor force an average of at least forty years. It takes that long for the consequences of dysfunctional education to have their full effect, and it might take as long to reverse these effects. For the time being we have a buffer. The United States has imported a large number of highly skilled technical and scientific workers, and is exporting an increasing share of the work they do to other countries.

It is not surprising that the majority of college graduates a few years later report that their college education was not needed for the jobs they have nor does the job make use of it [22]. Some eventually may end up in jobs that make use of their college education, but many if not most probably will not spend their working lives that way. Even then, they will do better on the average than those who never went to college. On the average they are smarter. But their gain is partly the result of educational discrimination by employers. Other forms of discrimination; sex, race, etc. are illegal, but education is not only allowed, but encouraged. Employers find it the only accepted way of profiling among multiple applicants. It is seen as an indirect indicator of desirable behavioral characteristics even if college education is unnecessary for the job. It is also a reflection of debasement of high school diplomas. The belief, or pretense, that the increase in general demand for college-educated workers has outpaced the increase in supply is based on inflated general educational requirements for hiring by employers, not because of a similar increase in occupational or job-specific knowledge or skills.

Most students, and parents, hope and expect that their education will lead to desirable jobs and good pay. Educational goals not focused on income and employment were fine when a college education was for the socioeconomic elite only, but not after it had become democratized. And part of the college structure and curriculum is still devoted to preparing students for desirable jobs. But the growing share of curriculum, and of faculty, have nothing to do with occupations and jobs and income, but with indoctrination, entertainment, and victimhood.

Higher education never was just about jobs and occupations, but its exposure to culture and civilization has become pop culture, passing fads and evangelization, of the secular species. Perhaps it can be viewed as preparation for the fourth great awakening. But there are unintended consequences, including unrealized expectations. We need to preserve the reputation of American colleges from a geopolitical standpoint. Think how many of the top leaders in third world countries have been graduates of American and British universities, and their role in modernization and democratization. - presidents, prime ministers and kings, and leaders in every field of endeavor.

The one healthy development is the growth of vocational programs in junior and community colleges. Their curriculum has shifted from academic to vocational. Between 1972 and 1981 the proportion of associate degrees awarded in occupational curricula increased from 40 to 70 percent. However, dropout rates are very high - little over one fourth of 1972 high school graduates entering two- year colleges completed an AA degree. One third later attended a four-year college, but little more than half of them completed a bachelors degree [23]. Kane and Rouse [24] found that less than half of high school seniors in 1982 who started in two-year colleges had earned any degree by 1992; 15% had earned certificates, 16% associate degrees, and 16% earned bachelors or higher degrees. Of high school seniors who enrolled in 1995-'96, 11% earned bachelors degrees, 17% associate degrees, and 11% certificates by 2001. The time spans studied are different, but if anything the trend is down.

COLLEGE COSTS

Equalization of opportunity for a college education has been pursued through government subsidies for lower income students, and price discrimination by colleges and universities. A high proportion of would-be college students simply cannot afford the tuition plus living expenses at most colleges and universities. With the large increase in capacity in higher education, and leveling off in numbers of the college-age population, without price discrimination colleges would face many empty seats and dorms and even higher costs per student. Colleges also must compete to attract promising students. As a result, a large proportion of students receive scholarships, fellowships, or subsidized student loans.

Colleges are not competing mainly on price or on quality of education, but on amenities, consumer goods and services unrelated to learning: athletic facilities, off-hours entertainment, luxurious accommodations. The college years are more about consumption and entertainment than intellectual inquiry [25]. Hence more money to subsidize college education simply increases the noneducational costs. It is no wonder that community colleges whose sole task is education can charge tuition which is a small fraction of that paid to most private and, for out of state students, public universities.

This strategy is costly, and must be complemented with other financial resources. There is a financial need for donations from alumni, other individuals and businesses, as well as sponsored research and government subsidies, quite apart from a race for prestige. Most colleges and universities would operate at a loss without external support. There are only a few private for-profit colleges that succeed by skimping on conspicuous consumption for students and on overhead costs.

The major shift of enrollments from private to public colleges and universities has been in large part a response to high tuition. It is a shift from the pockets of students and parents to those of taxpayers. Many students now enrolling in community colleges, saving on tuition and room and board, expect to transfer to four-year colleges in their junior year. But colleges and universities make money on enrollment in the freshman and sophomore years of large classes, a limited range of courses, and cheap faculty. They lose money in the junior and senior years of smaller classes, a wider range of courses, and more costly faculty. Thus the response of students to high tuition is likely to drive college costs per student even higher.

Student and parent competition to attend brand-name colleges is counter-egalitarian conspicuous consumption [26]. There is little relation between elite status or brand name and quality of undergraduate education or future prospects for the individual student, but prospective students and their parents think there is. Thus there is excess demand for high-priced universities, which enables tuition increases and higher admission standards. Universities down the line find that many of the students they accept go elsewhere, having applied just as a fallback option. They must accept too many, lowering standards, and guess at the yield rate. University elite status is based predominantly on graduate faculty, graduate education and research, on high admission standards, not on the quality of undergraduate education. Thus public and private subsidies for nonprofit educational institutions, and conspicuous consumption demands by applicants and their parents, drive up costs and limit the equalization of educational opportunity.

The college equivalent of the demand for smaller classes at the primary and secondary level is a reduced teaching load. When I first started teaching, the typical teaching schedule in most colleges was four courses per term. Now, whatever the formal course load, in many self-respecting universities, it is two per term, or some 5-6 hours in class a week, half of what it was when the baby boom generation went to college. Teachers need more time for preparation at the college level than at lower levels, especially for advanced and graduate courses. But most of the courses taught are undergraduate courses, with little need for preparation after teaching them several times. The reduction in course load means higher faculty costs. One response has been resort to lower-paid part time and nontenure faculty and the use of graduate students as teachers. Some do a very good job, better than some senior faculty hired, tenured, promoted without regard to their teaching ability or performance, but that is not what students and parents paid for. Part time faculty increased from 22.1% of the total in 1970 to 47.6% in 2005. Another response has been huge classes in introductory and survey courses, graded by student assistants.

The excuse for reduced teaching load is that courses take time and energy away from research. Faculty incentives in many universities are directed toward research and publication, not to better teaching. Reduced teaching loads are both incentive and reward for research. There has been a large increase in the number of professional journals to accommodate the flood of manuscripts vying for publication. Imitation down the hierarchy of colleges and universities drives faculty to write drivel to fatten their resumes. Much research publication is misdirected intellectual effort. Little of it is read. Time spent on specialized research detracts from keeping up with one's field. Faculty costs rise and students suffer neglect. There are better and much cheaper ways of judging whether a faculty member is keeping up with scholarship in his field and incorporating it in teaching. The number of publications is no measure of either.

A questionnaire sent to ten thousand college faculty in 1989 by the Carnegie Foundation for the Advancement of Teaching found that only 14% of faculty in doctorate-granting colleges and 38% in liberal arts colleges felt that teaching effectiveness should be the primary criterion for promotion. The proportion reporting that it was hard to get tenure without publishing doubled between 1969 and 1989. For doctorate granting universities, the increase was from 27 to 71%; for other universities, from 6 to 43%, and for 4-year colleges, from 6 to 24%. But except for doctorate-granting universities, the majority of faculty were interested primarily in teaching [27].

RETURNS TO INVESTMENT IN COLLEGE EDUCATION

The belief that achievement and income can be improved by education is well-founded in experience. The higher income of college graduates is the main parental and perhaps student motivation for college attendance. It is a major justification in promoting college for all. Education is not just about individual market skills, jobs, occupations, and income. Raising the floor on educational attainment and improving its quality contributes to productivity and levels of living and to non-economic aims of education. There is also hope that raising standards of education will reduce inequalities in achievement and income. For this the evidence is lacking; higher educational attainment has not reduced inequality.

Is higher education a good investment for the individual and for society? Both pay a high price for it, the individual in terms of tuition and other expenses, but mainly in terms of labor income forgone; the governments, in terms of a multitude of subsidies, tax exemptions, educational projects and programs. Do they get good return for their money? It is a question of how much education for how many; returns may depend on who and how many go to college. The upcoming generation deserves to know what it can expect from its educational decisions.

The private rate of return on investment in college education is based on the difference in lifetime earnings between those who went and those who didn't, net of the cost to the student of going to college, not just tuition and other expenses, but the additional income which would have been earned during college years had the student not gone to college. One can study 65-year olds and distinguish between the lifetime earnings of those who went to college and those who did not; but all this tells us is something about the private returns to education completed 40 or more years in the past. Or one can simulate lifetime earnings by constructing an earnings profile of workers today of different ages, distinguishing among them by educational attainment. Such a simulation sheds light on returns to college completed at different times in the near and distant past. Such data reflect the contribution of productivity gains and economic growth, and also the influence of demographic change (baby booms and busts) on the relation between education and income. But it is impossible to forecast lifetime earnings of those in college today, or even of recent graduates, never mind the difference in lifetime earnings between those who went to college and those who did not long ago..

The costs of education are borne up front, whereas benefits accrue over a lifetime. A dollar in hand is worth more than a dollar in the distant future. Benefits should be discounted by some rate, what rate is open to debate. There is no universally accepted single objective rate for discounting future earnings. Individuals, if they were to behave as rationally as economists assume, have subjective rates that vary widely: some are risk-prone, some risk-averse. Gratification deferment is a quality correlated with prolonged education and low discount rates. Or it was, when college was hard work, not good fun.

Rates of return should allow for variables believed to have an influence on earnings independent of education. These may include sex, race, parental education and income, and indicators of ability. Education itself can be stratified by quality and by field, in particular into growth-relevant and growth-irrelevant fields (or one might say instead, growth-influencing vs. growth-influenced fields).

The rate of return is an average of a wide variety of rates. It changes over time for three reasons. One is the changing composition of demand for skills which are acquired in college or for which college is a useful preparation, including the changing numbers of such jobs. Two is the changing composition of college graduates, whose share of the age group has increased greatly, and of those who finish high school but go little further, who are now the bulk of the age group, hence close to its average. Three is the relation between numbers of college graduates and the numbers of jobs in occupations which require a college education, or which in the past were associated with average educational attainment of 16 years or close to it. Even if there were no mismatch between distribution of majors and of job opportunities for new college graduates, there is now a disparity in total numbers.

Since educational attainment has become much more equally distributed, one might expect that earnings differences would have diminished. The reverse has happened. Wage inequality for the economy at large has been increasing. There was a large increase in wage differential between college graduates and others starting in the late 1970s, further widening in the 1990s and beyond. It did not begin earlier because the large increases in graduating classes in the 1960s and 1970s depressed the wages of college graduates. Also, selectivity of college admissions declined between 1961 and 1972, increasing thereafter [28] with a lagged effect on wages. The youngest cohort experiencing increased inequality would have been born in the late 1950s. Inequality of earnings by educational attainment and by level of ability continues to increase throughout working life. Hence this cohort should contribute to the increasing inequality that became noticeable in the 1980s until the 2020s at least.

The increase in inequality was attributable predominantly to a decline in real wages for less-educated workers, not an increase for college graduates. This suggests no shortfall in college graduates for jobs requiring college, but an excess supply of workers with only a high school education or less.Since returns are relative to those not going to college, they can be maintained even with increasing numbers of college graduates if earnings of high school graduates fall. Jobs and occupations once filled by high school graduates are now being filled largely by college graduates, downgrading the occupational distribution of the former.

Some of the increased wage inequality may be a temporary, decades-long adjustment to increased labor force participation of women. Only 43.3% of females 16 and older were in the labor force in 1970. In 2005 the participation rate was 59.3%, higher for every age group under 65, including females 16-19 years of age. If we have been witnessing a temporary adjustment, then we should have seen by now a phasing out of this adjustment, a trend toward reduced inequality of wages and incomes. Such a reversal is not in sight at this time.

The differences in ability between college graduates and high school graduates have widened. With higher rates of high school graduation, the average ability of high school graduates declined until it almost converged with average ability of the age group. Meanwhile college admission became more meritocratic, less socioeconomic. But the increased wage differential between college graduates and others cannot be explained by increases in standardized test scores of college graduates or in their high school grades, at least not for men. As the percentage of an age group completing college increases, one might expect this difference in ability to diminish.

So far I have not mentioned any number. Given all the considerations above, I don't believe that any one number is a good guide for either individual or for collective decisions on investment in higher education. For collective decisions, the relevant rates are social, not private, to be discussed in Chapter 5.

What accounts for the return? There are several possible explanations:

1. Differences in ability between college and high school graduates. If ability is broadly defined to include not just general intelligence and special talents but energy and drive as well, college graduates would have earned more even if they had not gone to college. Before the GI Bill of Rights, socioeconomic status was the main determinant of college attendance. Since then determinants of college admission and graduation have shifted to ability Greater equalization of educational opportunity in recent decades has enlarged the share of high-ability students who go to college and graduate. The large increase in the share of the age group entering college has had the opposite effect. But differences between college and high school graduates have widened because high school graduation has ceased to be selective.

2. Knowledge and skills acquired in college. This knowledge is not mere accumulation of information, much of it forgotten after final exams, but enhancement of cognitive skills in organizing and processing information, analysis and interpretation, inductive and deductive reasoning. A. N. Whitehead has noted that if universities only contributed information, they lost their raison d'être once printed books became commonplace. Skills and knowledge increase student productivity or other qualities valuable to potential employers. This is clearly the case in professional programs, such as law, medicine, engineering, whose graduates have completed a defined curriculum and have been tested on their achievement. Beyond any college accreditation, they must meet standards established by industry or professional associations in order to practice their profession. This is less true in many other areas, where neither a defined curriculum nor specific achievement standards exist. The amount of learning acquired in college, reflected in GRE scores, and in high school, partially reflected in SAT scores, has declined.

3. Privileged access to highly paid jobs and occupations, typically requiring skills and continued learning by experience and further training. Highly skilled work involves much more learning by experience than jobs requiring little skill, one reason why the earnings gap continues to grow throughout working life. Access may reflect greater ability, or working knowledge. Or it may be no more than a filter employers find

useful in selecting among job applicants. Access may be monopolized by law, as in the case of MDs and lawyers. The college degree does serve as an employment and occupational gatekeeper for nearly all students. For many majors, college provides little in the way of job-related skills. Its sole role is as gatekeeper. This is the sheepskin effect: college graduates make more than high school graduates regardless of ability or achievement by virtue of persisting and surviving four years of college. The diploma reduces uncertainty about the applicant in the mind of the prospective employer.

The sheepskin effect is across the board, but smaller now that college graduation is so commonplace and no longer reflects a common core of knowledge nor high standards of achievement. One result is the growing importance of "designer" degrees, diplomas from prestigious universities, which constitute a hierarchy of sheepskin effects. Regardless of the quality of their education, their students are a select group. The employer relies on the admissions officers of elite universities rather than on the sheepskin from just any college.

In the absence of specific educational requirements for a job or occupation, the differences in earnings between college graduates and others are in part, perhaps in large part, the simple result of hiring discrimination. High school graduates and college dropouts are pushed back toward the tail of the queue not because many of them cannot do the job but because it is a safe and simple way to narrow down a pool of applicants. There are legal risks or barriers in administering tests to determine their capability, so the diploma becomes a stand-in for job-specific tests. The college diploma is a protective tariff for desirable jobs and occupations.

Formal education, by restricting access to better jobs and occupations, guarantees a return to degrees, but it is a monopoly return only loosely related to the contribution of education to labor market performance. For occupations that require licensing, the success rate in licensing exams reflects gains from education, but limiting licensing to graduates excludes alternative means of acquiring knowledge or access: a double hurdle which further guarantees a return to diplomas and licenses.

We do not know for sure the relative importance of these three explanations. They differ by field of study. Ability is not easily quantified. Since it and education are highly correlated, it is impossible to distinguish confidently between their contributions to test performance or earnings. Relative earnings change somewhat over time in response to changing market forces. Thus the average difference in income between college and high school graduates tells us little. In particular, it does not justify a policy of college for all.

Other changes have affected the level of returns. Large increases in tuition and the large increase in the percentage of the college-age population attending and completing college, and of the working force with college degrees, tends to lower returns. Increases in subsidies: scholarships, fellowships, low interest loans, tend to increase returns; so does the shift in composition of the labor force toward managerial, professional and technical skills. Major changes in technology, including gains in productivity, tend to raise the incomes of all workers, not just college graduates. It is important to distinguish between differences resulting from the college education experience and those resulting from these trends.

The attribution of differences in earnings to differences in educational attainment ignores the demand side. Even with education as monopoly entry to particular jobs or occupations, if there is an oversupply of job seekers armed with diplomas, the return on education can be low or zero. The economist would argue that such surpluses are temporary, self-correcting. This is true, up to a point; undergraduates shift to different majors. But there are two constraints which limit such adjustment. One is the willingness or ability to shift to majors with academic requirements which students cannot meet and regard their acquisition a formidable barrier. This is particularly true of majors in the humanities and related fields, confronted with better prospects in the technical and scientific majors, who lack a math background,. Thus surpluses in humanities can go on forever. An overall surplus of graduates (the baby boom generation) may reduce college enrollment rates as expected returns decline. At best, adjustment takes years. Except for occupations with highly specific requirements, such as medicine and some technical and engineering fields, health and education, sophomore students' knowledge of prospects after graduation is vague, and foresight down the road is lacking. On the demand side, employers may inflate their educational expectations for new hires for jobs requiring no specific educational prerequisite.

In a few cases , such as medicine, the number of students is restricted to maintain the incomes of current practitioners and assure employment and earnings to new graduates.

Has demand for college graduates kept pace with the rapid increase in supply or not? The answer is yes, in the simple sense that relative educational attainment is a positive element in employer ranking of potential employees. But it may well be no, in the sense that the experience and learning gained in college are not required or important in work performance.

Job opportunities and earnings for college graduates are affected by the ratio of graduates to jobs available. If one third of the population finishes college, but only twenty percent of jobs truly require college training, the economist would argue that the system adjusts automatically: that college attendance decisions are based on expected returns, and if these fall, then enrollments will drop. The implicit assumption is that prospective college students are fully informed about prospective rates of return, which even economists cannot know. A second implicit assumption is that individuals base their expectations on overall averages, if they know them. Yet we know that millions are prepared to invest in zero and negative-sum games of chance in casinos and lotteries. A college education however is a positive sum game on the average. Since relevant expectations are long term, even lifetime, no one can know the rates or the probabilities, either on average or with reference to particular individuals. Decisions are made largely on psychological and sociological grounds; the main economic consideration is the ability to defer employment and pay the costs. The reality is that the rate of return may not fall enough to bring supply into equilibrium with demand for college-educated workers. What falls is job opportunities and earnings of high school graduates. The differential may be preserved by employer preference for sheepskins. It creates a disconnect between the number graduating from college and the jobs which can only be done well by college graduates.

INCOME DIFFERENCES AMONG COLLEGE GRADUATES

A doubling and tripling of the share of the age group completing college has inevitably increased the number and share of low ability college graduates, increasing inequality among graduates. With increased inequality in ability and achievement, it is reasonable to expect increased inequality of income as well. In fact nearly all the earnings differential of college graduates, the gains to a college education, accrue to the top quartile of college graduates as measured by academic ability. For the bottom quartile there is little or no return to a college education. Many earn little if any more than high school graduates. Blackburn and Neumark estimate that failure to consider ability differentials overstates the return to education by about 40 percent [29].

It is a deceptive simplification to estimate the returns to college education by aggregating all college graduates and comparing their average earnings with the average of all those who completed high school but did not go beyond. The individual rate of return on a college education varies widely, as a function of student ability, of choice of majors, and of the balance between jobs requiring a college education and the numbers of graduates available. A policy of college for all, or even college for most, based on an average expected return derived from the past, is deceitful as well as wasteful. It results in many wasting years of their lives and sacrificing income as well.

The changed sex ratio of college students is a factor. The beneficiaries of the GI Bill of Rights were predominantly white males. The biggest increases in college attendance and completion in recent decades have been females (who now outnumber males) and minorities. For a number of reasons: job and wage discrimination, younger average age than male workers, fewer years of work experience at a given age, and choice of majors leading to limited job opportunities and/or low wages, they may have contributed to wage inequality among college graduates.

College major, ability, type of college attended, and occupation are interrelated. Some efforts have been made to disaggregate returns. Kane and Rouse [30] estimate returns to college credits and diplomas for two- and four-year colleges, finding little difference once adjustment is made for family background. An early attempt to relate returns to different occupations in Canada found substantial differences, as well as sensitivity to the discount rate employed [31].

Grogger and Eide (1995) [32] found that the wage premium of college vs. high school graduates rose between 1977-'79 and 1986 by 13.5% for men, 7.7% for women. But the wage premium varied greatly by major, one indicator of skills acquired in college. For men, one quarter of the increased wage differential could be explained by changes to high wage-potential majors; for women, increased returns to math ability were important in explaining the increased wage premium. The large difference between men and women is partially explainable by choice of major. Rumberger and Thomas found that college major had a large impact on earnings for both men and women. College grades only influenced womens' earnings, and only for some majors. College quality helped explain differences in earnings, but not for all majors [33].

Even standardizing for occupation, major-specific wage premiums vary greatly. The trend away from low-skill majors such as education to high-skill majors such as engineering (Grogger and Eide's categorization) account for one fourth of the increase in the wage premium for men, and one third for women.

There is a large and widening gap between college majors in mastery of their subjects, as indicated by their GRE (Graduate Record Examination, taken by one third of college seniors) subject scores. Since SAT scores of college seniors plunged starting in the mid 1960s, one would expect a similar decline in GRE scores in the 1970s. In fact this is what happened. The differences between majors have widened. The largest declines were in history, political science, and sociology. But there were increases in math, sciences except geology, and engineering, whereas all others declined. Math majors scored 720 in 1989; the sciences (geology excepted), engineering and economics scored above 600. At the other extreme, sociology scored 425 and most of the humanities scored in the 400s and low 500s [34].

I am looking just at subject matter scores, what leaders in the field think of the competence of senior majors. Thus the numbers for different majors are not strictly comparable. Math competence is not all that important to humanities majors, and math and physics majors can get along without great mastery of English. The fact that the wage premium varies widely by major even after adjusting for occupation does imply that the differences in subject matter GRE scores by major are indicators of labor market-relevant abilities. There is another sharp dividing line between the high and the low scorers: all the high scoring majors except pre-law require some math; most of the low scorers require no math. The quality of math instruction in high school appears to be a major constraint on choice of majors in college.

Either the alleged return to a college education is actually little more than a return to differential ability (however defined) or to choice of major and subsequent occupations; but the last two are highly correlated. Students choosing majors leading to overcrowded occupations or to no occupation at all are concentrated at the low-ability end of college graduates. The implication is that their choice of majors and occupational preferences is not strongly market-oriented.

In sum, college is a good investment for some, not for others. From a national standpoint, a higher proportion of an age group completing college faces decreasing returns: at some point, too many will be going, the incremental benefits to the nation will become smaller than the incremental costs. One problem is that individuals and the entire society (or its governments) do not confront the same costs, or receive the same benefits. College education is heavily subsidized, hence individual graduates will benefit even with an oversupply. Benefits to graduates are paid for in part by nongraduates, whether by taxes or by reduced access to good jobs which are now monopolized by graduates. Hence both on the cost side and on the benefit side, there can be a persistent excess demand for a college education.

There is another perspective on differences in ability and income of college graduates. The huge increase in college enrollment has been accompanied by a change in institutional structure of higher education. The proportion going to private colleges and universities declined from 50% in 1950 to 25.5% in 2005 [35]. The proportion attending two-year colleges has changed from 18% in 1963 to 37% in 2005. The top colleges and universities are swamped with applications and have become more selective; the less selective colleges and universities have to scramble for students and have experienced a decline in ability of their students and low graduation rates. To the extent that individual returns to a college education depend on individual ability, the gap in earnings between higher and lower tier colleges and universities has widened.

MISMATCH OF MAJORS AND JOB OPPORTUNITIES

When 1993 college graduate workers were asked a year after graduation whether their job was related to their degree, and whether a degree was required for their job, 56 percent felt a degree was required, and 75 percent that their degree was related to their job [36]. But there was a big difference between majors in math, physical sciences, computers, engineering, education, and health sciences, who predominantly answered yes to both questions; and history, humanities and social sciences, the majority of whom said a degree was not required and nearly half of whom said their job was not related to their degree. Most business majors found their job related to their degree, but nearly half said the degree was not necessary. (When asked whether their jobs are possibly career-related, the differences between majors were much smaller; one wonders about the realism of expectations; but 'career' is an ambiguous term.) When 1993 graduates were asked again in 1997, the differences persisted. [36] In fact the percentage answering that their job was not closely related to their degree increased for all majors except math, computers and physical sciences. Surveys of graduates one year later conducted annually from 1976 to 2001 asked whether the job was closely related to the field of study but not whether a degree was necessary. The differences by major found for 1993 graduates persisted throughout this period, but the percentage answering no was substantially higher in 2001 than in 1994. Social sciences and humanities, plus health professions, accounted for all the increase in 'no' answers.

The large difference between majors in job experience after graduation suggests that there are too many majors in the humanities and social sciences relative to majors in math, the natural sciences, engineering, health services, and education. Even if there is no close match between many college majors and ensuing occupations, it appears that there is a large disparity between distribution of degrees by major and distribution of occupations in society. By implication, for many, there is only a tenuous relation between degree, jobs and wages. Part of the disparity, but only a small part, can be attributed to the shifting sex ratio in college; females who are now the majority are less likely to opt for math, science and technology majors.

Some of the mismatch between college graduates and jobs and careers is the result of unrealistic expectations of high school seniors. In 1976, 50.3% expected to earn at least a bachelors degree; by 2000, that number had grown to 78.3%, with 50.5% planning to go to graduate or professional schools. Occupational plans have also grown ever less related to reality. Whereas in 1976 41.2% of seniors planned to be working in professional occupations by age 30, in 2000 this number had grown to 63.4% [37], three times the actual share. The modal salary expectations of seniors at age 30 was two and a half times the actual average at the time.

A recent survey of 500 twenty-something college graduates by Insightexpress found that only one in three of those employed were satisfied with the status of their career; 36% had landed in careers they had planned for; 48% were not working on a career they envisioned in college; and four in ten, knowing what they know now, would have majored in something different [38]. Large differences in job prospects between majors tend to narrow as succeeding classes of college students switch to majors with better job prospects. Likewise, large differences in post-college pay between majors will be narrowed as succeeding graduating classes act on this information in their choice of majors. (Narrowed, not eliminated, since students have occupational preferences apart from earnings or job prospects.) There is something to this claim. But it assumes good information and a long time horizon, as well as an investor's rather than a consumer's mentality. And there are constraints to free choice resulting from poor background in high school. Mathematical competence appears to be a serious barrier to mobility that restricts choices to limited alternatives. Students who never mastered algebra in high school are not going to switch from majors in the humanities to the natural sciences, math or engineering just because there are better job and earnings prospects in these fields; their costs of switching are high. The competitive market model is applicable only within narrow limits. Large differences in earnings persist almost indefinitely.

In some well-defined fields the economists' conditions are met. Engineering enrollments in the past adjusted to perceived demand, via the so-called cobweb fluctuation. More recently one can observe adjustments in enrollments in business administration and education. But most majors lack a well-defined professional curriculum and job opportunity structure. What do political science or English literature graduates do? Apart from choices constrained by lack of background, market information is too uncertain to dominate academic decisions.

Long ago college was not viewed as employment-preparatory, but the democratization of higher education has created the expectation that a degree will lead to well-paid jobs. Nevertheless, most of the high-wage premium majors, with high probability of major-related jobs, have declined as a share of degrees awarded, in some cases in absolute numbers. It is the majors whose college training is least likely to lead to major-related jobs, whose wage premium is low, whose numbers and share of graduates has increased.

The proportion of bachelors degrees earned in mathematics has been declining since the 1960s, from a peak of nearly 4% to less than 1% since 2000. (See Table 4-1) In the physical sciences the same decline is evident. The percentage of bachelors degrees has declined from over 4% in 1960 to just 1.28% in 2004. In both math and physical science, the absolute numbers, not just the proportion of degrees earned, continue trending down despite large increases in total college enrollment and in the labor force. The actual number of degrees earned is down to less than half of what it was at its peak. The biological sciences show little decline, but this is a mixed bag which include health services as well as scientific disciplines. In general they require much less math than the physical sciences.

Math and physical and biological science graduates constitute the pool from which we should draw teachers of these subjects in secondary schools. They are also the pool of potential graduate students in these fields.

Engineering presents a slightly more favorable picture. Engineering graduates are the highest-paid occupational group. The proportion of bachelors degrees awarded has fluctuated widely. The long run trend is down but only slightly. The number of bachelors degrees awarded is somewhat below its peak, which came in the 1980s, not much earlier, as in math and physical sciences. The decline since is somewhat greater than indicated by the numbers in Table 4-1 because those numbers include an increasing proportion of foreign students. Some may remain permanently, others leave upon completion of their studies.

How do we know that poor preparation in high school, especially in math, is a major factor in the decline in college majors in math and science? One indication is the record of students in selective undergraduate colleges. As many as 20-25% major in the sciences, a higher percent than in comparable research universities and in contrast to a national average of 7%. In terms of PHD productivity in the sciences, 4 of the top 5 performers are liberal arts colleges; Reed and Swarthmore graduates earn PHDs at almost twice the rate of Harvard and Yale [39].

How do we know that we are producing too few mathematicians, scientists and engineers? It is not plausible to assume that we need fewer than we produced in the past, as well as a declining proportion of the labor force. It is more plausible to assume that the rapid technological changes in recent decades, still ongoing, would require an increasing number and share of technical and scientific personnel. In fact this assumption is a large part of the justification for increasing the proportion of the population completing college.

Can we assume huge overproduction in the 1960s? Even if so, they are now retirement age. What has been happening to the employment of mathematicians, physical scientists, and engineers? Many will be in management and other occupations which may use their training but not reflect it in their titles. So far as secondary schools are concerned, there is an acute shortage of qualified teachers in math and science.

For a generation there have been complaints about a surplus, not a shortage, of PhDs, including PhDs in the sciences and math [40]. Yet very few PhDs end up teaching high schools in their specialty. The coexistence of a shortage of undergraduate majors in science and math and an alleged surplus of PhDs is easily explained. A high proportion of graduate students in these fields, over half in some, are foreigners. Subtract foreigners, and there is a shortage, not a surplus. Further, the largest employers are colleges and universities. If there were more majors and minors in math and the sciences in college, there would be more teaching jobs for PhDs, and less need to import foreign students to maintain departmental enrollments. The reliance on foreigners will be discussed in the next chapter. It is incidental evidence of a shortage.

Table 4-1. Bachelors degrees in math, physical, biological sciences and engineering (percent of all bachelors degrees)

	Math	Physical Sciences	Biological Sciences	Engineering
1960	2.90%	4.08%	9.70%	9.60%
1970	3.46	2.71	4.30	5.61
1975	2.00	2.25	5.61	5.08
1980	1.19	2.52	4.99	7.41
1985	1.54	2.42	3.93	9.78
1990	1.44	1.53	3.54	7.74
1995	1.18	1.65	4.83	6.74
2000	0.98	1.49	5.13	5.86
2001	0.94	1.45	4.87	5.81
2002	0.96	1.38	4.66	5.73
2003	0.93	1.33	4.45	5.73
2004	0.96	1.28	4.41	5.59

Source: calculated from National Center for Education Statistics (2006) *Digest of Education Statistics 2005*. Washington, DC: U. S. Government Printing Office, Tables 249, 275, 281, 287, 288.

The decline indicated in Table 4-1 has clear implications for secondary schools, if not also for primary schools. Teaching fields should be closely related to college majors. High school math should be taught by math majors, although majors in physical sciences and engineering should be able to teach math too. High school chemistry, physics, biology should be taught by graduates in these majors. Teaching is a large share of potential employment for majors in some of these fields. High schools are faced with a self-reinforcing vicious circle: they cannot hire enough teachers who majored in math and science to teach these subjects because few major in these subjects in college and face a buyers market for jobs offering better pay and opportunity than teaching. Few major because most high school graduates have a weak preparation in science and math.

Supply does not create its own demand. Occupational distribution is determined by prevailing technology and the composition of final demand, which in turn are somewhat interdependent. It is not much affected by educational attainment or specialization; on the contrary, the occupational structure is the main influence on educational specialization. Higher educational attainment increases employment in the industry of education but creates few jobs elsewhere.

An advanced society, whatever its politics or ideology, is highly hierarchical. There is limited room at the top, much room near the bottom. This is just as true of public and nonprofit organizations as of business firms. All work is not equal; jobs and occupations vary in productivity, as do their occupants. This is the immovable obstacle to egalitarianism There is little, short of revolutionary technological change, that anyone can do about either hierarchy or occupational structure.

EDUCATION AND INEQUALITY

The motivation behind efforts to keep everyone in school through high school graduation, and to increase college enrollments, college for all, is twofold: improve earning and occupational choices for children of lower income parents, and reduce inequality of income as well. Many writers, starting with Horace Mann, have viewed democratization of education as an equalizer of economic conditions.That it contributes to social mobility is not questioned. The economic argument would be that a highly educated labor force will drive down the relative earnings of the high-wage occupations, most of which require a college education or more, and raise the relative wages of low-wage occupations, since few workers will lack the qualifications to compete for better jobs and occupations. Alternatively, these egalitarian objectives are based on two implicit assumptions: the fallacy of composition, that if some college-educated individuals become doctors and lawyers and make much money, putting everyone through college will extend the same results to everyone; and two, that the occupational structure adjusts to supply of appropriately educated individuals (and perhaps the earnings structure does not adjust, everyone will be well paid). Both are patently false. But facts are silent. Mobility is a two-way elevator.

Wage inequality has been increasing at least from 1973 while educational attainment of the labor force has become more equally distributed. The increased inequality has been concentrated at the upper end of the wage distribution [41]. Why? This question refers back to the sources of inequality of income among college graduates: ability, learning, and the sheepskin effect. Becker [42], writing in 1975, thought that ability accounted for a small proportion of the return to a college education, that learning was the principal factor. His information covered the third quarter of the 20th century. Major changes in enrollment, curriculum, grading suggest a decline in the learning component, an increase in the ability component of returns. It appears that less learning is required and probably less acquired in college now than a generation or two ago.

Perhaps the most compelling evidence is that future incomes of graduates are highly correlated with ability, not with college attended. Dale and Krueger compared students admitted to elite colleges and students of comparable ability not admitted. They found that students of comparable ability earned about the same whether they attended more or less selective colleges; that future earnings are explained by student ability regardless of the quality of the college attended. This does suggest that, on the average, private returns to college education are the result of ability, not educational experience (or that learning experience is determined by the student, not by the college). But children from low income families earned more if they attended selective colleges [43]. Hunter examined the contribution of cognitive ability to job performance [44]. He found that general cognitive ability is by far the best predictor for job training following hiring, for job performance, and for promotion. It is superior to specific aptitudes as a predictor of job knowledge.

The sheepskin effect is a significant contributor to the college earnings premium [45]. It is much larger than the effect of just additional years of schooling. The ranking of the college in prestige may be becoming a major factor. But prestige ranking is closely linked with admissions standards, i.e., ability. The correlation between ability, learning, and college prestige makes it difficult to isolate the separate contribution of any one factor.

How can reducing the disparity in educational attainment increase inequality of achievement? Inevitably, if it is accomplished via lower standards, as it has been. Then differences in achievement between schools increase. In every school some students will learn even if they don't have to; dumbing down increases inequality among students in any given grade, and that inequality in achievement continues to increase as students advance to high school graduation, then through college. Reduced inequality of attainment with high standards should have the contrary effect.

One possibility is that increased educational attainment, even with more equal educational distribution, itself promotes inequality. This is the theory that to those who have shall be given, that differentials in ability, interest, energy, associated with differential achievement are magnified in practice by additional education. In the words of St. Matthew 25-29, "For unto everyone that hath shall be given and he shall have abundance; but from him that hath not shall be taken away, even that which he hath." Ability increases the marginal benefit the individual acquires from schooling, one reason for the positive correlation between ability and educational attainment. This is consistent with a college/high school wage differential that has increased almost exclusively for the abler college graduates as earnings inequality among college graduates has widened. The inequality in performance (ability plus schooling) widens the higher the educational attainment of the population. Expectations of many students will not be realized, for achievement is often seen in relative terms, in comparison with one's peers.

The tortoise never catches up with the hare, and the longer the race, the wider the gap. If everyone left school after the 6th grade, the difference in knowledge and skills would be much less than if everyone stopped with a high school diploma. As more finish college, the gap in achievement is bound to widen. As the average level rises, an increasing share of the population bumps into its ceiling of capability. For them the only way to increase educational attainment is by dumbing down educational standards, the last ditch way of limiting inequality of achievement. We may not be able to increase the share completing high school much by other means, and may be close to the limit of population share capable of completing a reasonably rigorous four-year college program. This means that we are near the limits of attainable equalization of educational attainment, and any increase in average attainment will be concentrated on the abler part of the age group, contributing to rising inequality of achievement in terms of learning and labor market productivity.

In sum, the reduction in inequality of educational attainment should reduce wage inequality; but the higher average level of educational attainment and increased inequality in ability between college graduates and others contribute to increased wage inequality. I cannot quantify either effect, nor the net effect of their sum, beyond noting that wage and income inequality overall and by level of educational attainment have been increasing, not falling. They have been increasing in boom years and in recession years, and for a long time.

Finally there is the observation, and prediction, of Will and Ariel Durant, among others: "Every advance in the complexity of the economy puts an added premium upon superior ability, and intensifies the concentration of wealth, responsibility, and political power [46]. This view is independent of educational attainment and its distribution. It refers to the demand for ability and skill, whereas the previous changes refer to their supply. Technological advance increasing demand for highly skilled and able workers widens wage differentials by skill, occupation, ability, and education. It accounts for some of the increased wage differential accruing to abler college graduates, who are concentrated in the majors most affected by technological change. But technical change is a gradual continuing process, whereas educational attainment and the role of ability in attainment have experienced much more abrupt changes.

Can anything be done to reduce the inequality of earnings associated with increased educational attainment? What are the determinants of differences in earnings, other than the fortunate choice of parents and random dispensations of Lady Luck? Little can be done about the distribution of income-relevant abilities and propensities. A second determinant is promotion of abilities through education and training. There is much we can do individually and as a society, but the result could well be increased inequality. At some point, reduced inequality can only be achieved by lowering the marginal benefit of increased educational attainment, either by advancing those whose benefit from additional education is small, or by restraining further attainment for those whose benefit is large. This road to equality sacrifices efficiency and growth to the egalitarian God. It was another country that proclaimed liberty, equality, and fraternity. Meritocracy spells inequality.

Third, income and the way it is spent helps shape demand for diverse abilities and skills. Prospects of persuading consumers to spend less on doctors and lawyers and more on the services of high school dropouts are bleak. So are prospects for shifting spending from technical products and services to those of humanities majors.

Fourth, products and processes available through new technology influence consumer demand and determine the skills required to produce the goods demanded. Some say that technology is autonomous, that society has no control over changes in demand for diverse skills. Others deny this, pointing out that development of much technology responds to existing shortages of labor and particular skills, in the same way that students and workers adjust their education and training to perceived market opportunities. But new products: electronics, computers, pharmaceuticals, plastics, which have dominated technological progress recently, are not developed in response to labor force skills, though their production adjusts somewhat to labor availabilities, both here and abroad.

In the United States, new technology in the twentieth century increased the demand for new and high level skills, contributing to inequality. We do not know what future technology will imply for skill demands or wage differences. Past efforts to control the rate and direction of technological change have concentrated on protecting the jobs or wages of skilled craftsmen, or of low skill factory workers. They never succeeded in the long run. Today, efforts are directed to minimize social costs: the unintended consequences on health, environment, community. Any influence on occupational demands and inequality is incidental and its direction uncertain.

The skill requirements of new technology were major determinants of the occupational structure in days of protectionism and high costs of international transportation and information, but this is no longer true. The nation's ability to influence its occupational structure is much diminished in a world of open markets. The education industry is poorly adapted to provide students the opportunity to adjust their plans to opportunities in the market place. The two are related: an education industry more responsive to the needs of the economy would minimize the need to import highly skilled workers and to outsource production.

OVEREDUCATION AND ITS CONSEQUENCES

The United States has too many people receiving college diplomas. There are too many in terms of job and occupational opportunities related to their major fields of study; too many in terms of educational requirements for the labor market. Some mismatch between job and career opportunities and fields of study always occurs, but is largely self-correcting in the long run: student distribution by major adjusts somewhat, so does relative pay, and there is additional training and retraining. The oversupply to which I refer is a different situation: in overall numbers, a surplus which shows little tendency to self-correct even in the long run. Since most students do not pay the full cost of their education, they will exhibit excess demand for college. Or the demand is not so much a function of expected earnings and occupation as conspicuous consumption, status-seeking, that is unresponsive to higher tuition or even to economic rewards. Or they may be risk-prone, regarding lack of a degree as condemning them to low pay and low status jobs, whereas a sheepskin gives them a chance, whatever the odds. No doubt there is some of each motivation, plus plain ignorance.

Freeman [47], Berg [48], and other writers have been proclaiming since the baby boomers started entering the labor force that Americans are overeducated in the limited but important sense of unrealized expectations for jobs, occupations and earnings. Educational attainment has increased much more than needed to adjust for changes in occupational distribution from low-skill to high-skill occupations. Could it be accounted for by increased skill requirements for jobs within occupations?

Rumberger [49] estimated surplus schooling of workers, using workers' own views as the basis for establishing the education required for the occupation. He found that 20% of workers in 1977 had surplus schooling of 1 to 3 years, and 12%, of 3 or more years. The surplus was especially large for service workers and operatives. There has been little increase in educational attainment since 1977, but there has been some change in the occupational structure. Murphy and Welch [50] examined the changes in demand for skill due to changes in the occupational structure between 1940 and 1990. They found that the increase in demand for skill was little more than one third the increase in supply of skill as measured by educational attainment, or 1.4-1.5 additional years of education demanded versus an increase of 4.2 years supplied.

Hecker [51] found that the proportion of college graduates in jobs not requiring a college degree or unemployed nearly doubled from 10.7% in 1969 to 19.9% in 1990. Others have estimated that as many as one third of college graduates initially work in 'high school' jobs shortly after graduation. That share depends on the definition of jobs that can be adequately performed by high school graduates, if they are literate and numerate.

The fact that many recent graduates reported that their jobs did not require a college education and did not make use of their major is insufficient evidence that too many people are going to college in terms of labor market needs. Many who start out in 'high school' jobs may move up in time to jobs that require more than than a high school education. Some graduates are victims of a mismatch between choice of majors and labor market needs, which could persist whatever happens to the ratio of aggregate demand to aggregate supply of graduates.

Table 4-2. Educational attainment by occupational group

Occupational Groups	Median Educational Attainment			
	1948	1959	1975	1991
Professional specialty	16+	16.2	16.4	16.8
Executive, administrative, managerial	12.2	12.4	13.0	15.1
Sales occupations	12.3	12.5	12.7	13.0
Administrative support, inc. clerical	12.4	12.5	12.6	12.9
Service workers	8.7	10.1	12.1	12.5
Precision production, craft, repair	9.7	11.0	12.3	12.8
Operators, fabricators, and laborers	9.1	9.9	12.0	12.4
Farming, forestry and fishing	8.0	8.6	11.7	12.3

Sources: National Center for Education Statistics (1983) *Digest of Education Statistics 1982.* Washington, DC: U. S. Government Printing Office, Table 364. National Center for Education Statistics (1993) *Digest of Education Statistics 1992.* Washington, DC: U. S. Government Printing Office, Table 364.

Additional evidence is the change in educational attainment by occupation. The occupations which have the highest attainment and which most require continued learning through working life, professional and technical, have hardly increased their average educational attainment in the past 50 years (see Table 4-2). If one were to subtract doctors, lawyers, and college professors, the average of remaining professional and technical workers would be below 16 years. The occupations whose average attainment has increased most are executive, administrative, and managerial workers, and the occupations involving the least skill and the least need for continued learning after graduation, jobs many of which are performed by illiterates, some of whom scarcely speak English. Farming workers gained nearly four years between 1959 and 1991; unskilled and semiskilled workers gained two and a half years, as did service workers. Nearly all these gains were achieved by 1975. There appears to be an inverse relation between increases in educational attainment and occupational skill and learning requirements. It is difficult to claim that such an increase was not needed for professional workers, but was for other occupational groups.

Table 4-2 is an approximation, since there were reclassifications of occupational groups during the period shown. The increase in professional specialty is overstated (it no longer includes technical workers); that in administrative support is understated. In recent years the median is no longer reported; instead, a distribution of educational attainment for each occupational group is provided.

Further evidence of the overeducation of many workers is the wide dispersion of educational attainment within occupational groups (see Table 4-3). Professional specialty occupations have the least dispersion: 76.8% had college degrees in 2002; another 14.8% had an associate or equivalent degree; only 6.4% had a high school degree or less. There is much greater dispersion among other occupational groups. Among executives, managers and administrators, 22.3% had no college; among sales occupations, 36.5%; retail and personal services sales, 55.2%; among secretarial, 61.9%; service, well over two thirds. Within each of these broad occupational groups there are specific occupations requiring much more education or skills than the average. The point is that a high proportion of the jobs in all but professional occupations are being held by individuals who never went to college. If one had a breakdown by age group, no doubt the share of jobs in each group held by individuals who never went to college would be much lower for say 25-29 year olds than for 55-59 year olds. But that does not mean that the older workers could not do the work of the younger. More likely, the younger workers for all their additional education would not be able to do the work of the older very well if at all.

Table 4-3. Educational attainment, full time workers ages 25-64 (2002)

Occupational group	Less than High School	High School	Some College	College Degree
Professional specialty	0.6%	5.7%	16.8%	76.8%
Executive, administrative, managerial	2.6	19.0	27.4	51.0
Technicians and related	1.3	18.5	46.5	33.7
Sales occupations	6.1	30.4	30.4	33.1
Administrative support	3.8	39.1	40.1	16.9
Service occupations	19.7	41.3	28.7	10.3
Precision prod., craft, and repair	16.9	45.4	29.8	7.8
Operators, fabricators and laborers	22.8	50.2	21.5	5.6
Farming, forestry, fishing	29.8	25.3	21.1	12.6

Source: National Center for Education Statistics (2005). *Digest of Education Statistics 2004.* Washington, DC: U. S. Government Printing Office. Table 379.

The UK has also experienced a large increase in share of the age group going to college, and a decline in quality of university education. More than a third of 2000 graduates either could not find a job at all or had to settle for a low-skilled one. More than a quarter thought that their degree had not equipped them for the job market, and 40% thought it was more or less a waste of time, money and effort. There were sharp difference in wage premium: high in law, economics, and math, lower in social studies, close to zero in education and languages, and negative in arts [52]. Most other industrial nations are facing similar situations.

The most convincing evidence I know that college enrollments and graduates greatly exceed the needs of the economy is the example of Germany, with productivity comparable to that of the United States (higher per hour worked according to recent studies). In the 1990s it enrolled and graduated only one third as large a share of the college-age group as the United States. The Netherlands got by with little more than one half. Of course, Germany has an advanced system of vocational training and certification.

The usual argument for college for most is that since agents, managers, salespeople, technicians, clerks, aides who formerly had a high school diploma now flaunt a college degree, therefore the job has been upgraded in skill and educational requirements. This is a simple fallacy: post hoc ergo propter hoc. Where is the evidence that they do a better job today than in the past?

The need (economic demand) for more workers with college training increases but gradually. The existing labor force adjusts to these needs not by going back to college but by training and on the job learning, as it always has. Adjustment to technological change is largely by the existing labor force, not by the trickle of new entrants at the bottom of career ladders. The differences in formal educational attainment of the labor force in the United States and in some other advanced industrial nations, Germany in particular, were striking until recently. The supply of graduates was in advance of the demand for diplomas. A point was reached where there were not enough younger high school dropouts to fill all the jobs which required no more education and which dropouts had been filling in the past. Hence it became necessary to hire high school graduates, whose number had grown more than the number of jobs customarily filled by such graduates. The same process applied to college graduates, who came to do the work formerly done by workers with less formal education. Were it not for massive immigration of low skill workers, more college graduates would be holding "high school" jobs.

The large increase in educational attainment was concentrated in the 1950-1970 time period. It continues at a much slower pace, and cannot continue forever. At some point the costs of further increase exceed the gains. There are limits to the proportion of the population capable of completing an unadulterated college education. Assuming continuing shift in occupational structure toward jobs requiring college, one would expect the proportion of graduates ending up in 'high school' jobs to diminish slowly. This has not been happening. Perhaps the assumption of increasing educational requirements is wrong.

What are the consequences of too many graduates? The main one is disappointed expectations, frustration - one reason that rich societies are no happier than those only half as wealthy. People work at jobs which make little use of their college training, which do not require a college education to perform. In time, job and occupation educational requirements become inflated, extending frustration to those who do not finish, who do not go to college, for the jobs and occupations they might have held in the past are no longer open to them. A second consequence is the growth of graduate enrollments and degrees to achieve employment goals which once required no more than a bachelors degree.

The quantity theory of money, first enunciated by Bodin in the 16th century (also known as Gresham's Law, after Thomas Gresham), states that the value of money is inversely related to its quantity. But it is much wider in application: the value of any asset is inversely related to its quantity; thus the multiplication of college diplomas, regardless of the quality of education or the ability of graduates, debases their value. Hence the obsession with designer labels: degrees from elite universities, which retain value because their supply is limited.

Hence also the educational arms race; masters and doctoral degrees to move up the queue, to make up in quantity of education what has been lost in value of bachelors diplomas. Masters degrees were 18% of bachelors degrees in 1960 but rose to 40% in 2005; PHDs rose over the same period from 1% of bachelors degrees to 3.8%. Graduate enrollment is largely an exercize in one-upmanship.

Another consequence is the economic disfranchisement of those who never completed high school or who did not go beyond the high school diploma. They are deprived of some of the well-paid jobs which formerly were open to them, or are shoved down the queue of eligibles. Much of the increase in inequality observed in recent decades has been the result of a decline in real earnings of less educated workers. The causes are complex, including a flood of immigrants and changes in occupational demands, but bumping by college graduates cannot be ignored. This unintended consequence of more college graduates is in part attributable to the debasement of the high school diploma, because almost everyone gets it, partly because it is widely known that it is no longer an indicator of work-relevant abilities or skills, and high school offers less vocational training than it once did.

For many occupations there are tests of talent and preparation that are more reliable than a high school or a college diploma. But courts no longer allow employers to test high school graduates directly for competence. The Equal Employment Opportunity Commission decreed that employment tests would have to be validated by the government, and employers are hostile to that idea. The 5th US Circuit Court has ruled that it is improper to test clerk-typists for grammar, spelling and punctuation. Tests are discriminatory, that is their purpose. They may favor males, or large people, or smart people, or disciplined people; any test will favor some ethnic group more than another. The courts, or some judges, believe that Justice must be dumb, as well as blind. `

When there is a surplus in a particular occupation, there are several possible responses:

1. The supply of new entrants falls until the surplus disappears, and if there is a lengthy period of education and training before work, a shortage arises. Engineering education is a classic example of this oscillation between surpluses and shortages. These days, with foreigners filling many of the seats, it is less responsive to domestic fluctuations in demand than in the past.

2. Supply creates its own demand: this is the case of the health professions. A surplus of obstetricians results in a great increase in the number of Caesarian sections; a surplus of dentists greatly increases the number of braces, The customer or patient doesn't know any better.

3. Requirements for education and training are inflated, reducing supply because the cost and time for education and training is increased, whether or not standards are raised. This happened in the medical profession when a college degree became necessary for entry to medical school; when an MD became required for some specialties formerly practiced by technicians. More recently, the duration of internships for various specialties has increased by years; In teaching, normal school (two years of college more or less) was replaced by a college degree as a minimum requirement. In field after field, where once a college undergraduate degree in the appropriate specialization was sufficient for entry, graduate degrees become recommended, then necessary. In some, knowledge has grown enough that additional training time is required; in others it has not. Responses nos. 2 and 3 are means of

increasing the returns to education for students preparing for the relevant occupations, thus minimizing or eliminating response no. 1

The undersupply in some fields is not much of a problem. We simply import scientists, engineers, computer programmers from other nations. But schools cannot afford to do this at present, nor would most school bureaucracies allow it. Some less developed nations, such as India, have a "prestige project" approach to education, lavishing resources on universities before attaining universal primary school enrollment. Egypt until recently had a higher proportion of college graduates than Germany. They provide abundant evidence that supply does not create its own demand in the market for college graduates. But they can export graduates in technical and scientific fields to fill jobs for which the United States is not producing enough workers (as well as to keep American wages down.)

But American oversupply of college graduates is not so easily dealt with. There is no large overseas demand for graduates of American universities majoring in the humanities or social sciences. The distribution of graduates in terms of curricula and majors may be so poorly related to labor market needs that we need too many graduates. Perhaps educational investment in advanced countries can afford to be an end in itself, with little assurance of suitable employment or economic payoff.

Chapter 5

CONSEQUENCES FOR THE ECONOMY

FROM CLASSROOM TO WORKPLACE

Too many people are going to college in terms of the needs of the economy. Not enough are graduating with the skills needed for maintaining its forward motion. Our ability to in-source highly qualified foreigners to fill our gaps in human capital is eroding. The failure of our educational system places our future at risk.

This unhappy situation is the inevitable result of primary and secondary education in this country and its impact on colleges. Since anyone can get into some college these days (and two thirds of high school graduates do), the problem of poorly educated high school graduates is not college admission, it is debasement of the college curriculum and degree, and mismatch between education and labor market needs.

When college students graduate and seek employment, they face a discontinuity between the universe of education and the labor market. Competitive capitalism is meritocratic; employers are selective in job offers, and discriminate in pay and promotion on the basis of performance. Grade inflation in college and debasement of standards for graduation simply defer the consequences to the labor market, they do not prevent them. Egalitarianism in higher education complicates the employer's hiring efforts: how to distinguish between applicants with similar grades and recommendations. Prospective employers who have unreliable information on individual students may adjust by choosing schools before considering individuals (this is not new, but now more prevalent); and by upgrading minimum educational requirements (college, where high school was good enough in the past). Choosing schools before selecting individuals from those schools makes sense if graduation from a particular school, or its grades, or its recommendations are credible indicators of competence. Increasing educational requirements is more of a shotgun approach toward narrowing the pool of eligible candidates.

Employers will make more mistakes than in the past; there will be greater need to terminate new employees who don't pass muster. This will prove highly frustrating to graduates who on the basis of their college records thought they were very able and highly qualified. More money, time and effort will have to be devoted to on-the-job training and remedial education.

One can foresee growing efforts to export the egalitarian norms from school to office and factory, making it very difficult and expensive to terminate workers, as in some European nations. The result has been a combination of great reluctance to hire at all, with persistent high rates of unemployment, or the expansion of an underground economy violating or circumventing regulations: a dual labor market. The former response is prevalent in France and Germany, the later in Spain and Italy. These nations do not suffer from the burden of egalitarian college education or pre-college education largely dissociated from future employment opportunities, or nowhere to the same extent as American high schools and colleges. Still they are paying a high price for limiting the role of worker performance in labor retention decisions.

SCIENCE AND ENGINEERING SUPPLY AND DEMAND

Apart from the quality of the labor force, worker productivity, and the additional costs of training, there is the long run prospect for economic growth. Labor productivity depends not just on its education and training, but on the tools with which it works, and the products it delivers. Technological progress is the necessary condition for improved tools and new and better products. It is also essential to generate new jobs, as existing jobs are lost to nations with much lower labor costs, and as new technology itself permits us to economize on labor. Foreign workers have replaced American textile and clothing workers; higher productivity has reduced farm employment. New jobs in new industries were created, appropriate training was provided, employment and economic growth maintained. But there was nothing automatic in this process; inventions were made, and some of them were translated into new processes, products and services, creating jobs. Who does the inventing, and how does invention become job creation and economic growth?

Scientists and engineers do much of the discovery and inventing. New processes, new products often require technically skilled workers: a double role for workers with technical and scientific skills. One must think of their supply not simply in terms of the needs of the economy as it is currently structured, but in terms of generating the changes in the economy required to maintain employment and economic growth for decades to come.

Table 1 in chapter 4 revealed a decline in the share of bachelors degrees awarded to majors in the physical and mathematical sciences, a decline so large that the absolute number of new graduates in these fields has decreased despite a large increase in total bachelors degrees awarded and in the labor force. The peak year for physical science graduates in absolute numbers was 1982; for mathematical sciences and for engineering graduates it was 1986 and 1985. As physical and mathematical scientists graduating in the 1960s and 1970s retire, it does not appear that recent graduates will be able to replace them, much less maintain their share of the labor force constant. There appears to be a slight downward trend in the proportion of graduates in engineering. Too much should not be read into recent absolute declines for engineers since there are cycles in the choice of majors as a lagged response to perceived changes in market prospects. Nevertheless they are a warning of problems ahead

The situation is not any better at the postgraduate level. At the masters level, the peaks for masters degrees in physical and mathematical sciences were 1971 and 1972, for engineering 1994. At the doctorate level, the corresponding peaks were 1996, 1998 and 1996 [1], in spite of the fact that a high and rising proportion of graduate degrees is awarded to foreigners.

Table 5-1. Civilian employment of scientists and engineers (1000s)

Occupation	1983	2002
Engineers	1,572	2,028
Natural scientists	357	545
Mathematical and computer scientists	463	1,742

Source: U. S. Census Bureau. *Statistical Abstract of the United States 2003*. Washington, DC: Table No.615.

While the numbers of new graduates have declined, demand as reflected in civilian employment has grown considerably. The science and engineering work force is aging; the largest cohort is age 45-49 for graduate degree holders. There are not enough in the pipeline among younger workers to replace them as they retire. The number of graduates as a percentage of employment gives us a rough idea of the adequacy of the flow, assuming no growth at all in the future. Not all graduates in science or engineering will work as scientists or engineers, or do so all their working lives. The number of graduates in science and engineering has been about 3 percent of the number of workers; in math and computer science it has ranged from 1.5 to 2.5 percent. These numbers are insufficient even to maintain the current total employment. Yet the science and engineering labor force (or at least the demand for S&E workers) is projected to grow 13.4% for engineers, 12.2% for physical scientists, and 30.7% for computer and mathematical sciences occupations between 2004 and 2014 [2].

This picture, discouraging as it may be, is still too optimistic. It neglects the fact that an increasing share of our science and engineering graduates and labor force are foreign-born.

INTERNATIONAL BRAIN FLOW: SCIENTISTS AND ENGINEERS

Foreign Students

The current stopgap solution for graduate schools and for the labor market is through immigration. At the undergraduate level the proportion of foreign students majoring in the physical sciences, math and engineering is still small. but at the graduate level it has grown rapidly and has reached the point that universities have become dependent on foreign students in these subjects, and in many cases on foreign faculty as well. The majority of graduate engineering majors are foreign-born, and soon so will be the majority of engineering faculty. A similar trend is apparent in mathematics and the sciences.

A large mismatch between domestic supply and demand is found in most scientific fields once one excludes foreign students. What is rarely noted is that if there is a shortage of Americans for many of these jobs, there must be a surplus of college-educated Americans for non-scientific, non-technical jobs, given the large increase in college enrollments and graduation.

The representation of foreigners among science and engineering post-docs is even more striking. The post-docs are more workers than students. Some teach, but their primary role is as research workers. They accounted for 67 % of physical science, 54 % of mathematical sciences and 70% of engineering post-docs in 2003, all large increases over their share in

1977. The significance is that post-docs are a large share of the university research labor force. Graduate students also play an important role as research assistants [3].

Table 5-2. Degrees awarded to foreign citizens (percent of total degrees)

	Bachelors degrees		Masters degrees		Doctorate degrees		Post-Docs	
	1977	2002	1977	2002	1977	2003	1977	2003
Physical sciences	3.9	6.0	12.3	32.8	15.1	36.9	41.0	66.5
Mathematical sciences	2.8	7.1	11.3	44.9	17.6	44.6	37.2	54.0
Engineering	7.2	7.1	21.8	41.1	29.5	55.6	52.4	69.9

Source: National Science Board.(2007) *Science & Engineering Indicators 2006*. Arlington, VA: National Science Foundation, calculated from Appendix Tables 2-27, 2-29, 2-30, *and 2-35*.

It is not just the students needed to fill or even to offer courses who come from abroad, a rising proportion of the faculties in these subjects are also foreign-born. In 2003, 40% of engineering, 33% of math, 44% of computer science, and 25% of physical science doctorates employed in academic institutions were foreign-born. At the graduate level in the sciences and in engineering, universities are becoming institutions largely staffed by foreign faculty teaching largely foreign students.

Most foreign science and engineering doctorate recipients in the United States have plans to stay and work in the U.S. The proportion planning to stay rose between 1990-3 and 2000-03 from 69 to 79.6% for natural scientists, from 67.5 to 76.4% for mathematical scientists, and from 63.6 to 75.8% for engineering. It is 92.5% for China, 89.2% for India, 66.8% for Taiwan, and 69.6% for South Korea. These are the four nations with the largest number of doctorate recipients in American colleges and scientific and engineering workers in the labor force [4]. The proportion whose plans are firm is substantially smaller, but well over 50% in each field. This appears encouraging in terms of future labor supply.

The number of doctorates awarded to foreigners. peaked in the mid-1990s. Taiwan, India and South Korea have been sending far fewer students since the early 1990s.The numbers from China have also declined, but not as much. Comparing 1992-95 with 2000-03, the drop was 56.4, 32.7, 21.2 and 1.8% for these four nations respectively. For all countries, the decline in doctorates was 8.1% [5]. South Korea is said to have more PhDs per capita than any other nation, and one factor in its amazing progress in less than two generations from one of the poorest nations in the world, with few high school graduates, to income equivalent to poorer West European nations and rising fast.

These nations have built up their own universities. Graduates from American universities and universities of other advanced nations have contributed to the growth in numbers and quality of scientific and technical education in their own nations [6]. Many students who formerly would have sought advanced scientific and engineering training overseas now find it at home.

Table 5-3. Doctorates in physical and mathematical
sciences and engineering, selected nations

	1980	1990	2000	2003
China	0	1,013	6,790	6,996 (2001)
India	2,578	3,583	4,608	5,226
South Korea.	97	684	2,515	2,747(2002)
Taiwan	17	236	762	985

Source: National Science Board (2005). *Science & Engineering Indicators 2004*, Arlington, VA: National Science Foundation, Appendix Table 2-39. National Science Board (2007). *Science & Engineering Indicators 2006*, Arlington, VA: National Science Foundation, Appendix Table 2-43.

Escalating tuition costs in the U.S. could be a factor. India already had sizeable doctoral programs in the sciences by 1975, but the others did not. South Korea began graduating significant numbers of doctorates in natural sciences and engineering in the early 1980s, later in mathematical sciences. Taiwan's growth spurt started in the early 1990s. China was the latecomer, not taking off until the mid-1990s (see Table 5-2).

Economic progress in Asia has generated more jobs for scientists and engineers at home, reducing the number seeking education abroad as a stepping stone to jobs overseas. It has also led to the return of many who have worked for years in the United States to work, to establish new high-tech firms. Evidence that employment opportunities at home for foreign scientists and engineers have increased includes the rapid rise in the number of patents awarded by the United States to residents of Taiwan and South Korea (see below), among others. This is a development to be expected in many countries in the future, shrinking the inflow of students to American universities. Those who do come here now are more motivated by the desire to immigrate, with university study as a stepping stone, than to seek education not available at home. Some come here because they did not gain admission to highly selective universities in their own countries.

The number of foreign students in our universities is expected to continue declining, as is the number of highly-trained foreigners joining our labor force. A process already well under way was accelerated by the World Trade attack in September 2001, which raised barriers for admission of foreign students and workers.

A word about biological sciences. It is expected that an increasing share of discovery and invention in the twenty-first century will be in this area. Most of the degrees awarded in biological sciences, however, are for health delivery-related studies and occupations rather than research-oriented. Doctorate degrees are the exception. This is one field in which the number of doctorates has been increasing, from 3,484 in 1977 to 5,690 in 2003. It is also less dependent on foreigners, who constituted 9% of recipients in 1977, up to 31.5% percent in 2001.

Foreign-Born Workers

American leadership in science and technology is very recent and accidental. In the late 19th and early 20th centuries, Germany was the scientific and technical world leader. American engineering students in the 1930s studied scientific German, then the dominant language of scientific and technical research and publication. During World War II the United States catapulted from being one among several major nations to a world economic dominance unknown in past history. All advanced nations outside the Western Hemisphere and the South Pacific saw their economies in ruins, dependent on American aid for reconstruction and American military power for defense against the USSR. They remained free riders in defense for half a century, but their dependence may have been as much benefit as burden for the United States. Throughout history preparation for war and technological progress have been closely associated, and they still are. Before 1939, the United States received only 18 of 129 Nobel prizes awarded in physics, chemistry and medicine. Between 1945 and 1989, it received 26% of physics, 42% of chemistry, and 60% pf medicine Nobels [7]. But many of the recipients were foreign-born. And the United States has six times the population of the UK, and nearly four times that of Germany.

Through the rest of the 20th century and into the 21st, the United States has been the dominant scientific and technical leader; the world studies English, many scientific publications in other countries now use English only. But it cannot take full credit for this achievement. Major projects during WWII and shortly after, such as the Manhattan Project, relied heavily on foreign and immigrant physicists and engineers. Our space program, the landings on the moon, were led by German rocket scientist Werner Von Braun who earlier had designed the V-1 and V-2 rockets sent against England. This nation has always depended on foreign scientific and technical brainpower.

There is little awareness of our profit from the influx of highly qualified scientists and engineers from Europe just before and after WWII. That generation is gone. With the demise of the USSR and dissolution of the Soviet empire we have benefited from another smaller inflow. Although some brain drain continues from other advanced nations, recently most of the brain drain comes from the third world. Without this large scale brain drain over a period of some seventy years we could not have progressed technically and economically as we did. Today there is no large untapped pool of immigrant scientists and engineers anywhere on the planet.

Whether we look at research universities or institutes, or major research projects, foreign-born scientists and engineers are prominent. The role of the foreign-born scientists and engineers in the labor force is almost as large as in our colleges and universities. The higher the degree earned, the greater their share. This share has been growing In recent decades the main source of foreign-born workers has been through study in American universities, unlike the dominance of European-trained immigrants in earlier decades. But a substantial inflow of immigrants other than students continues. Public high schools, unlike universities and business, are not doing much to import themselves out of faculty shortages; they cannot compete in pay or professional opportunities.

Permanent visas to immigrants in scientific and engineering occupations have been growing rapidly. For engineers they doubled from 8.1 thousand in 1988 to 16.1 in 2001; for physical scientists, they quadrupled, from 1.2 to 4.6 thousand; and for mathematical scientists decupled from 1.2 to 12.7 [8]. Such increases suggest that domestic shortages are increasing. The current total of 65,000 H-1B visas for temporary employment in "specialty" occupations, predominantly science and technology, has been filled earlier and earlier in each successive year, by May in 2007. Since September 11, 2001, visas for students and for workers have become more difficult to obtain.

Table 5-4. Foreign-born U.S. scientists and engineers: percent of total (2003)

	Total	Bachelors	Masters	Doctorate
Physical sciences	23.0%	16.9	28.9	36.9
Mathematical sciences	25.8	19.3	40.4	47.5
Engineering	26.7	21.5	38.3	50.6

Source: National Science Board *(2007). Science & Engineering Indicators 2006,* Arlington, VA: National Science Foundation, Appendix Table 3-20.

Where do foreign-born workers with science and engineering and related degrees come from? The largest national groups in 2003 were India, with 448,700 and China, with 294,000. The Philippines, Germany, the former Soviet Union, Taiwan, the UK, and Canada each had over 100,000. Considering only foreign-born residents with doctoral degrees in science and engineering, of a total of 305 thousand, 62,500 were born in China and 41,300 in India, followed by the United Kingdom, the former Soviet Union, Canada, Taiwan and Germany in that order [9].

These numbers reflect two responses to an inadequate supply of American technical and scientific workers: retention of foreign students after graduation, and immigration of workers who received their technical and scientific training in other countries: "in-sourcing". India is the prime example: exporting graduates of top notch universities. At one time I read that 40% of computer specialists in Silicon Valley were from India. Some have created their own high-tech firms in this country; others have returned to India, and become technology entrepreneurs there

Is the U.S exploiting the rest of the world, especially less developed nations? Yes and no. Underdeveloped nations that produce more scientists and engineers than they can employ could be better off by exporting their surplus instead of having highly educated unemployed and underemployed workers in their midst. One can look at the brain drain in the opposite direction: the United States is financing the research facilities, the high tech enterprises, whose products become available to the rest of the world, many of them, such as valuable new knowledge, at zero cost. It is also subsidizing the higher education of foreign scientists and engineers who return home to create new enterprises and jobs and improve their universities.

Outsourcing

A third response to shortages of American technical workers is foreign "out-sourcing": an increasing share of software development and programming for American firms is being performed abroad, especially in India. Not just software, but biological research. Cost is a factor, but the inadequate domestic supply of highly proficient workers in these fields is important also. Even call-service out-sourcing is not exclusively a cost concern; quality of service can be improved. Who is more likely to give correct advice on income tax questions: IRS or an Indian tax preparation service? It is an open question. The United States has been outsourcing industries for a century: textiles, mining, steel, cars, computers. The difference today is that the industry being out-sourced is the engine of growth: the industry of discovery and invention.

Initially we in-sourced technical and scientific talent, not just through general immigration of workers and students but through the efforts of particular firms to hire individuals with particular skills and capabilities in foreign countries. Since in this country they received American, not Indian pay, it was not pay but scarcity that drove firms to hire abroad. We are still in-sourcing, but at a reduced rate. If there were a higher ceiling on visas for scientific and technical workers, there might be less outsourcing of work and jobs. In the past some American firms conducted research in Europe; now many firms have established subsidiaries in Asian nations not just for production but for research and development. Organizations in other countries, sometimes set up by technical entrepreneurs who had worked in the United States, have contracted to perform services for American firms.

Improvements in communication, especially the internet, bias the choice toward American firms outsourcing more and more of their technical work but retaining control through ownership rather than contracting out. Much depends on tax systems, property rights and business risks in the target countries. America retains a large institutional advantage, but will not have it forever. The main one is the rule of law, not laws as such but a society where laws are usually obeyed and enforced. Most important is the assurance of property rights, especially rights in intellectual property. Also important is the nature of the tax system, which limits property rights. A nation such as China, where everything once belonged to the emperor, later to the Party, is at a great disadvantage. Other nations, where the law is on the side of the party paying the highest price, also have a long way to go. From the rule of appropriate laws follows the incentive and reward for risk-taking, invention and innovation, and a supply of venture capital, both domestic and foreign.

Who needs competent American technical workers, as long as we can import them from other countries? We can maintain rapid productivity growth employing foreigners even if there are not enough Americans up to the job. But can brain imports continue indefinitely? Second, and far more timely, why import them when we can use their skills more cheaply in their countries of origin? The imbalance between domestic supply and demand for such workers will be eliminated not by perpetual brain flows from abroad, but by exporting jobs to lower-wage countries with an excess supply of such workers. India is the leading example, but job exports are under way to numerous other countries. Not low wage, low skill jobs, but technical and scientific jobs. Brain imports is not a permanent solution.

The problem with outsourcing scientific and technical work is that new knowledge does not travel well. Regional clusters of related economic and technical activity are important in offering quick access to information, skills, and business support. Such concentrations feature high rates of new business formation, innovation and productivity growth [10]. Patents in related areas tend to cluster geographically [11].

The U.S. share of global supply of scientists and engineers is declining on three counts: the declining share of Americans being trained in science, math and engineering; declining numbers of foreigners studying here and staying to work in the United States (with some reverse flow of science and engineering work in-sourced in the past); and rapidly increasing numbers of highly trained scientists and engineers in other countries. This nation's share of the global total of new engineering graduates, only 4.9% in 2002, is dropping rapidly [12]. So is the share of new graduates in the natural sciences, 10.8% [13]. Our universities have played an important role in increasing the quantity and quality of scientists, engineers, and computer scientists in developing nations. Their opportunities for employment at home have grown and continue to expand rapidly. This is in their interest and also in ours. This international redistribution of professionals trained to discover and invent is already having an effect on the international distribution of invention and on trade in high technology products and services. The ratio of U.S. high technology exports to imports has fallen from 2.4 in 1980 to 0.84 in 2004.

The concern is both 'short term' and 'long term'. The short term is the imminent retirement of nearly 3 million baby boomers in the physical sciences, engineering, and computer sciences. The proportion among them who majored in math and science in the 1960s and 1970s was much higher than it is today (see chapter 4 table 1) and there were more of them. The long term problem is the fact that only some 5% of US college graduates are earning degrees in engineering (contrasted to 20% in Japan, Germany, Korea and France, and 45% in China. A smaller disparity is found in the sciences. Most of the engineers currently being trained in China and India are poor quality, but this will change in time. The graduates in South Korea and Taiwan are better trained. The American demand for science and engineering workers increased four times as fast as the labor force between 1980 and 2000. From 2006 to 2016 it is expected to grow 10.6% for engineering, 15.7% for physical sciences, 19.9% for biological sciences, and 24.8% for computer and mathematical sciences occupations while the labor force is expected to grow 12.5% [14]. Supply may need to increase even more because of major changes in specialization within these broad occupational groups.

Without an increase in supply the market will adjust by shifting American demand to foreign shores. Many nations are educating far more engineers and scientists than they will be able to employ productively in their domestic economies. Intentionally or not, they are producing graduates for export. But they will not emigrate, as did the previous generation, which studied in the U.S. and remained there. Instead, American firms will deal with domestic shortages and high costs by shifting more and more of their research, development and testing to countries with rigorous graduate programs in science and engineering and a surplus of graduates, and invest in research facilities in these nations as well. The consequence is that more and more of the jobs resulting from new technology will be created in the nations where research and development is done, but many of the jobs lost will be in the United States.

It is not just a matter of numbers of scientists and engineers, but of quality. This is the essential human resource for discovery and invention. For decades we have been attracting many of the ablest and most creative to our shores. The disproportionate share of doctorates in science and engineering who are foreign-born suggests that we have been importing not just workers but talent. It is necessary to replace them with native-born equivalents to maintain the pace of creativity and economic progress.

Most outsourcing has little to do with discovery or invention or the individuals responsible for them; it is based strictly on cost of production. There are two major industries whose costs are running out of control, which incidentally are associated with discovery and invention. These are medical care and higher education. Whereas the cost of food and clothing has plummeted, and that of housing might have done so also had we not vastly upgraded our requirements for housing, health and education consume a large and increasing share of income. Part of the increase in health care costs can be attributed to technological progress, but this is not true of higher education. These two industries are prime targets for outsourcing. Both employ large numbers of technical and scientific personnel. Foreign MDs and technicians are already interpreting MRIs and other tests via the internet. Why not travel abroad for orthopedic and neurosurgery, cardiac as well? Most procedures costing in the five digits and up, many in four digits, are ripe targets for outsourcing. Some patients are doing this already. Select hospitals and clinics overseas can compare with the best in America. Nursing care would be better. Patients and insurance companies would eliminate one digit from their bills. What is now a trickle could become a flood.

Another possibility for outsourcing is the four-year liberal arts college. Medical schools catering to Americans already are in place in the Caribbean and Central America. With many private colleges and universities charging tuition, room and board well in excess of $30,000, and many state universities catching up for out of state students,, the potential for large savings is there. Some foreign localities offer ample opportunities for entertainment which U.S campuses charge astronomical prices to provide. Such colleges would have no athletic scholarships, no large stadia. Internet can provide for much of student library needs, for students who read. Faculty would be hired for ability to teach, not write unintelligible research papers on trivial topics. There would be no tenure. All courses would be taught by faculty, not graduate students. There would be huge savings in tuition, even including travel expenses. Many undergraduate students already spend a year abroad, why not four? They might learn a foreign language if they wish, and experience true multiculturalism instead of the ersatz variety manufactured in American schools.

DISCOVERY AND INVENTION

In the long run it is not education but invention and innovation that keep the economy growing. Inventors can be found in every field, every occupation, every level of educational attainment. But if there is one occupation trained to invent, it is engineering, whose job is problem-solving, whose principal work is process and product design and improvement. Although one can find inventors in every walk of life, it is the engineers and applied scientists who dominate. (I am using the terms invention and innovation interchangeably, although in some technical literature innovation is reserved for adoption of inventions, a process without which inventions are meaningless).

Discoverers and Inventors

The inventors and innovators, the Watts and Wrights and Bells and Edisons and Marconis, are the engineers, and biologists and other applied scientists in fields ripe for invention. They are not the Newtons and Einsteins, who are discoverers rather than worldly inventors. Very soon if not already, India and China will have more highly trained engineers than the United States. Japan and Russia already have more, but Japan is a senescent society and so is Russia. In another generation, Brazil and perhaps additional countries will have more engineers than the United States.

We need both discoverers and inventors. If the engineers are the typical inventors, the physicists during the 20th century were the archetypical scientific discoverers. In this century they will have company: the biophysicists. Long ago inventors and discoverers might have gone their separate ways, but no more. Today, the physicists and theoretical biologists depend on the instruments and facilities designed by the engineers, without which science could not advance. The engineers in turn convert discoveries into useful products, such as microwaves into wireless communication or tools for medical diagnosis or convert the properties of silicon into computers or genetic knowledge into pharmaceutical drugs. Without continued discovery, the inventiveness of engineers would decline.

The aging of scientists and engineers raises another question. For whatever reason, creativity peaks early and declines with age. I suspect it is the curse of specialization that dictates diminishing returns. Perhaps pressure to make tenure is a factor, among faculty. There is pressure to perform also among others whose job security is low in their early working years and whose prospects for promotion diminish with age. Is our aging stock of inventive talent and scientific explorers yielding diminishing returns?

The physicist and the engineer are very different in their ways of thinking, in their motivation and goals. Some cultures are congenial to physicists, to abstract thinking, to scientific discovery; others are congenial to engineering, to improvement, problem-solving. The Greeks were physicists, philosophers, mathematicians; the Romans were not, but they were great engineers. The United States is an engineering culture. Americans are not deep thinkers, they are doers. They deal with the concrete, not the abstract. This is a nation of tinkerers. Year after year, many of the Nobel prizes in the sciences are awarded to scientists working in the United States, but most years (2004 was an exception) the majority are foreign-born, some still foreign nationals. I suspect this will continue although to a lesser extent. America may always need some help with discovery from foreign-born scientists. But there is no cultural reason, other than the failures of our system of education, why we should not generate all the engineers and applied scientists we need, both in numbers and in quality.

Discoveries, unlike inventions, are broadcast worldwide, not hidden or protected by law. Nevertheless the nation that has the discoverers as well as the inventors has a lead on the rest in developing new products.

The not so Far East will produce the physicists and engineers in which America is deficient, and which Europe, facing demographic suicide, will soon produce in smaller numbers. Will they be driven to discover and invent? They can do this when immersed in Western culture, with its ideology of progress, its insatiable curiosity, its individualism and tolerance of risk. But will this culture prevail in the nations of Asia, will their potential discoverers and inventors be driven to venture into the unknown, or be satisfied to replicate a static culture generation after generation?

Sometime in the future the world center of invention is likely to move west, to East Asia. By the end of the current century, perhaps much earlier, East Asia, with its empirical, pragmatic cultures, will dominate in invention and innovation, the domain of engineers and applied scientists. Not right away, perhaps, for engineers will be very busy for a while building the infrastructure which is already in place in advanced nations. We have seen this transition in Japan then in South Korea and Taiwan, now in China. The culture of this area is practical, applied. Thinking is situational, problem-oriented, empirically minded. Already Japan is the leading nation in foreign patent applications in the US; Taiwan is number 3, and its applications and patents, as well as South Korea's, are increasing at a very rapid rate.

On the other hand, the discoveries, the scientific breakthroughs, the Nobel prizes are likely to be centered in South Asia, India in particular. Why India? China may have more engineers and technicians. It is a matter of philosophy, cultural values. The Indians have a tradition of abstract theoretical thought, logic and mathematics; they may find a scientific attitude and scientific method more congenial than do the Chinese [15]. The data on doctorates awarded in their own countries tell the same story. In China, Japan, South Korea and Taiwan, as in the United States, the number of engineering doctorates greatly exceeds the number of doctorates in physical and mathematical sciences combined. It is exactly the reverse in India, which produces fewer engineering doctorates than either Taiwan or South Korea. This Indian preference cannot be explained in economic terms. On the other hand, Japan is second only to the United States in output of patented inventions, but a laggard among advanced nations in Nobel prize winners in the physical sciences.

Western Europe has dropped behind the United States in productivity and economic growth. A similar change of fortunes can be expected for the United States, although more slowly, given the underdevelopment of the East and South Asian continent. The loss of European leadership was its own doing in two world wars. American decline will also be of its own doing, but by peaceful means: disregard of the conditions for invention and innovation. Whether the relative decline of the United States is small or large, slow or rapid, depends mainly on its own educational achievement in science and technology.

It is not just that we do not educate for math and science, but that we overeducate for law. Derek Bok, former president of Harvard, complains that too many of our brightest college students end up in law school. Some lawyers are necessary for the maintenance and improvement of the legal infrastructure of our society. But our excess supply of lawyers produces no good and little service; their main work is redistribution, not production. It is a diversion and a waste of talent better employed in more productive endeavors, quite possibly a negative contribution to economic progress. Pre-law students are the only majors in a field not requiring math who score high on achievement tests as seniors. The abilities and interests of lawyers are comparable in level to some of the sciences. Some professions require deductive reasoning; others require inductive reasoning, not that each profession cannot benefit from both kinds of logic. Lawyers must be good at deductive logic; so must mathematicians and physicists. Engineers must be good at induction, so must be many applied scientists. The cognitive requirements for a good lawyer are not unlike those for a creative scientist: logic, evidence, proof.

Research and Development Expenditures

Invention takes money and time, not just scientists and engineers. The United States is spending nearly 3% of its GNP for R&D. This share has ranged between 2.34 and 2.82 over a twenty-year period. Japan caught up in 1989 and has been spending a slightly larger share since. Germany is in the same ballpark, with France and the United Kingdom not far behind [16]. Aggregate numbers tell us something, but do not reveal the allocation of research effort by field and project, nor the quality and efficiency of the effort.

Nearly all research and development is conducted by industry, but the federal government is a major source of funds. The amount of federal funds changed little from 1985 to 2002 in real dollars, whereas the amount financed by industry more than doubled. Industry now accounts for some two-thirds of research spending [17].

The composition of American R&D is different from that of these other nations. A large share of R&D in the United States is directed at national defense needs. These needs divert money and scientific talent from research aimed at commercial markets. In nondefense R&D

spending as a share of the GDP the United States has lagged behind Japan and Germany for the past twenty years and is roughly on a par with France [18].

There are spillover effects from defense R&D to the civilian economy, but these are uncertain, and may involve long lags. On the other hand, defense research often leads commercial research, whereas in the past it followed. One upon a time the military adopted, adapted civilian technology: telegraph, radio, steam engines and internal combustion engines. But first with the aeroplane, more recently with communications and information technology, the military (and space exploration) has led, with perhaps unintended spillovers into the commercial market. Radar led to the microwave oven. New materials developed to withstand temperature extremes, stress, pressure, conductance, to deflect radiation developed for military purposes have found commercial applications. Communication via earth-circling satellites, global positioning technology, are byproducts of the space program. On one hand, research is funded before it is commercially feasible, on the other hand, its productivity may be low compared to research conducted by business with its own funds. Defense and space research is conducted without regard to potential commercial uses. It is limited in range: sensors, robotics, communications, information processing, specialized propulsion requirements, not pharmaceuticals or energy or industrial machinery.

One could regard 'basic' research as the effort to discover, and 'applied' research and development as the inventive process. Basic research has been financed predominantly by the federal government since the 1960s. Nonprofits, especially colleges and universities, are major performers. Some federal government research facilities also play a significant role: the National Institutes of Health, NASA. Applied research and development is the domain of industry. The role of government is more as a source of funds than as performer.

Another way of looking at research and development is in terms of employment of scientists and engineers. Some R&D requires a great deal of capital, other kinds of R&D are predominantly technical labor. By no means are all inventions made by workers whose primary task is research and development, but the number of such workers is an indicator of the resources devoted directly to discovery and invention. In 2003, over one million (1,116 thousand) scientists and engineers were employed full time in research and development. This was more than double the 469 thousand in 1980 and a significant increase over the 787 thousand in 1992 [19].

Patents

A very rough measure of inventive activity is the number of patent applications and patents granted. The proportion of patents applications to the U.S Patent Office by foreigners is slowly creeping up, as is the proportion of patents granted. The United States has been the world's largest national market for more than a century. Inventors in other nations have had an incentive to apply for patents from the U.S Patent Office. Patents granted to foreigners serve as an indicator of international trends in invention. Between 1963 and 1977, an average of 27.7% of patents went to nonresidents. Since then their share have increased gradually, ranging in recent years from 45 to 48 percent [20].

Most patents are awarded to corporations, not individuals. The proportion going to foreign corporations between 1953 and 1977 was 27.2%, but has ranged since from 37 to 50%. One problem with the numbers awarded to US corporations or individual residents, is that we do not know how many, what share, are the product of foreign-born inventors. On the basis of the proportion of scientists and engineers, especially those with advanced degrees, it should be large. It is a share which is sure to decline. Another is the increasing share of patents awarded to American corporations developed in their foreign research facilities. Friedman mentions large numbers of patents and patent applications from American firms in India [21], a country which barely shows up in patents awarded to foreign corporations.

The national distribution of foreign patent recipients is changing dramatically. West Germany was the leading nation until the mid-1970s, but was been replaced by Japan, which recently has been receiving three patents for every one awarded to Germany. Taiwan, which was number 28 just behind Luxembourg in number of patents between 1963 and 1977, has moved up to number 3. In patents per capita Taiwan is now far ahead of Germany and closing in on Japan and the United States. South Korea, twenty eighth in the early period, is now fourth, just ahead of Canada, France, and the United Kingdom. In 2004, the ten firms with the largest number of U.S. patents included five Japanese and one Korean firm.

India and China and the Russian Federation are invisible, respectively nos. 19, 21, and 24 in number of patents in 2003, behind Singapore. Hong Kong is no. 22. But this is temporary. Russia certainly has the human resources and infrastructure, it just lacks the sociopolitical conditions. India and China are relying for the time being on abundant very cheap labor rather than process and product improvements, on lower costs rather than on new or better products. But they are beginning to follow in the path of Taiwan and South Korea, which have advanced from toys, textiles and apparel to their own brand of cars, computers, and sophisticated electronics. India is already a major player in software and pharmaceuticals; some of its abundant cheap labor is highly skilled.

Let us admit that this is both inevitable and desirable. As other countries rise in income and educational attainment one should expect an increase in the number of scientists and engineers, in research and inventiveness. Technological progress, wherever it originates, benefits all nations, although there are always some losers - individuals who lose their jobs. The issue is whether the United States is doing enough to increase the benefits and to minimize the costs of progress.

As in the case of R&D spending and employment, patent numbers tell us something, but much remains unsaid. Patents vary widely in economic significance - most of them have none. There has been patent inflation, patenting standards are said to have fallen. Some adjustment for quality of patents can be made by noting the extent to which patent applications cite scientific literature. By this indicator, patents from Europe are more significant than patents from Asia. Nevertheless it is clear that foreign corporations and foreign resident individuals are increasing their share of total patents and that Asia is gaining patent share rapidly.

Trade Balance in Royalties and Fees

Another indicator of the competitive position of the United States in technology is international royalty and fee payments and receipts. Receipts still greatly exceed payments, but the ratio is declining. Back in the period 1967-1977, the ratio ranged between 8 and 10. In 1987, it was 3.66; and continued dropping to 1.9 for 2000-2003 [22]. These receipts and payments are a lagged indicator, reflecting inventive activity years, even decades in the past.

The surplus is still rising, but the decline in ratio of receipts to payments can be expected to continue, and the rise in the surplus could soon be reversed.

There has been a major shift in the distribution of both payments and receipts by country. On the U.S. receipts side, Europe was dominant in the earlier post-WWII years, but Japan has` been a larger payer than all of Europe since 2000 and South Korea the second largest. On the U.S. payments side, Japan replaced Germany as the largest recipient in 1993.

INVENTION, EMPLOYMENT AND ECONOMIC GROWTH

The United States is unique among the large industrial nations. All the others face a decline in population. The coming decline in the ratio of workers to retirees dooms their social welfare systems and threatens a decline in per capita income. The United States on the other hand will continue growing for the foreseeable future. The decline in the ratio of workers to retirees will be much smaller and the welfare system is much less generous than in Europe. Furthermore, much of the American welfare system has been private. There is growing realization among beneficiaries that some past commitments are untenable and some movement toward adjustment. Firms that can no longer pay pensions or health benefits can go bankrupt and wipe clean the slate of obligations.. But government cannot go out of business. The United States exports and imports a smaller percentage of its GNP than other industrial nations (Japanese imports excepted), thus a decline in its competitive position - in the value of the dollar relative to other currencies - results in a smaller increase in its cost of living than in other nations. The threat here is different. The engine of growth is slowly running out of fuel. That fuel is the flow of new discoveries and inventions.

In previous centuries the United States became richer by exploiting abundant natural resources and by reaping economies of scale as the nation grew. It was less dependent on invention and innovation for economic growth than it is now. Those sources of growth are over. To grow, even to avoid a possible decline in its current level of living, it must rely almost exclusively on technology: improved processes of production, new and better products. A nation as large as the United States can maintain rising incomes and high employment only if it remains at the frontiers of science and technology on a wide range of industries. It must keep creating new products, industries, and jobs, as productivity gains cut employment in older products or other nations become competitors and gain market share.

Today, when the ratio of workers to population is expected to decline for the next half century, when in-sourcing of highly qualified foreign workers is hampered by security concerns, is not a good time to lose technology leadership. Some economic consequences of playing follow the leader could be chronic high unemployment and a lag in real incomes behind more innovative nations. It may be no coincidence that the nations with the highest per capita number of patent applications to the US Patent Office, and those with the mostly rapidly increasing numbers, are those that have experienced the most rapid economic growth in recent decades.

Agriculture during the 20th century declined from 30% of the labor force to 2%. The United States lost market share in some products, such as wheat and beef, now soybeans, but remains the largest agricultural exporter in the world, and its output continues to rise. Enormous productivity gains permitted agriculture to remain internationally competitive in most crops. Most agriculture-dependent workers never set foot on a farm; they produce farm machinery, fuel and fertilizer, pesticides, they transport and process farm products. Manufacturing initially absorbed many of the workers no longer employed in farming. But it has been declining in share of employment for decades; in the last few years the number of manufacturing jobs declined and is not expected recover. Still, manufacturing output continues to rise.

The prevailing attitude toward the economic impact of new technology since the days of the Luddists has been that it poses a threat to employment [23]. This of course refers to process technology increasing productivity, not new products. There has been little awareness that without new technology there can be no continuing growth; that there will be a loss of jobs as other nations adopt new technology, lowering the cost of their products below ours.

The role of technology in creating new jobs is more important for the future than it has been in the past. Freer trade is one factor limiting ability to preserve jobs in some industries facing low-cost foreign competition, while it promotes exports and jobs in others. Some industries, such as textiles and apparel, have migrated to low-wage nations. In others, employment has declined because of great increases in productivity, despite continuing rise in output. New industries, such as computers and electronic products, have grown, and biotechnology holds promise for the future.

It makes a difference what kind of innovations are made. They may be cost-reducing, thereby improving our foreign trade position and diverting income to other uses. In the absence of expanding foreign sales, such inventions are likely to lead to a loss of jobs, unless consumer demand is highly sensitive to their prices. Or they may be product-substituting, or product-adding. Product-substituting inventions may increase or decrease demand for labor, and any decrease could be either domestic labor or foreign labor. It is the product-adding variety which is most important in maintaining employment and economic growth.

Most inventions are a mix, perhaps there is no purely product-adding invention. The motor vehicle was a substitute for the horse and buggy, and for railroads. It cut time and cost by a large factor for many activities, it generated multiple related inventions: batteries, windshield wipers, and infrastructure investments: highways, filling stations. The same is true of the personal computer. It is the mix of these diverse effects that matters for employment. The PC has displaced the typewriter industry and reduced Post Office and library employment, but opened many new uses.

The mix of inventions is influenced by the composition of scientific and technical workers. Discoveries and the scientists who concentrate on them are more likely to create new opportunities for product-adding inventions than the tinkering of technicians or the problem-solving mentality of engineers. But new discoveries are unpredictable in timing or consequences, and their lead-time to marketable products is very long.

What does it matter where inventions are made? That is where the jobs they create will be filled initially, that is where the training for these jobs will first be established. That is why we are in-sourcing Indian computer programmers to Silicon Valley, in-sourcing scientists from Europe and elsewhere to university faculties, foundations and business firms. Students from all over the world come to our universities. Soon enough our huge competitive advantage will dwindle; either we train Americans for the jobs filled by foreigners or both invention and the jobs they generate will decline at home. Our competitive advantage has already degenerated substantially. We keep running huge trade deficits. But for huge inflows of capital from the rest of the world, new investment would be down and unemployment would be up.

It is more important now than ever before to maintain a constant stream of job-creating innovations because free trade, cheaper transportation and communication have reduced inventor nation advantage in creating the resulting jobs. The loss of our textile and apparel industry did not become important until more than a century after its establishment in New England. The domestic motor vehicle industry started losing market share in half that time. The IBM personal computer was introduced in 1980; within a decade most computers were imported, and some electronic inventions made in this country were first manufactured overseas.

What does it matter whether the United States continues to grow in output and income? It is wealthy enough, although there are issues of distribution of income and wealth. Why should it care whether or not it remains no. 1? It is not just about employment, nor about continued overconsumption. Since 1939 the burden of world history has weighed heavily on American shoulders, and the country is fated to continue bearing it for an unknown future. Until then it must generate the resources to make that burden bearable. It is a task not of its choosing, but it must finish the job. For this reason alone it needs to maintain technological leadership a little longer.

Institutional Climate

A supply of creative scientists and engineers is a necessary condition for continued growth, but it is not sufficient. In other respects, the United States is well-endowed. First, it is by far the largest market in the world, three times the size of its nearest rival, Japan. National markets still matter, for despite much reduction in trade barriers, many remain, if not in the form of tariffs or quotas, then in regulations and obstructions of bureaucratic ingenuity. This advantage of market size is due to disappear in another generation.

Second, the American legal system: property rights, patent, trademark, and copyrights important among them, reduces the risks and uncertainties facing inventors, innovators and entrepreneurs. These rights offer potential rewards, incentives which can justify the risks of investing in research. In this regard we may not be much ahead of Europe, but a light year ahead of China, whose tradition is that everything belongs to the emperor, be he named Ming or Mao. It will take more than passage of laws to create the trust that exists here. India is a different matter; its adoption of an English legal system provides the foundation for an environment favorable to invention and innovation. It is only a matter of enforcement, of minimizing the corruption, as well as reducing government obstacles to foreign investment and technology transfer which prevailed in the past.

Third, as a consequence of both market size and a favorable legal system, venture capital is available to finance new ideas and products, not only from within the country, but from throughout the world. This is not the kind of capital that is pouring into China at this time, but China, India and other nations could attract it in the not so distant future.

Fourth, a decentralized government sector and competitive market system provide many potential sponsors for research and innovation. Authoritarian regimes limit opportunities, as did imperial and Maoist China, and to some extent the USSR. It is still possible to invent a paper clip on a park bench, but most technological inventions require tools and resources far beyond the capability of individuals. Institutions, both public and private, are needed to provide equipment and support services for working scientists and engineers. This country retains a large advantage in this regard, one reason why so many Nobel-prize winners work here, but it is bound to diminish over time.

Finally, the rule of law prevails. This is not the same thing as the legal system. Nations with abysmal societies, governments and economies can point to magnificent constitutions and legal systems. Words are not enough. There must be a presumption of proper behavior, a climate of trust, an obedience to economic laws (no corruption, no conspiracy) as well as to the legal system.

Beyond institutions, there is the American belief in progress, in the superiority of the new over the old, in the willingness to bear risk and uncertainty and accept novelty. This mentality perpetuates a market for novelty, an incentive to invent, and underlies the availability of venture capital and entrepreneurs.

The United States will continue to lead in providing the climate and the resources for invention and innovation, but not the inventors and innovators. The implications of poor training in math and science should be clear from past history. Margaret Jacob [24], in studying the origins of the industrial revolution, asked why was it that England led the way. A major part of the answer is that it had a large number of crafts workers and entrepreneurs who mastered the applied science and technology of the day, and schools which taught the new science and technology to the next generation. Schools on the continent lagged a generation or more behind, and so did workers and entrepreneurs. The rapid catch-up of the Germans in the 19th century, and Japan in the 20th, is no secret. Education and training in science and technology was essential. The lack of an appropriate infrastructure helps explain why China, as technologically advanced as the West long ago, came to lag, never produced its Watts; why India, which gave the West key mathematical and logical concepts, was not the home of a Galileo or Newton. Apart from legal and economic infrastructure, there is a political, cultural and intellectual one as well. This is not the place to consider their interconnection. Tyrannies, dictatorships, theocracies are not good at discovery or invention.

The Middle East and Southwest Asia are an object lesson. Despite ancient civilizations, in many cases a literate, educated populations, countries in this area have lagged behind the rapidly advancing economies of east and southeast Asia. And they are in a constant state of unrest. Lewis [25] points to unemployed young males as a central aspect of unrest and stagnation. This is a problem in particular when the unemployed young males are educated, college graduates. Some East and South Asian countries are dealing with this problem partly via emigration of their well-qualified workers, viz. India, the Philippines. Countries in the Middle East and Southwest Asia have been less successful. Why the difference? Look at the content and method of education in much of the Middle East. The substance is in large part a version of the Koran, the method is rote memory. Graduates in many cases have no useful market skills. Lewis [26] notes the lack of research workers in these countries, the historical absence of translation of works in other languages. By contrast, students in South Korea, Taiwan, also India, China, and other nations in East and Southeast Asia master knowledge more useful in the context of modern society, economy, and technology. These nations are growing rapidly. If there are not enough jobs at home, their educated young adults are employable elsewhere. A second advantage over the Middle East is the availability of educated and trained women for the labor force and for rearing the next generation. Invention does not thrive in backward-looking societies.

The lesson for the United States is that this country too is graduating large numbers who have not mastered the basic knowledge needed for functioning in modern society and economy, who lack employable skills. We adapt by attracting immigrants who have these capabilities (so do some Middle Eastern countries with the oil wealth to hire them). But we cannot expect developing nations to continue subsidizing a country whose educational system is out of step with the needs of its economy. As to our unemployed or underemployed young males, the better-educated are into demonstrations and "causes", the less educated are selling drugs, committing crimes to buy drugs, and highly over-represented in the prison population of some two million.

Paths of Growth

Historically, growth has come in spurts, driven by a major innovation which required many decades to work out its full impact [27]. In the last half of the nineteenth century, it was the steam engine on wheels, which led to the construction of railroads all over the nation, the expansion of the steel industry and coal mining, which in turn lowered transport costs and altered the location of population and economic activity.

In the first half of the twentieth century, the major innovation was the internal combustion engine on wheels, the automobile, which led to decades of highway construction and great expansion of the cement and petroleum industries and eventually reshaped our cities. Electric power was a major parallel invention, turning night into day, requiring the building of power plants and transmission lines everywhere, adding to the demand for coal and oil, steel and copper.

The next major innovation, in whose wake we find ourselves was in information technology, primarily the computer. The first working computers were built in the 1940s, during WWII, to manage information and calculate the trajectory of missiles. It took decades to progress from a machine the size of a house consuming enough electricity to light a small town to a laptop whose computing power far exceeds that of the original monsters. It also took decades for the impact of this new innovation to become evident. Until the mid-1990s, economists were asking, where is the productivity jump long expected from the multiple uses of computers and associated information technology? It has finally arrived. The point is that it took a long time, that growth paths following major innovations are measured in generations, not years, and that the consequences throughout the economy and society are unpredictable. Without the internet the computer would have been just a much better office machine.

There is a big difference between the earlier "long waves" and the current tsunami. Steam engines and railroads were built in this country, the jobs in coal and steel and lumber were American. This was true of automobiles, until the 1970s, when Japanese imports became important, and so did the importation of oil. Today, our computers are made in Taiwan, China, components are made in Malaysia, Much of the software is still American-made, but not for long. Globalization means that the need for inventions is greater than ever if the United States is to maintain rising or even stable personal income. The need is also the result of the changing nature of innovations. Advances in information, electronics, biology have only a transitory impact on domestic jobs compared to the impact of railroads or motor vehicles or electricity. Only invention and innovation in space exploration and defense retain a long term advantage for the United States, largely because of the enormous investment costs involved. But these industries cannot serve as the main basis for generating employment. What this means is that the United States must run faster to stay in place, it must increase its pace of discovery, invention and innovation, at least until differences in costs between countries with the capability to produce the resulting goods and services are greatly reduced. The need is for quality, not quantity, but graduates in science and engineering are the pool in which we fish for talent. A bigger pool contains more talent.

Until recently only a small proportion of world population lived in economically advanced nations with high income, high educational attainment and a supply of technically trained workers that could generate inventions and readily adopt techniques developed elsewhere. Soon the situation will be reversed: most of the world population will be in countries with an abundant supply of scientists, engineers and technically adept workers. What will happen we can surmise from considering what has already happened early in the twentieth century in the case of Japan, later with Taiwan, South Korea, Singapore. As they acquired first the ability to adopt foreign technologies, then to adapt it and to develop their own, their income and educational attainment converged toward those of the nations that first industrialized.

It will take much longer for China and India to approximate the income and education of the advanced industrial nations than it took Taiwan and South Korea. It is this convergence period that poses risks to the economy of the United States and other advanced nations. For decades China and India will have a large absolute cost advantage not only in low skill labor but also in high skill labor. This is the period of potential stagnation and high unemployment, for which accelerated discovery and invention are preventives or cures. The United States would gain through the lower costs of imported goods and services, but skilled workers here would receive lower real wages. If the dollar is substantially devalued, the country could face both higher costs of imports and lower wages [28].

It is an unprecedented situation. The rise of Germany and the United States to challenge the preeminence of the United Kingdom following the Industrial Revolution was never based on cheap low skill labor. The early twentieth century rise of Japan as an economic competitor was initially based on cheap low skill labor, but its competitive edge in high skill labor did not come until two generations later, after it had lost comparative advantage in low skill labor.

The explosive growth of South Korea and Taiwan in the past half century could be easily accommodated because of their small size. But when a nation of over a billion - and there are two of them - follows in their track, the situation is without parallel (other than the United States itself in the twentieth century). Currently most people in both giant nations live not much above the subsistence level. Were they to approximate the levels already achieved by the Asian Tigers, just their demand for numerous materials - not just oil - would exceed current world supply. Major technological innovation will be required if the world is to avoid an inflationary scramble. These giant nations will not be able to achieve first-world living standards through export-led growth, as did their much smaller neighbors and Japan earlier. China will find that export markets are not big enough to accommodate such a policy, nor will its competitive advantage persist much longer. India, which followed a policy of autarchy into the 1990s, is much less dependent on export markets. There is more time to adjust than projections from the recent past would indicate.

There is much concern these days about the loss of manufacturing jobs. Most people blame it on imports. This is a small part of the explanation. Rapid productivity growth means that fewer workers can produce more goods. The import of goods and the export of jobs would have been greater had productivity gains been smaller. Eventually costs in low-wage countries will rise, their currency will appreciate relative to the dollar, and some equilibrium will be reached, but with fewer jobs remaining in old industries at home. The United States would depend on a comparative advantage in capital, perhaps in agriculture, and the legal and economic infrastructure favoring productivity and invention.

Economists might say, no problem, if China and India have a large advantage in labor, both low skill and highly skilled, all that means is that the dollar is overvalued. A decline in the exchange value of the dollar will reduce America's disadvantage in labor costs, and increase its advantage in capital and legal structure. As of today, the dollar has been overvalued, and declined substantially relative to many other currencies. But China is not playing by the economists' rules, keeping its currency pegged to the dollar, despite allowing a minor revaluation. This will change. The equilibrium foreseen is not a happy one: import costs and cost of living will rise, unemployment will be kept in check only if real wages decline. In fact, real wages for much of the labor force have not increased in decades. One factor delaying a further decline in the dollar is the fortuitous fact that other nations, including China and Japan, hold very large reserves in the form of U.S. Treasury securities. They do not wish to see a large drop in the purchasing power of their reserves.

The eventual result will be a great diminution in comparative advantage among the majority of the industrialized countries - it will not be much cheaper to produce most goods in any of these countries than in any other. All will compete for diminishing supplies of cheap low skill labor in a shrinking number of countries, whose labor costs will escalate as a result. Natural resources are a small and declining source of employment for the nations that have them in abundance; low transport costs makes them available to all. Capital flows more freely than ever between nations; differences in the infrastructure that promotes investment and keeps capital costs low will diminish.

A major determinant of competitive advantage and trade balance in the second half of the century is likely to be neither resources nor skills nor capital, but demography. The ratio of workers to retirees is expected to drop to two in many countries, a consequence of increased longevity and sharp drop in birth rates. Public responses to aging population will differ among nations. National differences in tax burdens on workers and business firms may become the principal determinant of competitive advantage. Nations with high female labor force participation rates, late retirement, high ratios of workers to population will have a competitive edge. Nations that neglect their elders will have an advantage over those that cater to them, but not those that neglect their children.

CHANGING SKILL REQUIREMENTSS

The effects of technological changes on skill requirements is a subject of debate and disagreement. There are instances of de-skilling, instances of increased skill requirements. What matters is changing skill needs in the future, and no one can predict the net impact of future technological change on needs for skill, or for that matter on demand for labor. Technological change is not the only consideration; where will the new or higher skills be employed, where will low-skill workers be displaced if not retrained? We cannot assume that any country is self-contained. Whatever our estimates, there are three possible responses. One is different education, another is more education, which implies difference; the third is training of workers. The appropriate response depends on the particulars.

The prevalent belief, relentlessly promoted by the educational lobby, is that the skills required to succeed in the labor market have increased dramatically, and are still rising. By implication, so are the requirements for education. Both statements have a grain of truth, little more.

Even the least skilled occupations now have much higher educational attainment than in the past because so do available workers. But millions of workers in these occupations manage with little education and little English. Higher education and marketable skills have grown apart, as indicated by reliance on foreign students and foreign faculty in math, natural sciences and engineering.

One should distinguish between change in educational needs resulting from a change in occupational structure: a higher proportion of workers in occupations requiring high levels of education or high skills; and changes in education and skill requirements within occupations [29]. The first justifies more people getting a college education; the second justifies more education and/or training for the same number of people.

Formal education cannot prepare graduates for work requirements decades down the road; it only prepares them to work at the time of graduation, and provides the skills for learning in the future. On the job learning and occupational training throughout working life is the only way to adjust to changing job requirements. More years in college cannot do this. Do not go to an MD who graduated first in his Harvard class 40 years ago and has learned nothing new since. Thomas Friedman [30] recommends that most workers remain in contact or have occasional contact with a campus. Over a working life most skill requirements will change, whatever the job or occupation. Workers need retraining or keeping up to remain employable. An implicit assumption is that alternative institutions for training, retraining, updating skills are not up to the job. The apprentice route is passé. At one time some unions did a good job of this. With the decline of unions, the burden is on the employer. Some large firms do a good job. But in a competitive environment there is no tenure, no lifetime employment; employees are mobile. The firm that trains and retrains its workers may be subsidizing its competitors.

Estimates of changing demand for skill rely on indirect measures. The best indicator is the change in occupational structure. The implicit assumption is that the average skill of workers in a specific occupation does not change. But as indicated above, rare is the occupation whose skill needs have not altered. One question is whether workers in occupations whose skill requirements have risen indeed have higher skills than in the past. Widespread complaints by employers about poor preparation and performance of workers suggest that requirements are not being met. Declines in standardized test scores among high school seniors and among college seniors raise the possibility that even if skill requirements of specific occupations remain unchanged, the actual skills of workers may decline. Our managers are much more schooled than their predecessors, but are they any better? What about occupations whose tasks changed little and with which we come into frequent contact? Does anyone think that salespeople or clerical workers today are more knowledgeable, more skilled than their counterparts forty years ago? Rare is the occupation for which the number of years of schooling is a good indicator of job preparation. Occupational skills are often specific, one does not master them in a liberal arts curriculum. If skills have changed in an occupation, years of school rarely address that change. Curriculum content would be a better indicator.

The argument that so many jobs are so much more technical than in the past is grossly exaggerated. New technology is often a way of making a job easier, not more difficult. Millions of jobs require less skill than in the past (many such jobs have been lost as well). Every major technological advance has involved large scale de-skilling. The industrial revolution displaced many highly skilled craftsmen. The workers who toiled in the Ford assembly lines in the 1920s and 1930s were definitely less skilled than those who built horseless carriages, the auto workers of the first decade of the last century. A secretary no longer needs to be a good speller, nor a good typist; Spellcheck can substitute for the first deficiency, and corrections on a PC are simplicity itself contrasted to the whiteout or retyping required in the past. An even touch went out of fashion with the electric typewriter. Multiple identical copies are easily made at the push of a button; who remembers carbon paper? The telephone records the number of the caller, and accepts messages. A sales clerk today does not need the skills required by an earlier generation. Sales personnel can be innumerate and close to illiterate as well, and many of them are. Bar codes read prices, software calculates sales taxes. Mysterious machines check credit cards and avoid the need to make change. Printed instructions, ingredients and warnings accompanying the product are substitutes for knowledge of products and services. Inventory management is largely automated. Millions of jobs can be performed and currently are held by illiterates and inumerates. They will not disappear.

Levin and Rumberger [31], using Bureau of Labor Statistics forecasts of occupational composition, concluded in 1987 that educational requirements would actually decline from 1982 to 1995. The greatest shortage in our complex society, in every type of organization, is competent management, and it cannot be eliminated by piling degree upon degree.

Cappelli [32] studied the increase in skill requirements in manufacturing between 1978 and 1988. For production jobs, most of the increase was within jobs, not shifts in occupational composition. But for clerical jobs, upgrading and shifts in occupational composition were equally important. However, he did not know what jobs were contracted out, what were the effects on other jobs, and to what extent nonunion jobs were redesigned.

Howell and Weiler [33] examined changes in demand for skills. They question the belief that decline in wages of low-skill workers was the result of decline in demand for low-skill workers. In manufacturing, nearly all the shift in occupational composition from production to no production workers occurred in a 3-year period, 1980-'82. In transportation, communication and utilities, the shift to higher-skill occupations was reversed after 1983. In trade and miscellaneous services, the share of skilled workers rose slowly, but there was no change between 1988 and 1996. They concluded that decline in wages of low-skill workers was largely a response to increased competitive pressures, not the consequence of skill restructuring.

Table 5-5 shows the change in share of employment of the most educated and least educated occupational groups. (Note that there are two numbers for 1975; they represent, in order, the old and the new occupational classification. Another reclassification was introduced in 2003.) Most of the increase in share of professional occupations occurred between 1950 and 1970, from 8 to 14.2%. But this increase accounted for only a small part of the increase in median educational attainment during the same period. Much of the increase in professional share was the result of the rise in educational attainment of the large baby boom generation as it entered school: primary and secondary school teachers, college faculty and staff. Employment of the least educated group, operators, fabricators and laborers, has declined substantially as a share of the total, but that of service occupations, almost as low in educational attainment, increased slightly. These are the two groups that experienced the largest increase in average educational attainment.

Table 5-5. Employment in the most and least educated occupational groups
(percent of total)

Occupational Group	1960	1970	1975	1975	1980	1990	2002
professional	11.4	14.2	15.0	11.5	11.9	13.3	16.1
managerial	10.7	10.5	10.5	11.5	11.9	12.5	15.1
Service	12.2	12.4	13.7	13.5	13.2	13.5	14.1
operatives	18.2	17.7	15.2	19.4	18.1	15.2	13.0

Source: U. S. Department of Labor, Bureau of Labor Statistrics. *Employment and Earnings.* Washington, DC. Government Printing Office.

The largest increase in professional specialty employment was concentrated in mathematical and computer scientists, whose number employed more than quadrupled between 1983 and 2002. A large share of these workers are foreign born, and much outsourcing is likely to be in this type of work. One might conclude that this huge increase in employment in professional specialties justifies the current high rate of college enrollment. Unfortunately, the scientific occupations which have experienced large increases in employment, such as mathematics and natural sciences, have had large relative and some absolute decline the number of college majors - modest for the sciences, very large for mathematics. Engineering is better off - the increase in employment was about 30%, whereas degrees have declined only slightly in recent years. As to computer science, whose employment grew from 418 thousand in 1983 to 1,986 thousand in 2002, the closest bachelors degree classification is computer and information sciences, degrees in which exploded in the 1970s and early 1980s, but hardly changed thereafter, averaging around 25,000 until 2000 when they began an upward climb to over 47,000 in 2002, still far short of the percentage increase in the number of jobs. Many of the degrees in "information sciences" may be faddish rather than functional.

A disproportionate share of the managerial, professional and technical labor force - the baby boom generation - will be retiring in the near future, imposing exceptional replacement needs in these occupations. There will be more than enough college graduates to replace them, in terms of numbers alone.

If one were to define skill requirements for an occupation in terms of the educational attainment of its workers, the largest increase has been for unskilled and semiskilled labor, the smallest for professional and technical labor. Obviously this makes no sense. Educational needs for professional and technical labor are probably changing more rapidly than for any other occupational group. But they need not imply more years of school, just a change in what is learned and how. The huge increase in educational attainment of farmers and unskilled and semiskilled workers has little if anything to do with technological change or educational requirements.

Level of education is a poor measure of labor market needs. Education in what, for what, is more relevant. Jobs are being created and destroyed every day. So, at a slower pace, are occupations and industries. Forecasting job openings by occupation involves assumptions about the growth and decline of industries, including the rise of entirely new industries, and the changing occupational distribution within industries.

We must consider the possibility that demand for educated workers may not increase in the future, as all educators and government officials assure us it will. The assumption that only low-skill jobs are lost, and new jobs are all high-skill, has some basis in recent history. But during the nineteenth and early twentieth centuries, much new technology had the opposite effect. History is no sure guide for the future - which history? The potential for outsourcing highly skilled jobs, for downgrading the occupational structure, exists now not for the first time.

Ours is predominantly a service economy, and service jobs requiring some literacy and numeracy are fast disappearing. I go to the subway, there is no one there to sell me tickets or tokens, or to see that I pay admission, just a phalanx of machines that must be occasionally restocked and a gate that demands my token or fare card. I go to the bank; there are a dozen windows for tellers, but only two have a human being, and neither has a line of customers. There are ATMs everywhere, I can make deposits, pay bills, withdraw cash without ever setting foot in a bank. The blood I donate is analyzed for dozens of substances by an elegant machine, not by a battery of human chemical analysts. I want information but don't have to go to a library, I can find it on the web. I can read newspapers and articles in hundreds of magazines without ever buying or borrowing a copy. I can look up airline schedules and buy a ticket without contacting a soul. Some day I will not to have to hunt through the shelves in drug stores and groceries. New jobs are created to manufacture, stock and maintain all these machines, but they are few compared to the number they displace, and they may be in another country.

It is consumption that has become much more complex. New products and new versions of old products offer multiple options unknown in the past, each with its own rules and daunting user's manual. Even in simple items there are dials and buttons and knobs and rings the user must decipher. Watches no longer just keep time. TVs, portable phones represent a higher order of complexity and versatility. They all require literacy but otherwise their mastery is unrelated to formal education or training, just lots of rote memory. For the consumer, much retraining is waste. There is calculated obsolescence of products and incidentally of user skills, built-in incompatibility with older models to sell more computers or software. Almost every consumer product undergoes the same process. How do I set the alarm on my new wrist watch or the focus on my new camera? How can we minimize the consumer and worker cost of competitive war? One question bothers me: how much of the training and retraining needs of industry and of consumers represents costs of technological progress, how much is waste associated with competitive pressure to innovate products and processes?

NATIONAL RETURNS TO COLLEGE EDUCATION

If there is a disjunction between education and the needs of the economy, what does the return to education have to do with economic growth? Private returns are relative: higher attainment is correlated with higher earnings. The college graduate gets better jobs than the nongraduate, has better opportunities for advancement in jobs, occupations, careers. This is true whether the economy is expanding, static, or declining, whether the college graduate's income is increasing or not, whether it is higher than that of previous graduates or not. High private rates of return have been found in countries doing well and in countries doing badly.

In recent decades there has been a shift in composition of graduates away from majors with high earnings, tending to widen earnings differentials. There has also been a shift from the subjects whose masters are most likely to discover and invent. Meanwhile, the value of a diploma has been degraded either as an indicator of ability or as an indicator of learning. This is the result of college admission to nearly all high school graduates who wish to pursue higher education - the majority - and curriculum diffusion and debasement. Nevertheless, private returns have not fallen.

The screening role of college admission, and of college graduation, has been severely undermined. Only by ranking degrees by college or university is it possible to restore a useful screening or predictive role for the sheepskin. Essentially colleges are ranked by their admissions standards, which are easier to compare than their instruction processes. The degree screens, but for what? College graduates with different majors have a different mix of ability, learning, and monopoly rent. Who is screened out, who does not graduate? Is it ability, effort (learning), socioeconomic status, behavior and personality?

Education is a good investment for many individuals. But is it a good investment for the society that demands it and the economy that subsidizes it? Does the taxpayer pay for too many graduates in some fields, too many overall?

Social Returns, the Traditional View: A Critique

Private returns to additional education are better jobs and pay (net of taxes), minus costs borne by the individual or family. But what is the "social" return to society? Social rates of return as typically calculated are simply private rates of return adjusted. Social costs are calculated by adding all other costs to those borne by the student and family. Social costs are invariably greater than private costs, since college education is subsidized, most heavily in public institutions. They include the loss of the student's potential earnings from full time employment while in school. On the benefit side, the incremental income taxes paid are added to private benefits. Social benefits also include the impact of higher productivity of graduates on that of other workers, promoting economic growth. Other proposed benefits, such as reduced the crime rate, improved health are hoped for, but none are reliably quantifiable. The social rate of return as usually defined can be high in countries advancing rapidly in productivity and income per capita, and in countries that are static or even declining in productivity since it is an addition to private benefit of graduates. Given the negative rates of growth observed in numerous countries, plus pursuit of questionable educational policies: large subsidies, excessive enrollments in higher education in terms of the needs of the economy, it is truly amazing that all social rates of return as reported in the literature are positive and most are large! This makes no sense to me. But if the social return is simply the private rate adjusted for educational subsidies plus taxes paid by educated people, that is what we get. It is used to justify ever-increasing public subsidies to higher education with no end in sight, since such investments need never face diminishing returns.

Estimating social rates of return to education by making adjustments to private rates assumes that the private rates reflect gains in individual productivity associated with investment in education. However, as discussed in Chapter 4, some returns to college education are attributable to the information provided to prospective employers about the capabilities of the graduates, which makes a contribution, although a smaller one, to productivity. And some of the returns are monopoly rent, a protective tariff for high-paying occupations and jobs, whose contribution to social returns is negative, not positive. Only incremental returns reflecting the learning and behavioral outcomes of education are properly returns to education. Thus estimated rates of return, both private and social, are too high, by how much we do not know. They result in misguided recommendations and policies.

Social returns as conventionally defined contribute to economic growth/productivity gain only under restrictive, unrealistic assumptions: that differential private returns faithfully reflect differences in productivity, and that incremental education for some does not adversely affect the return to anyone else. Social return should reflect the loss of income involved in deferring entry into the labor force. But it should also reflect the loss of income to high school graduates who do not attend college, and to college dropouts who are screened out of jobs they could perform. Social rates of return as adjustments to private rates implicitly assume that occupational distribution and corresponding economic structure adjusts to changes in the number of college graduates, and does this rather quickly. (Otherwise, increases in number of graduates could reduce job and income opportunities for nongraduates.) Such an assumption is reasonable for a single individual, but not for the group. For a nation, it represents a fallacy of composition.

Another implicit assumption is that investment in education is the efficient cause of economic growth. There is evidence that the causal relation is the reverse: growth leads to increased investment in education, not the other way around. Bills and Klenow [34] examine the impact of schooling on the growth of human capital and on the growth of technology, then examine the impact of expected growth on schooling, and conclude that the predominant relation is that of growth on schooling. Hanushek and Kimko [35] examine the relation between education and subsequent economic growth for many nations. Using 8th grade test scores in math and sciences as indicators of educational quality, they find that quality of education is important, whereas the proportion completing high school is not significant. Labor force quality, indicated by tests of math and scientific skills, accounts for 40% of the variation in productivity. However, their analysis neglects higher education, which is important for growth of more advanced nations which rely on scientists and engineers for ideas and inventions.

South Korea and Taiwan were well on their way to advanced nation status before any significant gain in educational attainment of their labor force. It does take a decade or two for increased educational attainment of new generations to upgrade the labor force. On the other hand, nations with high educational attainment, especially in scientific and technical areas, such as Russia and some states formerly part of the Soviet empire, have not done very well. To some extent this is also true of some nations in the Middle East. There is much more to productivity and growth than educational attainment.

Differences in individual productivity are mainly an attribute of jobs, occupations, organizations, industries, only secondarily of the job performance of individuals. Thus it can be plausibly reasoned that individual returns are a function of social returns as well as the reverse. The structure of society and economy engage or constrain the efforts of educated workers.

Can we say that the large increase in numbers, and percentage of the age group, finishing high school in the 1940s and 1950s, finishing college between 1950 and 1970, increased the growth rate of the economy? That the stagnation in these ratios and numbers since has slowed the growth rate or hindered its increase? The growth that matters is in productivity or output per worker. Productivity growth, which had been rapid in the 1940s and 1950s, was very slow in the 1970s, 1980s and the first half of the 1990s. Then the rate of productivity growth rose abruptly, and has been well above historical averages since the late 1990s. There does not appear to be any relation between trends in higher education and lagged trends in productivity. What has driven productivity is investment in new and improved technology, not more college graduates.

Numerous articles and doctoral dissertations have been written on the social (and private) returns to education. They would be harmless, if useless exercises in numerology were it not for the tendency of analysts and policy makers to use them as indicators of the inadequate level and allocation of resources to education. Social rates of return as usually defined are no such thing, and numbers resulting from numerous studies are neither comparable nor suitable as guides for educational policy.

The simple conclusion is that the social rate of return as conventionally measured has little to do with economic growth. A more complex reaction is to ask, what is the growth baseline? What would have happened had there been less education, or more education? This baseline is not the same for every country, or every time period. Sometimes it is zero, sometimes negative, sometimes positive. Ours has been positive for a long time as a byproduct of population growth and resulting economies of scale, among other factors. There are numerous variables affecting growth rates, such as property rights, natural resources, public policy; education is but one among many.

If growth in GDP per capita is unrelated to rates of return to higher education, what are the possible partial explanations? First, earnings do not reflect individual productivity, nor do differences in earnings reflect differences in productivity. The most persuasive evidence against this hypothesis is the age-earnings profile, which suggests differences in productivity grow with age. Even here one may argue that differential access to training and experience, rather than educational attainment, accounts for the steeper age-earnings profile.

A second explanation, in support of the first, is that access to higher education (in many countries to secondary education), has little to do with individual ability, much to do with the wealth, status, influence of parents, friends and relatives. Access to well-paying jobs is likewise determined, with higher education a dependent, not an independent, variable. This inter-generational effect is less important in this country than in most others, and less today than in the past.

Third, productivity may not be a function of individuals but of the organizations in which they work; more educated individuals are employed by more efficient organizations. This is undoubtedly true, but raises questions about the direction of causation. Another consideration is that productivity is a function of the resources supplied to the workers, not that of the workers themselves. A man with a plow is more productive than the same man with a hoe; a doctor with a team of nurses and technicians is more productive than a doctor working solo. But then what accounts for efficient organizations, or for superior productive resources?

Fourth, as incomes rise, education becomes more and more a consumption good rather than an investment. A rising share of curricula are productivity and economic growth-irrelevant, hence one would expect a decline in private and social rates of return if in fact they reflect productivity gains. This has not happened. What is undoubtedly true is that there must be diminishing returns from increasing educational attainment. At some school-leaving age, if not 21, then perhaps 25, additional educational costs begin to exceed additional benefits. Education needs to change with the structure of the economy, but change does not always imply more.

Social Returns to Education and Economic Growth

I would define the social costs of investment in education in terms of the costs to the economy, i.e., private costs to students and their families plus costs borne by governments and various donors. But the benefits have little to do with returns to educated individuals. As a counterpart to the private rate of return, the social benefit is not the pretax incomes of graduates minus subsidies, but much more widely distributed. Social returns of college education should include not just the productivity gain of educated individuals but also their impact on the productivity of others, the contribution to economic growth/productivity gain. If there is a surplus of college graduates, private returns will be positive, but social returns of additional education can be negative. There are additional costs, but no additional benefits. Social returns may also refer to quality of government, improved health, reduced crime rate, an informed and considerate society, apart from any impact on productivity and growth. These benefits are not limited to members of the labor force, but accrue to all. Unfortunately these qualitative returns largely defy measurement.

Of the three major determinants of private returns, only economically relevant learning is part of national return. Differential ability (broadly defined to include whatever is pertinent to performance) is not part of the social return unless magnified by learning or simply identified via graduation. The sheepskin as monopoly return is no part of national return; it may reduce it. To the extent that educational restrictions on access to jobs are unrelated to quality, or are excessive as quality controls, they increases the private rate of return, but reduce social rates of return by shifting resources from production to education and by misallocating workers. But the sheepskin as information is a plus.

We need to distinguish between static and dynamic social returns to investment in education. In the former case we look at differences in income associated with differences in educational attainment at a point in time: social returns as private returns adjusted. In the latter case we look at the differences in income associated with differences in educational attainment at different points in time: changes in educational attainment and in per worker output growth. Much of the lifetime return to more education is not the result of the education as such but of increases in productivity of the economy over the individual's working life. The distribution of these gains is influenced by many variables, among which the formal education of the worker may be a minor factor.

From a static standpoint, educated highly skilled workers retire and die and must be replaced. The level of educational attainment consistent with the structure of the economy and a constant private rate of return should be maintained if per capita national income is not to decline. If population is growing, then the numbers of secondary school and college graduates must grow in pace.

One cannot infer from the fact that college graduates earn much more than high school dropouts in a static economy that therefore expansion of investment in college education yields a positive macroeconomic return. This could only be true if it should lead to increased productivity, to growth. An increased proportion going to college can only result in macroeconomic benefit if the economic and occupational structure of society has changed in such a way as to increase demand for the abilities and skills of the college-educated, provided that the increase in graduates is related to the unmet needs of the economy. Change in the occupational structure can be the result of new technology, or of changing international competitive position. In neither case does it always result in an 'upgrading' of the occupational structure.

From a dynamic standpoint, new or improved processes and products must be discovered, invented, innovated. This requires creativity and enterprise. And it requires time; the process of inventing and introducing a new process or product can take decades. There are other sources of productivity growth. Reduction of trade barriers and enforcement of competition improve the allocation of resources. Tax systems can be designed to encourage or discourage investment in research and new products. But these other sources tend to be self-limiting.

The principal determinant of productivity gain in the long run has been technological change. Many nations can maintain forward motion for generations simply by playing catch-up. The United States did that in the eighteenth and much of the nineteenth century, but now it is the turn of others. An economy that is already on the frontier of economic development has no place to go. It must create new opportunities via discovery and invention, not by following the leaders. A small country, an underdeveloped country, can advance without its own industry of discovery and invention, as long as it has the skills needed to adopt technologies developed elsewhere. But a very large nation, one at the forefront of technical progress, cannot advance in copycat fashion; it must generate much of its own new products and new technologies.

Technological change is not the result of the number of college graduates, but of the invention and innovation of individuals, most of whom are graduates, but most of whom are technically trained: applied scientists and engineers. It follows that returns to education of most workers in the long run depend not just on their ability and achievement, but on the creative contribution of the discoverers and inventors. In a competitive world, the discoverers and inventors are essential to maintain the value of the human capital stock.

Inventions and innovations may or may not require adaptation of the labor force via education of the next generation of workers; they may or may not need an increase in educational attainment. But almost invariably they require training of the current labor force. It is the change in industry and occupation mix that raises productivity, skills facilitate the change, and education follows. Change is accomplished by the existing labor force, only gradually can it be supplemented by the educational system, which is not a substitute for specific training or learning on the job. The motive power of economic growth for a large nation on the frontier of science and technology must be the creativity mainly of engineers and applied scientists generating a continuing stream of inventions and innovations. It is not the result of rising average educational attainment, which obviously cannot rise indefinitely.

Is the pace of creativity related to the number of scientists and engineers, or more closely to their quality – the number with doctoral degrees? Are there diminishing returns – natural limits to what humans can accomplish in particular fields? We do not know. Particular technologies have limits, but new technologies have replaced them in the past

There are consequences beyond the economic that follow from slower growth and loss of scientific and technological leadership. This nation, because of the size of its economy and inventiveness of its people, plays a unique role in the world culturally and politically. It is the exceptional nation, and at this time the indispensable nation. One need only think of what the world would have been for the past 65 years, would be today, had there been no United States. It bears the heavy burden of history and cannot shift it to other shoulders. Continued growth makes the burden bearable.

Economic Impact of the Industry of Education

One can view the economic impact of the "industry" of education from different perspectives. The first is the allocation of resources to education, resources that might be productively employed elsewhere. One consequence is a smaller labor force because of delayed school-leaving. A second perspective is the impact on the labor market and on the functioning of the economy of successive generations of graduates. Do schools produce graduates trained in basic skills and the right numbers with occupation-specific knowledge? Poorly educated workers impose costs of remedial training on business and government, contribute to low productivity and low potential output and income. How much do schools spend, and how well do they spend?

Inefficiency and Resource Waste in Education

Perhaps the largest cost and loss to the economy is that of keeping nearly all of the 5-17 and much of the 18-21 age group in school full time, producing nothing, learning so little in the first twelve years of school that a large proportion of high school seniors are semi-literate and have problems with basic arithmetic. Many students enter first grade able to read, why should it take many others an additional 12 years? What do they learn during this long sentence of benefit to them, in return for what we pay? Or are schools merely institutions for communal confinement and deferment of labor force entry? The waste is not graduating such a large proportion of the age group, but a combination of low standards and low achievement, and failure to address the needs of students who are not or should not be college-bound but are or should be work-bound. The outcome is lack of skills, lack of direction, and lack of information for potential employers, as well as for college admissions officers. Many colleges in turn enroll and retain students who lack the elements of a minimal education; and provide a watery soup of recondite material pretending to be useful learning for the next four or five years for those not determined to master useful knowledge. College admissions officers make too many mistakes, given the lack of standards and reliable information on high school student achievement. Colleges invest large resources in remedial course work. The attrition rate is very high, despite easy grading and wide choice of courses, a waste for the student and for the taxpayer and philanthropist. The student benefits little from an incomplete college career, either in future income or in job prospects, and suffers the income foregone by not working full time.

The college degree does serve as an employment and occupational gatekeeper for nearly all students. For some majors, college prepares them for on the job training after graduation. But for many majors, college provides little in the way of job-related skills; its sole role is as gatekeeper. (College is not just about preparation for work, but that is the function relevant to estimates of rates of return to a college education). It deprives individuals who do not go to college of opportunities for jobs they would be perfectly capable of performing, depressing their earnings. Appropriate tests would be a better means of selecting suitable employees for many jobs, at a tiny fraction of the cost of a sheepskin.

Let us call higher education for what it has become: investment for some, entertainment, procrastination, consumption for many. Whether that consumption be intentional: cultural or conspicuous, or simply misdirected investment, it is a waste of resources from the viewpoint of the economy. Perhaps the society does want to delay entry into the full time labor force until age 21 or later; perhaps it wants most or all its citizens to have the opportunity to learn whatever they wish until then. It may be a better use of abundant resources than mindless overconsumption. But let us not pretend that handing out college diplomas to an ever growing proportion of the population is an economic investment for them or for the government that subsidizes them.

College entry and completion may implement social goals of equality of opportunity if not equality of outcomes. But it does not enlarge the universe of opportunities. To the extent that the result is excessive admissions and/or inadequate quality controls for graduation, the value of information provided by degrees, grades, letters of recommendation is compromised. Employers face higher costs of information about job applicants and/or higher costs of training.

There is a profound misunderstanding of the role of formal education in an advanced economy. College degrees do not produce full fledged members of the productive labor force. All they can to is provide capable trainees. Most of the skills are acquired through training and experience, on the job. They are specific to tasks, occupations, organizations. Professional schools and certificate programs are a very partial exception. The greater the skill level of an occupation, the greater the rate of growth in productivity, the greater the need for worker learning, training and retraining, throughout much of a working life. Yet first in high school, now in college, the process of education has minimized the role of trainee preparation, replacing it with a menu of consumer choice.

The mediocre quality of American public school education, in particular the low quality of technical and scientific education, slows future productivity growth, undermines future employment prospects, and threatens our levels of living. A surplus of graduates does not stimulate the growth and change required to absorb the surplus.

Labor Force and Wage Effects

Sixteen million college students are spending on tuition and living expenses, and receiving learning, some of which is convertible eventually into well paid jobs, but some of no economic and little if any social value, plus entertainment, which is consumption, not investment. Income foregone by not working during the years of college attendance is a major cost of education. Social income foregone is not simply private income plus tax revenues foregone. College enrollment of 16 million is equivalent to 12 million workers, assuming a labor force participation rate of 75%. This is roughly 9% of employment. There are some 4 million 18 year olds, 4 million 19 year olds, etc. Changing college attendance by one year would change the labor force by 3 million workers, or 2.2%. This is an overstatement, since many college students work part time, some full time. Such an increase could be achieved not by reducing college attendance rates but by completing high school in 10 or 11 years instead of 12, or by completing college in 3 years, as some do by attending summer sessions or taking extra courses during the academic year. Accelerating educational attainment pre-college involves minimal reduction in the labor force, hence it is much cheaper than doing so later. It affects the entire age group, instead of just the share that goes to college.

If twelve million college students were to become full time members of the labor force, there would be downward pressure on wages and possible increases in unemployment rates. Thus some of the return to college education is the higher wage levels associated with a reduced labor force. Much of this "return" accrues not to college graduates, but to other workers, since there is some competition between graduates and nongraduates for jobs. The college student confers this benefit on workers while absent from the labor force, and when working after college receives this benefit thanks to later cohorts of college students who continue to hold down the size of the labor force.

One could argue that even without any impact on occupational distribution, more years of education will increase labor productivity enough to compensate for the decline in working years plus the diversion of resources from production to additional education. This might happen, but it is in the realm of hopeful speculation. A further consequence of increases in average educational attainment is a reduction in the quality of education. There is some tradeoff between quantity and quality. This would have to be subtracted from any increase in individual productivity resulting from additional education in the absence of occupational consequences.

In the long run, everything depends on isolating the contribution of four years of education as distinguished from that of superior ability, energy, motivation of college graduates, and the sheepskin effect on employer hiring discrimination. College admission and graduation is still a selective process, which would be associated with higher incomes even if no one learned anything in college, if no one experienced any improvement in work-related abilities as a result of the schooling. For individuals, learning and consumption benefits can be added; for society, adding production and consumption is double-counting.

Delayed entry into the labor force, if not compensated fully by delayed retirement, aggravates the problems of Social Security and Medicare. Increased life expectancy has reduced the ratio of years worked to years in retirement. Any policy that further lowers this ratio is to be avoided if possible. In the past the typical retirement age for blue collar occupations was younger than for white collar occupations. If additional years of education for an individual means access to an occupation with higher average retirement age, then there is no reduction in the labor force and could conceivably be an increase. But to generalize this finding assumes that more education generates more jobs that require the additional education. There is no justification for a supply-side effect on demand for graduates. Thus beyond a certain number of graduates, the excess must work in jobs which require the same kinds of physical capabilities which prevail in jobs held by non-college workers. If the occupational; distribution of the labor force (education industry excepted) is not affected by the additional education, then there should be no change in the average retirement age.

It is not only the surplus of college students that would enter the labor force, increasing employment and output, damping wage increases. The industry of higher education would shed many workers, including many highly trained professionals, who would be available for work other than training students for jobs in excess of labor market requirements. Their skills might find more productive uses elsewhere as demand is reallocated from colleges to the rest of the economy.

Occupational Structure

An advanced society, whatever its politics or ideology, is highly hierarchical. This is the unavoidable condition for industrialization and high productivity. There is little room at the top, much room at the bottom. This is just as true of public and nonprofit organizations as of business firms. There are few employers, many employees. The distribution of occupations is determined by technology and by final demand, which in turn are somewhat interdependent. It is not much affected by educational attainment or specialization; on the contrary, the occupational structure is the main influence on educational specialization. Higher educational attainment increases employment in the industry of education, most of which is public. There is little that egalitarians can do about either hierarchy or occupational structure.

Even if all had the same ability, achievement, and education, the occupational hierarchy, whether defined in cognitive and skill requirements, status, or power, would remain. Perhaps a lottery would be needed to decide who goes to graduate and professional schools. Or everyone could go, then a lottery could decide who gets what jobs in which occupations. Or, for occupations that can be practiced by individuals or small groups, everyone could put out a shingle, and let consumers decide who practices. We would have a great surplus of MDs, many of them with only part time work, as Italy had for years, and necessarily a great shortage of some other occupations. Even if a maternal state were to assure everyone equal incomes, the occupational structure would persist. We would be flooded with odes to the common man, but few would pick up the garbage. Work assignments might require a lottery and a draft.

It is the independence of the occupational structure from the level of educational attainment and the distribution of graduates by field of specialization that sets limits on economic gains from increasing educational attainment. Supposing everyone completed college, what would everyone do? How would universal graduate study improve economic growth? If everyone were well-trained for high-skill jobs, occupations, careers, the result would not be that everyone would succeed in work. Instead, the relative pay of such high-skill, high-status jobs would decline, that of low-skill, low-status jobs would increase, and a large proportion of those trained for high-skill jobs would spend frustrated working lives in humble occupations. This is already happening; only the large inflow of low-skill immigrants, legal and illegal, keeps low-skill wages from rising, despite the poor preparation of so many of our high school graduates and dropouts

The occupational structure is a major aspect of social status. Current concerns about the near-absence of net upward mobility in terms of "class" reflect the stability of occupational structure. Social mobility is still a positive-sum game: someone need not move down for everyone who moves up. The net upward mobility reflected in change in occupational distribution is less than it seems. At the high end of the job market, some of the upward mobility reflected in the growth of scientific and technical occupations is the result of an inflow of educated immigrants. Education and training of more Americans in these occupations would on one hand reduce the in-sourcing of foreigners, on the other might reduce the out-sourcing of jobs. At the lower end of the occupational distribution, net upward employment. In the middle, the encroachment of college graduates into occupations formerly held by high school graduates lowers the ceiling on upward mobility for many.

On the hopeful side, occupational skill requirements may continue rising while the proportion completing high school and completing college seems on a plateau. The surplus of college graduates could fade away, provided the disparity between choice of majors and occupational needs is reduced. But there is a real possibility that with a decline in international comparative advantage in highly skilled jobs and occupations, mobility will become at best a zero-sum game.

Education as a Positional Good

Fred Hirsch [36] once wrote a book, *Social Limits to Growth*, that described the growing importance of socially limited goods - goods and services that cannot be indefinitely reproduced, whether it be an Old Masters oil painting or bucolic cottages on empty beaches or the presidency of the United States. Some are physically limited, others generate negative externalities undermining their own value: the beach becomes crowded, noisy and dirty.

Education is also subject to absolute limits if viewed not as an end in itself, a consumer good, but as a means toward other ends, as a capital good. As a means toward higher income and access to desirable jobs, occupations, and careers, it too is a limited good. Even as a consumer good, as numbers of graduates increase, it loses its badge of distinction, degrading from luxury to necessity. Beyond some point perhaps already reached, more education becomes a socially counterproductive treadmill. High school graduation for all, now college attendance for all, later college diplomas for all merely requires an explosion of graduate enrollments and graduate degrees, well under way, raising the age of labor force entry and over-expanding the inefficient industry of higher education, wasting years and resources in positional struggle. Since the cost of more education eventually includes a reduced number of years working and earning, there is a problem of diminishing returns. At some school-leaving age, additional educational attainment becomes a negative-sum game. For many individuals it is a lottery. The house always wins, no wonder it promotes gambling.

It may be true that any individual can increase annual income as a result of obtaining more education. It is a positional good: the benefit to the individual depends on his attainment compared to that of others. Workers as a whole cannot gain. The main exceptions are the jobs and occupations associated with an expanded education industry: faculty, administrators, staff. What is limited is not the educational attainment, quality aside, but the supply of desired occupations. We already have many unemployed lawyers and underemployed dentists. Were we to double the capacity of medical schools, we would end up with many unemployed doctors.

For lack of adjustment at the bachelors level, in some fields the positional struggle for new entrants into the labor force has advanced to graduate study. This has happened not in the professional schools such as law and medicine which long have been the gatekeepers to these occupations, but masters degrees in a wide variety of fields with an overabundance of graduates and/or whose undergraduate training lacks focus or rigor or occupational counterpart. In 1950, masters degree recipients were 13.4% of bachelors degree recipients; by 1960, they had risen to 27%. Since then, masters degrees have crept up to 40% in 2005 [37].

Teaching vs. Research

Another source of waste is the college faculty tenure and promotion system requiring publication at the expense of teaching. Many universities and some colleges pretend that they are centers of scholarship rather than teaching institutions and seek to emulate the few that are indeed centers of scholarship by hiring faculty on the expectation of research and publication and rewarding them with promotion and tenure on that basis. Time and effort devoted to research is time and effort not available for teaching and students. In order to encourage research and publication, universities have radically cut teaching "loads" for their tenure-track and tenured professors. As a result, there are too many faculty members. The stress on research and publication accelerates the trend toward narrow specialization.

Lotka's Law tells us that creativity any field is extremely unequal in distribution. For example, one percent of the workers in a field may account for half the contributions, the next five percent for nearly all the rest. The most creative scholars in every generation probably end up in faculties or foundations. Their research output is largely independent of priorities for research vs. teaching. The number of college faculty has more than quadrupled since 1950. With pressures to publish or perish, formerly limited to leading universities, now exported to four-year colleges and through much of the industry of higher education, the quantity of published research has increased many times over, accommodated by a multiplication of journals to publish them. One would expect an explosion of new findings. Where are they?. The advancement of knowledge is not a function of the multiplication of researchers in most fields. The same model of research productivity is applied to every subject. There are fields where research output does advance knowledge, others where it simply adds publications, compositions, objets d'art. Science and technology advance in stepladder fashion: today's achievements are based on yesterday's accomplishments. But today's literature does not replace Homer, or advance on Shakespeare; it just adds to the volume of available reading. Research is an appropriate interest in the former, much less so in the latter. One contributes to the structure of knowledge, the other just adds to the stockpile.

Much academic research is not a contribution to knowledge or asset in teaching, just a means of tenure, promotion, ego enhancement, and when funded, profit to non-profit institutions. Knowledge grows through interconnection, not multiplication. Enough is enough; more is waste.

Today there is a prevalent belief that teaching detracts from faculty research, but I have not seen credible evidence to that effect. For some faculty, course preparation and teaching generate much of their research ideas and contribute to the research process. Perhaps there is no strong inverse correlation between teaching load and research output. There is some evidence that teaching contributes to research [38]. Whatever the case, there are research institutions, in the private sector, in government, within universities, where qualified individuals may devote full time to advancing human knowledge without conflicts of interest. They may get ideas from each other rather than from course preparation and teaching. The primary purpose of most universities is and should be the production of educated and trained graduates, not working papers and publications.

The stress on research and demeaning of teaching is to some extent the self-serving belief of faculty and administrators who went through the rigors of a Ph.D. program, which is a research degree. It is a fairly recent development. Surveys in 1969 and 1989 by the Carnegie

Foundation for the Advancement of Teaching found huge increases in the proportion of faculty who believed it difficult to gain tenure without publishing. In particular, only 6% of respondents in 4-year colleges and universities not granting doctorates thought so in 1969,, but 24% in colleges and 43% in universities thought so in 1989 [39].

The cost to the economy is not just that of faculty overstaffing and neglect of students, but the potential output of highly educated and able individuals were they engaged in other occupations. A surplus of college professors, like the surplus of lawyers, is a lost opportunity.

Chapter 6

SIMPLE 'SOLUTIONS'

Why are our schools so bad, and what can be done about it? One should recognize that comparisons of high school student achievement today with 50 years ago are imperfect, for two reasons: 50 years ago, most never finished high school; graduating classes on average were abler than they can be today. (This does not apply to elementary school.) However there is no weaseling out of the fact that American students at various ages score poorly in comparison with students in other nations with universal elementary school attendance and rates of high school graduation near or exceeding our own. Second, curricula have changed, or at least curriculum requirements should have changed. There were no computers, they are ubiquitous now. Knowledge of foreign languages was considered more important than it is today despite all the promotion of multiculturalism. Needs for mathematical competence have grown.

There is much concern about the quality of education and much controversy about causes and cures. Many perceive that education is in crisis. Americans believe that all problems have solutions. Many are addicted to single causes and simple solutions. What about class size and teacher pay? Are they self-serving proposals or important policies?

CLASS SIZE

Smaller class size is one 'solution' popular with educators. By implication, classes are too large. Smaller class size requires more teachers. The practical problem is the current shortage of qualified teachers, and the rising average age of faculty, which promises to worsen the shortage. Even if class size is an important determinant of quality of education, in the short run, smaller class sizes require lowering standards for hiring and retention of teachers. One unintended consequence would be some reduction in teacher quality. It is unrealistic to expect otherwise. With smaller class sizes, fewer would get the better teachers, whereas with large classes, more could benefit. Smaller classes also require an increase in the number of classrooms. Whatever the policy, there are tradeoffs.

Smaller classes - smaller than what? How small? These questions are rarely asked. Is there an optimum class size, could it be the tutor-pupil one to one relation of earlier times, limited to wealthy aristocracy, now approximated with home schooling by educated parents?

There have been many hundreds of studies of the effect of class size on learning. Ehrenberg et al. [1], in a recent assessment of their findings, conclude that smaller class size in the early years can have lasting effects especially among disadvantaged students. But they do not find that the evidence supports a general policy of reduced class size in terms of learning, even without considering the costs and unintended consequences of such a policy. As to cost, there may be better ways of using the money to improve learning. More teachers are a major component of increased costs.

In elementary schools with a high proportion of students in poverty, and/or a high proportion consisting of minorities, smaller class size does make a difference. Ferguson and Ladd [21] find no advantage in class sizes smaller than around 23-25 for reading, but do find that classes smaller than that improve math achievement.

The relation between class size and student performance depends in part on the subject being taught, the grade level, the style of teaching, on the teacher as well as on the students. The maximum class size compatible with effective teaching and learning varies especially with class composition. If students of a wide range of ability are grouped in the same classes, teaching is more difficult and class size should be smaller than if students are sorted by level of ability/achievement. The case for smaller class size cannot be dissociated from the issue of tracking. According to Hallinan and Sorensen [3], with ability grouping there is no relation between class size and achievement in reading or math. Where the curriculum is well-organized, even dictated at the national level, and teacher-directed, larger class size is more feasible than when there is a great deal of give and take, student-oriented subject matter and learning procedures.

Class size above some critical number alters the nature of the learning experience. The class society becomes hierarchical: a few students tend to dominate questions and answers, some students are overlooked and others become slackers. Student attitudes and culture matter. Teachers often handle large class size by grouping students so that they help each other, no one gets lost without being noticed. This is done effectively in Japan with its other-oriented society, not as well in an individualistic, self-oriented one, where free riding is a problem. It also depends on the organization of subject matter

Bill O'Reilly of the O'Reilly Factor recently confessed that he attended elementary school in a class of 60. Who knows how far he might have gone had the class size been 20! I had a respected colleague, Ivy league PHD, who attended a one-room elementary school with all six grades in the room, and a single teacher. There is no such thing as an optimum class size. classes can be too small for some. One cannot draw conclusions from anecdotes. Much depends on the individual student and on the individual teacher.

The distribution of class size remains an issue. Policy should not aim to reduce average size, but target selectively by school, grade, subjects and students most likely to benefit. This means that additional teachers must be hired who fit these needs. Targeted reduction in class size may not be achievable by simply redistributing teachers, increasing class size where size does not matter. Teachers are not all-purpose, interchangeable. We have enough teachers to attain a satisfactory average class size. But are they the right teachers, and in the right place?

What has been happening to class size? Since 1960 the student/teacher ratio declined by thirty five percent for high schools, and by thirty eight percent for elementary schools. The ratio of high school students to teachers fell from 21.7 in 1960 to 14.1 in 1999. For elementary schools the drop was from 28.4 in 1960 to 17.6 in 1999. (The ratio has scarcely changed since, but recent numbers are not consistent with the previous time series.) Half of this decline has been translated into reduced class size in elementary schools, but very little in secondary schools. Average elementary school class size has declined from 29 in 1961 to 21 in 1986 - seventeen percent, where it remained in 2000. For high schools, class size declined from 28 in 1961 to 23 in 1981, but rose to 31 in 1995, then back to 28 in 2001.

Table 6-1. Student/Teacher Ratio and Average Class Size

Year	Student/Teacher Ratio(Fall)		Average Class Size(Spring)	
	Elementary	Secondary	Elementary	Secondary
1960-'01	28.4	21.7	29	28
1970-'01	24.3	19.8	27	27
1980-'01	20.4	16.8	25	23
1990-'01	18.9	14.6	24	26
1995-'06	19.3	14.4	24	31
1999 -2000	17.6	14.1	21	28

Source: National Center for Education Statistics (2001). *Digest of Education Statistics* 2000. Washington, DC: U.S. Government Printing Office, Tables 65 and 69.

These numbers overstate reduction in average class size because of the increase in the number of students in special education classes, which are smaller than average classes. The reduction was largely an unintended consequence of decline in enrollments after the baby boomers had graduated, and the reluctance to cut faculty, rather than deliberate policy. Class size is smaller than in most of the countries at the top of the heap in student performance.

The average number of students taught per high school teacher per day declined from 138 in 1961 to '94 in 1993 and 86 in 2001 [4]. These numbers imply that teachers were teaching 5 classes in 1961 but were averaging just three classes in 2001. It seems that most of the increase in ratio of teachers to students resulted not in smaller classes but in fewer classes per teacher. That is the arithmetic implication of teachers' own estimates of average class size and number of students taught. Presumably teachers have become involved in more and more meetings and non-teaching monitoring assignments. Whether this is the best use of the large decline in students per teacher is an issue not addressed by proponents of smaller class size. Neither is the issue of quality of teaching as a function of number of classes a teacher meets per day. The decline in number of students per teacher and in average class size has not been correlated with increased achievement.

Class size varies too widely by school, region, grade, and subject for an overall average to mean much. But the number of teachers tells us what are the total teaching resources available. Unfortunately kindergarten and high school physics teachers are not interchangeable, whatever the class size or the student/teacher ratio.

One should also look at the proportion of school employees who are teachers. The United States in 2001 had more employees in schools from kindergarten through high school, 116 per thousand students, than the OECD average of 99.5. But little more than half of them, 51%, were teachers. Other instructional staff - instructional aides, guidance counselors and librarians- totaled another 16%. The educational bureaucracy in this country appears to be top-heavy, even realizing that our decentralized system with some fifteen thousand school districts may require a higher ratio of nonteaching employees than the centralized systems in most OECD nations. There are opportunities here for reducing educational costs, shifting resources from nonteaching to teaching, possibly shifting some employees as well, reducing class size.

What was class size when student performance was better, or believed to have been better? The answer is, larger. In 1950 there were 27.2 students per teacher for elementary and secondary schools combined; this ratio dropped to 17 in 1988 and has remained much the same since. This is not the same thing as average class size but either they are very closely related, or teachers are spending much more of their time not teaching and we should ask why. Reducing class size is not a prescription for high quality education, whatever its merits in particular cases and places. Reducing size is a mechanical diversion with no promise of payoff.

What are class sizes in the countries whose 9, 13, and 17 year olds do so much better than American students, especially in math and science? The number of students per teacher is larger, much larger in the case of South Korea, always at or very close to the top. Classes are larger. There are some European countries with fewer students per teacher, but many, and all high-performing Asian nations, have more students per teacher than the United States. Japan and Korea have large class sizes, but after school and on weekends a high proportion of students continue studying with private tutors. It is a question of family commitment to learning, and of strict performance criteria for admission and success in college.

We will always hear that present class size, whatever it may be, is too large and should be reduced. Complaint is an excuse for failure. Smaller class size is a subterfuge for lower teaching load. Teachers now average less than two thirds as many students as they did in 1960, yet they complain of overwork. It is true for many, but because so much of their time is now devoted to school activities that have no academic, cognitive, or educational content. Reducing average class size by hiring more teachers is by far the most expensive and inefficient way of reducing teacher workload. If there were less diversity of achievement within schools and classes there would be no case at all for reducing size.

MORE TEACHING

An alternative solution is not smaller classes, but more classes, longer school days and school year. Students in no other advanced nation spend so little time in class or at study. Americans spend 180 days in school; This has not changed in decades, although the number of nonteaching school days has crept up, from 4 to 7. Japanese spend 240 days in school. The solution is simple: air-conditioning in many schools, larger payrolls for longer school years, more money for maintenance. Few students are needed for spring planting or fall harvest. There would be adjustment problems, not least among students, who would see summer vacations truncated or (for older students) summer jobs lost.

Length of school year is only one approach to more teaching. Another is length of school day, or rather increased time devoted to the academic curriculum. More teaching relevant for cognitive development and preparation for college and employment could be achieved within the current school day and school year. It would involve redistribution of student time away from sports and recreation activities in school and from time spent in social engineering, in loco parentis instruction, and ideological indoctrination. Many students, after hours of sporting activities. are too tired to do their home work and short of time for it as well. These alternative uses of school time have exploded in recent decades. They have infiltrated many standard courses as well. But that is not a simple "solution"; it borders on the revolutionary.

Whether the teachers engaged in these activities can be converted to academic pursuits is an open question.

The tradeoff between time spent in school and at home depends on what students can be expected to do away from school supervision. If either parental supervision or students' motivation were to lead to home study, there would be no need for longer school days. But today these conditions are missing in particular among those students who most need extra class and study time. The practical problems are the same as those confronted by policies to reduce average class size: more teachers and/or higher pay for extra teaching. But perhaps not. As noted above, apparently there has been a large reduction in the number of classes taught by the average teacher, in the number of students with whom the teacher has contact. There has been no corresponding improvement in student performance. It is not that the teacher is idle but that teacher time has been redirected to nonacademic student activities, meetings, paperwork. Cut these back, and many teachers can shift some of their time and effort to the academic component of the school day.

Another proposal, and trend, toward more teaching is an earlier start, head start for everyone. It implies hiring more teachers at a time when one problem is not enough teachers. Whatever its merits, it is a diversion. Other nations whose students outperform American students do not get an earlier start; many of them have a later start. In this country, nearly all students now go to kindergarten, and an increasing proportion to all-day kindergarten. Pre-school enrollment has also risen markedly. Realistically, these trends have little to do with correcting school deficiencies, everything to do with working mothers. Some are educational enterprises; many are baby and child sitting enterprises. Their growth has not prevented a decline in achievement. It coincided with theories about reading-readiness, anything-readiness, justifying non-achievement. Even Head Start has not proven to have lasting effects.

Increasing teaching, whether devoting more hours per day to learning, or longer school year, overlooks the ineffectiveness of schools. Quality of teaching is far more important than quantity. More learning need not require more time. Unfortunately, teaching is also up to parents and learning to students. Teachers can't do everything.

SPENDING PER STUDENT

School administrators, teachers unions, schools of education, the education lobby, will always demand more money. That is their nature, it is also their leading excuse for failure. Schools are not spending enough per student. It is a mindless proposal: spending for what? How much more? What is enough? In fact spending per student has been rising, not falling. It has more than doubled in real terms since 1970. But this spending has not been translated into superior achievement. More spending can be a catchall for higher teacher pay, better teachers, more teachers, smaller classes, bloated bureaucracies.

Comparing spending per student and achievement is meaningless because the alleged causal variable, dollars, is heterogeneous. Only if spending is restricted to particular ends: smaller class size, better paid teachers, etc., can it be related to achievement. There is another reason to question many efforts to relate spending and achievement: often spending is the effect of underachievement, an effort to correct it, hence low-achieving schools may spend more per student. That does not imply that spending less is better. Since schools, and students, vary widely in achievement, any attempt to relate spending however allocated to achievement must refer to subsequent increments in achievement, not to the levels themselves.

Greenwald et al. [5] performed a meta-analysis of 60 studies on the relation between school resources and student achievement, concluding that resources are not only positively related, but large enough to be important. They look at spending per student; teacher ability, education, experience and salary, class size and school size. However, for each of the variables except spending per student, teacher ability, and school size, the number of non-significant studies is at least twice that of significant studies. And some of the significant studies, including teacher graduate degrees, have negative values.

I am more impressed by Hanushek's rebuttal [6], and his own previous work. He finds no systematic relation between expenditures and performance; any relation disappears once allowance is made for student family background. What this means is not that resources don't matter, they have to matter, but that they are so inefficiently used that more resources overall make little difference. They are no sovereign solution, whatever their value in particular schools and districts.

Blau [7] also finds no significant effect of resources on achievement after controlling for family background. However, school quality (socioeconomic character of the student body) is a factor. Schools whose students are well-to-do can have a higher achievement per unit of resources than schools for minorities and the poor.

Childs and Shakeshaft [8] analyzed over 400 publications on the relation between expenditures and achievement. They considered 13 types of expenditure and 37 of achievement. They found a decline in the relation over time, as though there may be some level of spending above which there are no additional positive results. Each subclass of expenditure was more significant than overall spending. Instructional costs - teacher salaries and instructional supplies - were the most significant factor. Greater gains were obtained from additional spending on math and science than on language arts. Overall, however, the relation between spending and achievement was minimal. How money is spent is more important than how much.

Some would spend money to improve achievement by providing a computer for every student. They really think that students will use them for educational purposes! Schools that don't have computers for everyone are considered inferior. Go back a couple of decades, and no schools had computers for anyone. Computers are more likely to become problems than solutions; the evidence is beginning to mount [9]. This is exactly what happened to TV, once heralded as a great new teaching tool. They are great tools, but greater toys. Giving every student a computer is worth perhaps two sentences. This is the second one. There are no mechanical or electronic solutions.

Real expenditures per pupil have more than tripled since 1960. Part of this is the increased high school graduation rate and the higher cost per student in higher grades. Part of this growth is the large increase in teacher/student ratio and the reduction in teaching load per teacher and in average class size. But this and other increases vary by school, system and region, perhaps providing some basis for estimating the productivity of various kinds of expenditure. It is around 1964 that student SAT scores began a steep decline. It does not follow of course that class size is too small or that spending per student is too high. But it does follow that these were not major factors in student achievement during the past half century.

Table 6-2. Current expenditures per student, elementary and secondary public schools

Year	2004-'05 Dollars
1949-'50	$1,767
1959-'60	2,541
1969-'70	4,298
1979-'80	5,823
1989-'90	7,804
1999-2000	8,691
2003-'04	9,516

Source: National Center for Education Statistics.(2007) *Digest of Education Statistics 2006.* Washington, DC: U. S. Government Printing Office, Table 167.

It should not come as a surprise that the United States spends more per elementary school student than any other country, and is second only to Switzerland in spending per secondary school student [10]. Yet US 15-year olds ranked 19th in math, 14th in science, and 15th in reading in 2000 [11]. More money is certainly not the cure for incompetence. "More" is not a solution.

The answer is not more spending, but better allocation of existing resources, and greater efficiency in their use. The District of Columbia school system spends more per student than any state, almost three times as much as the state of Utah, but many of its students have no textbook. The problem of allocation is aggravated by the local and state character of the American educational system. High student turnover is also a liability.

PUBLIC SCHOOL TEACHER PAY

A third solution, one version of more spending per student, is increased teacher pay. It is viewed as a means of increasing the supply of teachers via both recruitment and retention, and also increasing the quality of the teachers hired. The question of teacher pay is not simple. For starters, teachers do not work 50 weeks a year, but 40 or less. The average teacher works little more than 180 days. The full time full year worker puts in between 230 and 240 days. Thus for comparative purposes teachers' salaries should be increased by at least one quarter. Some choose teaching because they want the long vacations. Other teachers may work at summer jobs. Public school teachers have greater job security and better benefits than the average college graduate. A direct comparison with full time full-year workers cannot be made. As workers age, their average pay increases; the average age of teachers is higher than that of the labor force, and higher than it was in the past. Thus dollar comparisons overstate relative pay, both relative to teacher pay in the past, and to pay of others.

The case against salary increases as a solution is simple. It is not true that public school teachers are underpaid compared to other college graduates. (See Table 2-1 in Chapter 2.) It is true for males, but false for female teachers, who constitute some three quarters of all teachers. They earn as much as female college graduates. Formerly they earned much more, but the difference has been eliminated as formerly all-male occupations have opened up to females. Nevertheless, the decline in relative pay and the low rate of new hires at a time when many more teachers will be needed, suggests that pay should increase at some point. In particular the rate of increase in pay with age and experience is smaller for public school teachers than it is for non-government workers Temin compares pay of female college graduates with that of female teachers age 35-44, finding a rise in the ratio from 0.88 in 1979 to 1.12 in 1999 [12].

In comparing pay of public school teachers with that of other occupations, the poor quality of majors in education must be kept in mind. Pay should be compared not with all college graduates, but with graduates with similar average levels of ability. There is more direct evidence on the poor quality of public school teachers than their standardized college test performance: the abysmally low minimum standards set for teacher qualification. About half the school jurisdictions set passing scores below the national 25th percentile in reading; only Virginia sets a minimum passing score at or near the national median score for reading, writing, and mathematics. We should expect teachers, all of them, to be *above* the national median. Since no one wishes to perpetuate the low quality of public school teachers, pay should be sufficient to attract higher quality, not to maintain the status quo. The problem is not low pay but low quality, and increasing pay under current institutional constraints on hiring would accomplish little.

One indicator of adequacy of starting pay is ability to recruit. By this criterion pay is too low; not enough teachers have been entering the profession in recent years - little more than 3 percent of the total each year. But the shortfall is not across-the-board; it is severe for math and science teachers, much less so in some other fields. Accordingly, increases in starting pay should be selective.

Another indicator of the adequacy of teacher pay, not starting pay, but pay structure, is the ability of schools to retain teachers. The overall teacher turnover rate is higher than the average of all other occupations combined. The fact that pay for college graduates in the private market increases faster with age and experience than it does for public school teachers is a factor. But nearly half the turnover consists of movers rather than leavers. There is greater comparability of institutions and jobs in teaching than in most other occupations; they can be found almost everywhere. Changing jobs is easy. Many movers simply take equivalent jobs in other schools in the same school system. The reasons for leaving schools in high poverty urban areas are first, poor administrative support, and second, lack of faculty influence. In suburban schools, half the leavers mentioned salary as their first reason, poor administrative support as their second. Turnover is highest for science teachers, high for math teachers [13].

On the other hand, pay of unionized teachers is higher than that of non-union teachers (private schools). Limiting the supply of potential teachers largely to those who have received a bachelors degree in education must further increase pay needed to hire the requisite number of able teachers. The inference is that public school teachers should be overpaid because they must meet this requirement.

Private schools pay less yet achieve better results. There is little difference in turnover rates between public and private schools. The superior private performance is attributable to three factors: market pay, merit pay, and a wider pool of potential teachers. Private schools do not follow a policy of one paycheck fits all, with starting pay and annual increases the same for good teachers and bad teachers alike. They are free to differentiate pay according to market conditions, to hire teachers with degrees in math and science without the necessity of raising the pay for other teachers or requiring that they meet school of education requirements. By differentiating pay by field, they can hire better faculty. By awarding pay increases related to teacher performance they cut down on turnover among the best teachers. And they do not offer job security regardless of performance. Bad teachers do not have their contracts renewed. Public schools have the equivalent of tenure without the rigorous trial period found in colleges.

Private school parents pay tuition, suggesting a level of concern about the quality of teachers that may not prevail in public schools. Many parents have a choice of private schools, exercising a degree of quality control absent elsewhere. Private schools have to compete for students and revenues; public schools at best compete for school district budgets. All the more reason why public schools need an entry pay system that reflects the market, and pay increases based on merit.

The superior achievement of private school students cannot be attributed entirely to better teaching; some is attributable to a different mix of students, and of parents. Evidence in this regard is that students in Catholic high schools in urban areas do much better than those in public high schools, but that there is little difference between private and public suburban high schools [14].

What about the effect of pay increases on the quality of teachers? It is not clear that a sizeable increase in pay would do much to improve the average quality of teachers. It is likely that any benefit would take much too long to take effect. The problem is the unintended consequences: higher pay would induce teachers, good and bad alike, to stay longer. The number of openings for new teachers would be reduced. This in turn would lower the probability that an applicant would receive an offer, discouraging those applicants with attractive alternatives. Higher pay should be targeted only to the better teachers.

Having compared teacher pay to pay for other college graduates, public versus private school pay, and noted recruitment and retention rates in public schools, where does this leave us? We cannot say that average pay is x percent lower than it should be, in order to attract and retain the teachers needed. What we can say is that pay structures of public schools, in combination with their retention practices, will never succeed in attracting and holding the quality teachers needed, at any feasible average pay. Differential pay reflecting alternative jobs and earnings opportunities, and teaching performance, *including pay cuts* is part of the answer. It would be much more cost-effective than an across the board raise. It would increase the retention of good teachers and the turnover of bad teachers.

In sum, class size has fallen substantially, and spending per student has increased a great deal, without improving student achievement. There is no evidence that average class size is too large, although individual schools and school districts may be understaffed. School financing is more than adequate, although in many cases funds are very inefficiently allocated. There is little evidence that the teachers we have are underpaid on average, but we get what we pay for, and teaching salaries are very badly distributed. There is no obvious need at this time to increase average pay, only to change the pay structure. Pay is a stopgap recourse; in the long run other means must also be found to improve the attractiveness of a teaching career for able college graduates.

Chapter 7

MULTIPLE RESPONSES TO COMPLEX PROBLEMS

INTRODUCTION

What if anything should be done? People of many points of view agree that something should be done, although they may disagree on why and on what. Promoters of self-esteem should recognize that self-esteem is a consequence, not a cause of achievement. Teaching methods that focus on learning do more for self-esteem than those that stress self-esteem. Egalitarians should support change, because the current egalitarian agenda has actually increased inequality of achievement by lowering standards and stakes. Underperforming pedagogies should be abandoned. Only those whose interest in education is the promotion of ideologies and secular religions might resist change, for their agenda has had some success and any alternative would pose a threat.

But what change, and how much change? On this there is bound to be disagreement, deriving from different concepts of the purpose of public education. At the heart of controversy is the choice between meritocracy and egalitarianism. It is also a choice between public wants and private needs, between democracy and a competitive economy. Democracy is egalitarianism unqualified. A competitive economy only thrives on the selective principle of meritocracy. For what are public schools preparing students? Not for citizenship - civics is grossly neglected and history is badly taught. Not for economic success - the basic learning tools of language and numbers, in both of which performance has lagged. I see no reason why public schools cannot do both; the adult is both a citizen and a worker.

To speak of solutions one must define the problem. There is no consensus on what schools and students should accomplish, nor on the adequacy of current achievements. Millions, in particular those engaged in the industry of education, see little need for higher achievement, or what is the same thing, see no problem that cannot be solved by pouring more money down a bottomless maw: higher salaries, smaller classes, computers for all. They oppose every other proposal to change the status quo. Most do see a problem, but there is a variety of views, disagreements, on the proper content of achievement, on the desired level of achievement, even on achievement for whom.

In this chapter I assume that the purpose of educational reform is to improve learning to empower the individual as a worker, and maintain national economic growth via economic efficiency and leadership in innovation. This is not, never has been, the only purpose. Some may care nothing about economic prospects for students or for society; they may prefer other purposes and propose a different set of reforms. Accordingly the following proposals should be viewed as possible components of diverse strategies for raising achievement, however defined, rather than "solutions" to a "problem." They are diverse: some refer to incentives, others to penalties, yet others to quality and efficiency concerns, to competition, to information.

Americans like single 'causes' and simple solutions, and prompt, even immediate results. The failures of our schools started early in the twentieth century, those of our colleges go back a half century. There is no way of reversing course in a decade, of restoring a healthy system of learning in just a single generation. Some policies can yield prompt results, others require a generation or two. Both are needed.

We know that there are many factors influencing outcomes, that some of them are beyond the control or perhaps even the influence of school systems and teachers and outside their responsibility. Some factors are interdependent, so that looking at just one cannot tell us the magnitude of its contribution. It is possible that the popular variables are not important; they are superficial at best. Factors not measured by class size or teacher pay or spending per student, such as teacher quality, are more fundamental. And not much improvement in teacher quality is possible in the short run; it is nearly impossible to terminate bad or mediocre teachers, and impossible to hire large numbers of superior teachers in some subjects, even with substantial increase in salaries; the supply isn't there.

The large number of proposed policies to improve learning in public schools are not a menu; they are not alternatives. They serve different purposes. Most policies have unintended consequences; some are quickly implemented, others take a long time. There is an optimal sequence of policies. The first is information.

How can radical improvement be brought about? Many things need to be done. But what are the priorities? What is the sequence? To hire and retain much better teachers it is necessary to bypass schools of education and teachers unions. A salary scale that reflects the market and rewards merit must be instituted, over the opposition of the teachers unions. Curriculum and pedagogical reform can only follow from staffing schools with teachers who were not mindwashed by schools of education. Vouchers and other means of compelling performance from public schools are likewise adamantly opposed by the industry itself. Under these conditions the proper strategy is to concentrate on information. Parents, and students, must be made acutely aware of the failings of their schools, in providing basic learning skills, in preparing them for college, for jobs. At present too many parents of students in failing schools are pleased with their children's' high grades and many honors. Freedom of information is the necessary condition for genuine reform. Without information there is not enough pressure to adopt a reform agenda; even if such an agenda were adopted, it would not be implemented.

I consider first, the key obstacles to reform of public schools, which are the monopoly of public education, the teachers unions, and the schools of education. Then I focus on the substance of reform, its core objectives, which are better teachers and a radically improved curriculum, which combined imply pedagogic reform as well. Only then can the numerous policies be considered, together with their interaction and appropriate sequence.

Many private schools suffer from the same handicaps and shortcomings that beleaguer the public school system. But they are only one tenth the enrollment, parents have a choice of schools, and change must come one school at a time, whereas in the public school system much change can be at the district and state level, and some at the national level.

PROBLEM: THE THREE MONOPOLIES

There is a widespread belief that public schools are under local control. This may have been true several generations ago, but not any more. The administrative units, school districts have become larger, enhancing the power of administrators relative to individual schools, teachers, or parents. Funding, 83% local in 1920, is now only 43% local. Regulation is increasingly federal. Perhaps more important in redistribution of power is the indirect role of schools of education and their products, who dominate the teachers unions, in shaping textbooks and curricula. The dominance of unions traces back to the 1960s.

The fundamental problem is monopoly, not a single monopoly, but three. The first monopoly is that of public schools. The vast majority of parents and students have no alternative; even those who can afford private schools are heavily discriminated against. They pay taxes for public schools, but receive no subsidy if enrolled in private schools. Public school monopoly limits accountability; parents are uninformed and schools are unresponsive to their wishes, to the needs of students in later life, and to those of employers.

The answer to this monopoly is obvious: subsidy for students enrolling in private schools, somewhat less than the cost of attending public schools, but sufficient to give most students and parents a choice. This is the political argument. The economic argument is that extensive subsidies would introduce effective competition in the market for education. There may be undesirable consequences of course, but they must be balanced against the indubitable gains. In large cities there are possibilities for limited choice and competition between public schools, which raise some of the same problems as do vouchers for private schools, to be discussed later.

The second stage monopoly is that of labor unions that control the market for public school teachers and have much influence on curricula and other aspects of public education. These unions oppose standardized testing or almost any kind of independent evaluation of achievement, i.e., they oppose information. They oppose market-based starting salaries and merit pay; and they oppose hiring of teachers with majors in the fields they teach without a prolonged detour in a school of education, i.e., they oppose competition. It is in the nature of any union to stress inputs: more money, higher salaries, smaller classes without regard to their effectiveness, and to avoid stress on outputs: student achievement, teacher merit pay.

Teachers unions have a role, but they should not rule. The professional association, or even the medieval guild, whose primary concern is quality of service, should be their primary function. Because the public school system is so decentralized, they exercise power over the salary structure which they should not have. Teacher pay that reflects both market and merit is incompatible with the egalitarian structure which unions require for their own survival as labor unions. It is for management, not labor, to decide on salary structure consistent with recruitment and retention of able teachers, and management responsibility to seek the necessary funds.

The primary purposes of unions – to provide job security for employees, to assure acceptable working conditions, including pay and workload, and to provide a mechanism for handling individual complaints, have been largely met by the teacher unions. But nature abhors a vacuum, so they are spending most of their time and their members' contributions on activities unrelated to the justifications for their existence. The National Education Association is neither a professional association nor a labor union, but a doctrinaire political lobby and ideological propaganda mill with little interest in education and of negative value to public schools. All one needs to do to verify these charges is to look at the resolutions of any recent NEA annual meeting, and at how teachers' contributions are spent. Phyllis Schlafly [1] summarizes the 2005 meeting, noting that the large melange of resolutions did not include improved teaching of basic math or phonics, and contrasting it with the NEA of 1951. To be fair, most teachers would not support many, perhaps most, of NEA resolutions. The American Federation of Teachers at least remains a labor union.

Unions cannot be abolished. Can they be reformed? If they were flooded with new teachers possessing high IQs, with majors in the fields they teach, without going through the obstacle course of schools of education, union attitudes and behavior might change for the better. They might behave more like professional associations, as the NEA once was. But this is unlikely, and at best would take decades. In the meantime, an increasing number of teachers - some ten percent of the total - have resisted pressure for union membership and joined new professional associations whose sole concern is education, not politics or ideology. At least 20 states have such associations, and in three their membership outnumbers the NEA and the AFT [2]. Perhaps these states can lead the way in teacher qualifications, in realistic pay systems, in curriculum reform, imposing competitive pressure on adjacent states by hiring and retaining the best teachers. It is a trend to be encouraged. Teachers should have a professional association.

The third stage of monopoly is schools and departments of education. Their quasi-monopoly on public school staffing, exercised indirectly via unions and public school administrators, must be eliminated. There are many majors in history, English, social sciences, some even in the natural sciences, who cannot get jobs in their chosen fields but who are blocked from teaching to protect the graduates of schools of education. Gross notes that the first President Bush, Yale Phi Beta Kappa, was denied a teaching job in Texas [3].

Nearly three out of four school districts "require" that teachers be graduates of a teacher education program; two out of three require a college major or minor in the subject taught, a double requirement impossible to enforce if recruitment needs are to be met. In fact these requirements are often "met" not in arts and sciences departments, but in departments of education. How many will obtain degrees in education and also major in math or science, or almost any other field, just for the opportunity of teaching in public schools? Most districts however do not require that teachers pass state tests of basic skills or of subject knowledge.

Schools and departments of education try to maintain enrollments by perpetuating a monopoly over the supply of teachers and by pressuring teachers to acquire masters degrees in education. Since they have no monopoly of subject matter, they concentrate on methods, on know-how, absent know-what. Their faculties are mainly drawn from the same poor quality pool of students who staff our elementary and secondary schools.

The issue is not just the low quality of many teachers and the lack of command over the subject matter they teach. It is also their concept of learning and pedagogy, inculcated in schools of education: ideology, subversion, confusion and irrationality. The current primary and secondary school faculty should be turned over as rapidly as possible to eliminate intellectual abuse of children, and the schools of education that train them should be bypassed as rapidly as possible. There is no prospect of reforming schools of education, or most of their products now teaching. They need to be replaced. They are what they are, and cannot change identities [4]. Even with the best of intentions at the top, there is no prospect for meaningful reform in less than a generation. Current college faculty are not going to jettison what they regard as their intellectual capital. Tenure plus an end to compulsory retirement assure their continued employment. Gross [5] recommends that all undergraduate degrees in education be abolished. He would also abolish the Ed.D. think he goes a little too far, but in the right direction. We still need a few graduate schools of education of high quality for training and research, provided most of their faculty have doctorates in fields other than education.

Colleges and universities with degree programs in education could apply the same standards to such programs, their majors, and their faculty, as they do in other fields. The number of students and the number of programs would dwindle rapidly, and those that survive need not be an embarrassment to a self-respecting university. Schools of education are dysfunctional. They missed their opportunity decades ago when applicants were at their peak. Now with a decline in enrollments they cannot resist the pressure to accept all applicants and graduate all majors. It is a matter of self-preservation. As to universities, and this is plausible speculation, they need enrollments and tuition revenue, particularly from departments whose cost of instruction is very low. Schools of education have no high-salaried staff, no expensive labs. Their standards are low enough to retain tuition-paying students who might not survive as majors in other departments. It is too much to expect states to impose test requirements for public college graduation such as they are imposing on high school seniors.

The influence of schools of education can be undermined by changing requirements for teacher certification. Current teacher certification standards are little more than job guarantees for graduates of schools of education. If the standards for secondary school teachers were the equivalent of the GRE subject matter tests, they would end the monopoly of schools of education and force surviving schools to shape up.

Objectives of education other than command over subject matter and development of cognitive skills, such as socialization and value formation, are properly subjects for study in departments of psychology, sociology, philosophy. Theories of learning should be left to psychologists. For teachers aspiring to administrative positions, business schools can offer appropriate instruction.

Some states and school systems are weakening the monopoly over teaching jobs exercised by schools of education and teachers unions dominated by their graduates. But allowing a math major to teach provided that individual takes a year's coursework in a school of education is not much of a chink in the monopoly armor. Why should a math major whose market alternatives are better than teaching pay incur the additional cost of a year of schooling for the right or privilege of teaching high school mathematics at the same pay as a major in education, or English? It is a barrier that does not exist for college professors, who are not expected to take any courses in education.

The monopoly power of education graduates over public school teaching can be undermined also through competition: vouchers, charter schools. The constraints on reform imposed by unions would be relaxed as a byproduct. But first there must be irresistible pressure for change on the demand side; it is not there yet. In practice, the number of students earning degrees in education is far below that needed to replace teachers who are retiring or leaving. Change is coming from the supply side, but it needs to be accelerated.

The power of these monopolies should not be underestimated. Complaints about public school curricula and pedagogy go back more than half a century; complaints about student achievement go back almost as long. But little progress has been made, and reforms are often challenged in court by the very organizations that should be leading reform.

OBJECTIVES

Teacher Quality

Many million Americans are keenly aware of differences in school quality: those who send their children to private schools, those who home-school, those who favor vouchers, those who decide where to live on the basis of their perception of the quality of local schools. It is true that the meaning of quality education varies widely among them, but they know that schools matter. Amount spent per student, class size, teacher/student ratios do not appear to matter much if at all. These just happen to be factors easily quantified. Other factors must matter a great deal. The quality of teachers is one factor everyone agrees matters. Perceptions of quality of teaching are as varied as those of quality of schooling. Ability as indicated by standardized test scores is only a partial indicator. Skill at interpersonal communication is important, almost essential in the early years of school. But teacher cognitive ability and subject mastery become increasing important as students advance through secondary school grades.

In the long run, better teacher quality requires an increase in the supply of potential teachers by improving the attractiveness of teaching as a profession for individuals who have majored in subjects other than education. The fundamental obstacles are: 1. the low status of teachers, 2. the egalitarian philosophy dominating educational circles and organizations that rejects market forces and refuses to reward merit in salary policy, and 3. the barriers to entry and competition erected by the industry of education.

We suspect that a large proportion of those currently teaching in public schools are not good teachers. The unsatisfactory student performance on standardized tests, and their low ratings in international comparisons, imply as much. Perhaps Asian and European teachers are better than American. In science and math, no doubt they are. More direct evidence is the performance of education majors on SATs, and on GREs, which is and has remained always at or near the bottom in comparison with majors in other fields. These are the college graduates who have become the teachers of our children today, and perhaps were our teachers some time ago. By contrast, teachers in countries whose students score highest are recruited from the top tier of college graduates [6].

Some lay the blame for low quality and low standards on the influence of teachers unions. I see them more as agents than as principals. The core of the problem of quality is schools and departments of education.

There are two basic requirements to improve the quality of teachers. First, all teachers in public middle and high schools, eventually also many elementary school teachers, should have a degree in the subjects they teach or a close equivalent (a physics major should be able to teach math). It should be possible for individuals to be certified who can demonstrate their mastery of a subject at the level of a college graduate major regardless of formal education. Second, current certification standards are a bad joke and must be replaced.

Education is not a subject; it is a process and an institution. Learning is a subject, properly studied in courses and departments of psychology, biology, neurology. Students with atypical learning processes may benefit from specialized attention and instruction. They may be able to learn through eyes alone, or ears alone, or have difficulties in inter-sensory interconnections, or problems with memory imprinting or retrieval, or a variety of cognitive specializations, whether deficits or extraordinary abilities. With improved instruments for deciphering mental processes we are learning how better to deal with unusual students. But little of the research or the know-how is the work of individuals with degrees in education.

Requirements for a bachelors degree in education, or at least a year's course work in education for those with degrees in other fields, is best viewed as a high protective tariff. In the first instance it protects schools of education, assuring them a near-monopoly of teaching candidates. In the second instance, it protects hundreds of thousands of teachers with a degree in education but not in the subject they teach from competition with teachers majoring in the fields they teach – a competition in which they would be at a disadvantage. In the third instance, the protection afforded teachers unions is more complex and speculative. Too many new teachers who have not been ground in the same educational mill could threaten the tenure of union officials. More relevant for union members is the threat new members with a different orientation pose to union ideology: unbending opposition to vouchers, to standardized tests, to merit pay (including the fear that teachers with bachelors degrees in education would be at the bottom of the pay scale). There would be increased pressure for reform of the curriculum in many subjects, including new and better textbooks and other teaching materials.

A degree or even course work in education should no longer be needed to qualify for any teaching job. Would-be teachers might participate in summer workshops led by master teachers in their subjects, or take an appropriately designed course in college psychology departments. There is no reason why most pedagogic knowledge useful in teaching courses in middle school and high school cannot be presented in a single one-semester course. Curriculum content of such courses must be reviewed to eliminate their current bias and fashion. The special needs for teachers of the very young could and should be met more effectively and efficiently by psychology departments: child psychology, the learning process, teaching methods.

A degree in the subject to be taught would automatically increase average ability of applicants for teaching certificates, because nearly all subject matter departments have higher standards for their majors and graduates than do schools of education. One result would be a rise in the prestige of teaching, one reinforcing the other. This is not going to happen overnight. But as states alter their requirements for the education of teachers, it will come to pass.

These educational requirements cannot be made retroactive, or many schools would have to close. To impose it on all new hires implies elimination of requirements for extensive course work in education, otherwise the supply of new teachers would plummet. Of course it is possible to master a subject without majoring or even minoring in it. Any individual who demonstrates the requisite knowledge could be hired. The appropriate test might be something like the subject GRE test administered to many college seniors. It cannot be a test given or selected by the public school system. Such a test should be taken by all applicants for teaching positions in the subject they are to teach, because a college degree is not always a guarantee of major subject mastery.

Standards for public school teacher certification are abysmally low in many states. We do not allow medical schools to decide who is qualified to practice medicine, or law schools to design their own bar exam. Teacher certification should be the function of professionals in the subject to be taught who are independent of the school system. Such a system would greatly reduce the number of newly qualified teachers, unless there are accompanying changes in salary levels and schedules. In some fields it would take a decade or two even with pay adjustments. To avoid shortages, raising standards should be an effect of improved teacher quality, not a causal factor. What should come first is elimination of current barriers and obstacles.

Our decentralized system of education allows individual school systems and states to raise their own standards, applying public pressure on others to follow suit

One field where a college major may not be important is foreign languages. Many of the teachers of foreign languages learned them as children; they are their native languages. For them some training in teaching methods, not in the language, may be appropriate.

Teachers who never took courses in schools of education do as well or better as those who received degrees in education. Teachers with masters in education - the majority - do no better than those who have only bachelors degree. Alternative certification is available in most states, but significant in only a few, although such teachers are better than those certified the standard way [7]. In sum, the years teachers spent earning those degrees appear to contribute nothing to the education of the young. I am not saying that an education major cannot gain the command over the subject equivalent to that of a major on his or her own initiative. It happens, but not often enough.

Schools of education will never be able to attract the quality of students needed to teach in our public schools. Grudging alternative certification in subjects in critical shortage to attract teachers who did not get a college degree in education is not the answer. Private schools do not have to have teacher certification that excludes many potential teachers, do not require coursework in schools of education, and therefore can draw on a larger talent pool, one reason they do better than public schools at lower cost. Unions would survive if degrees in education were no longer required, but most schools of education would not. A degree in education is occupation-specific; a degree in most other majors opens up a wider range of job and occupational opportunities.

The decline in the number of education graduates fortunately forces schools to hire more teachers who never majored in education. For the past decade an average of 106 thousand bachelors degrees in education have been awarded every year, little more than 3% of the total number of teachers, while leavers are roughly twice that number. The shortfall is even larger, since a high proportion of graduates in education never teach. Schools will have to rely more and more on new teachers who do not have a bachelors in education. This in turn will reduce the attraction of schools of education as privileged access to teaching jobs. Sprinkling elementary and high school faculties with more majors in fields that score at or near the top in SATS and GREs would have a leavening effect.

It is not enough to upgrade teacher certification standards. A salary structure is needed that will attract well-qualified individuals to teaching positions, and retain them. The pay structure for starting teachers must reflect the market, which pays more for math majors than for English majors. Teaching would become more attractive for a double reason: the prestige of teachers would rise, and qualified teachers would have employment options outside of the school systems. Across the board pay increases are not the way; the cost is too high, and would preempt other uses for educational funds. It would reduce openings by reducing turnover among good and bad teachers alike. Ballou and Podgursky [8] estimate that even with a 20 percent across the board increase in pay, average cognitive ability of teachers would remain below the mean of college graduates, and it would take ten years to obtain even half of the final improvement. And it is possible that there would be no improvement, since higher pay reduces turnover of bad teachers as well as good, and reduced turnover in turn limits the opportunity to hire new teachers, held to a higher standard.

Pay differentiation reflecting demand and supply for different specialties is what we find in private schools, colleges, and the private economy at large. There is no other way to hire the teachers needed. Since most teachers have degrees in education, they have nothing to gain from a wage policy reflecting market opportunities and pay for those with degrees in math and science (the stress is on math and science, but applies to every subject taught in secondary school). Individual public schools typically have little say on salaries for new hires, not much on pay increases

The current civil service salary schedules must go. Equal pay and equal increases amount to institutionalized unfairness. Merit pay involves subjective judgments and the possibility of favoritism, but nothing like the wholesale unfairness of the current pay system. Merit pay provides incentives now lacking for attracting good teachers and for self-improvement and retention slanted toward the better teachers.

Teaching performance is not easy to ascertain. One difficulty is comparing merit across specialties with allowance for circumstances: differences in community and parental support, student preparation, student ability. It must be assessed in terms of incremental learning, not levels of achievement. Teachers may not trust the ability of principals to make fair distinctions. This means that merit pay may create morale problems [9]. Public schools need more good principals at least as much as good teachers. Evaluating merit is a heavy burden. Principals too should get merit evaluations and pay. Merit is not self-defining. To reward on merit assumes that the principal and other school and district administrators agree that merit means scholastic achievement, not student self-esteem, teacher popularity, or student indoctrination. With current administrators this is not assured. But the new regime of annual testing could provide a benchmark.

One 'merit' aspect of pay structure is pay increase for those teachers who earn an advanced degree. Hanushek [10] sees no merit in more education for teachers. Greenwald [11] examined numerous studies of the relation between teacher education and student achievement; six of thirteen studies of teacher education finding a significant relation show a negative impact on achievement. They shed no light on the difference between more teacher education in the subject taught vs. more years in schools of education. Advanced degrees in education contribute nothing to performance, hence they should not be encouraged by pay increase, which are just an unmerited subsidy for schools of education. It may still be desirable to provide incentives for advanced training in a high school teacher's subject, whether it be science or history or English. Educational administrators might earn graduate degrees in management.

The situation in public schools is quite different from that in much of the rest of the economy. In a private firm, or government agency, the better workers are promoted to different jobs; the higher pay is associated with the different type of work done, of responsibility assumed. In schools there is minimal hierarchy: there are teachers, and a principal, an assistant principal. All teachers are alike, and differences in pay increases are entirely personal distinctions. The absence of hierarchy means that pay tends to rise less with experience than is typical in the larger market. All the more reason for merit pay to retain the best teachers.

Pay differentiation should not be limited to subjects taught and teacher performance. Working conditions and teaching difficulty vary by location. Teachers in problematic school districts or schools should be able to start on a higher pay schedule than in desirable schools and school districts. The market for elementary school teachers and their skills is different from that of high school teachers with majors in their subjects. On average they require less pay.

Getting state educational officials to press for these changes requires political pressure. National standardized tests of educational progress, revealing how poorly students are achieving, and state tests as a requirement for high school graduation imposing consequences on bad education, help provide this pressure. But they must be publicized, at the level of the individual school as well as state-wide. States should be denied the opportunity to improve achievement by lowering standards. We see this now. In state after state, over eighty percent of 4th and 8th graders are meeting state math proficiency standards but only some twenty percent meet federal standards [12]. Without adequate publicity, states with low standards look good. Adequate publicity would compel some upward convergence in standards and avoid the need for national standards and tests.

There is a way out. It is enough to have a small minority of school districts or states adopt a market wage structure reflecting differences in demand for different skills. That combined with inter-district and inter-state mobility of would-be teachers will gradually undermine the current egalitarian structure. There would be unintended consequences: some districts or states would find it difficult to finance the resulting increases in salaries and would need help. But this is nothing new; many face that problem today. The wage level for high schools would then be significantly higher than that for elementary schools. School funds would be redistributed between elementary and high schools. Salaries would rise in schools with large concentrations of poor and minority students.

As long as public schools are regarded as a sacred monopoly of schools of education, imposing burdensome education requirements on those with degrees in other fields, they raise the salary requirements for hiring math and science teachers, among other fields, aggravating their shortage. All this does is protect teachers who are poorly qualified to teach these subjects, and penalize their students. An alternative way of improving quality is to lower the costs of acquiring teaching credentials, the obvious candidate being the elimination of a degree or extensive course work in education. The sad fact remains that even this approach, so adamantly resisted by the public education establishment, would take a long time to make much difference. The only way to speed it up is to increase the turnover among the worse teachers, creating more new vacancies. That too is anathema.

There are not enough trained people who majored in some subjects to meet the needs of the economy and the schools. Few college students major in math and the physical sciences. In 2004 only 2.2% of bachelors degrees awarded were in these fields.. As long as they are few, job opportunities other than teaching are more attractive. Some states now allow or require teachers to major in the subjects they teach, but national implementation of such policies is impossible in the short run.

Back in the 1960s we faced the problem of a shortage of scientists and engineers as we mounted a race to the moon and expanded defense research efforts. The expectation then was for a ten-year lead time; the process had to start in middle school, with improved math and science teaching, to generate the college majors in scientific fields. We were nowhere as deficient then in terms of Americans majoring in science and math or in the supply of teachers as we are today. The need was largely political, not economic. That crisis was short-lived, and we have managed in the meantime by in-sourcing scientific and technical talent from the rest of the world. Today the timing is just as pressing and the need is economic, the preservation of American jobs and incomes. Better high school math and science teachers need not be rocket scientists, but the lead time may take 20 years, for first we must train the teachers who will educate the future scientific and technical workers of America

The decline in share of college students majoring in math and the natural sciences has consequences for the supply of new PhDs in these fields, generating another vicious cycle. Good teaching in math and the natural sciences requires an adequate number of PhDs. College teaching is the largest employer of PhDs. But the limited number of undergraduate majors on one hand reduces the stock from which graduate students are recruited, and the decline in academic demand for PhDs further reduces the number who choose to pursue postgraduate degrees. Converting this circle from vicious to virtuous must be done at the elementary and high school level by improving student mastery of math and science before admission to college.

There is one way of accelerating the needed increase in the supply of math and science teachers and perhaps in some other subjects. As an accelerator, qualified English-fluent teachers from other countries could be imported. In other industries we rely heavily on immigrants to supply the skills which our colleges are not producing in adequate numbers. India trains every year more very able people in math and science than it can employ; people who speak good English. It has provided much of the Silicon Valley computer manpower. Indian teachers in the United States would benefit both countries, India by reducing the problem of highly educated workers with no suitable jobs at home, the United States by filling the shortage of qualified teachers. The Philippines is another potential source of English-speaking teachers. Seven million Filipinos work abroad, some could teach here. Another possible recourse is graduate students in subjects short of teachers, some of whom have worked as teaching assistants and might be able to teach their subjects on a part time basis. These short term partial solutions are not possible with current teacher certification requirements in most states. Another way of accelerating the process is reliance on audio-visual techniques to magnify the impact of the best teachers. Passive listening and viewing is not enough, but it can help

Hiring better teachers is only part of the agenda. We need to eliminate bad teachers, incidentally creating the opportunity to hire more good teachers. Teacher valuation of job security and teacher shortages militate against discharge of bad teachers. More important perhaps, we need to eliminate elementary school teachers indoctrinated in schools of education to employ ineffective techniques - particularly in reading and math instruction, or retrain them to employ more effective teaching methods. Methodology has been waylaid by ideology.

It is also a question of altering priorities. A straw poll of high school teachers' concerns listed self esteem, grooming, job prospects, ethical character, absence of drugs and alcohol, political activity, social consciousness, dress, but hardly any educational desiderata [13]. Teachers' beliefs and values are hard to change [14]. They influence their judgments of merit and achievement. Administrators should go who impose inappropriate curricula reflecting current fashion of cultural, social, and political correctness with no value for further learning or for future employment

In addition to the general problem of teacher quality is that of distribution by schools and school systems. The average performance of African-American high school seniors is four years behind that of whites. Schools with a high minority, high poverty student body have teachers who are less qualified than schools whose students are mainly white and affluent. They should have the best teachers,. but prevailing salary structures guarantee that they don't. Its equal pay for unequal work. The teacher seniority system perpetuates this inequality. Seniority among public school teachers offers not prospects for promotion but greater freedom to choose the easy and the pleasant assignments – to work less.

Schools of education are not limited to teacher training. Many offer graduate programs for school principals and superintendents. According to Arthur Levin, President of Columbia Teachers College, the quality of graduate training for principals and superintendents in schools of education ranges from the inadequate to the appalling [15]. The quality of the students is scraping bottom, faculty have no scholarly interest, and most programs are inadequate or worse. Hess and Kelly [16] examined 11 of the most popular textbooks for training prospective principals and finds them unsatisfactory for management training and somewhat ideological. They also examined 210 course syllabi from 31 different graduate programs of education administration and found them inadequate particularly in managing for greater academic achievement [17]. Neither texts nor syllabi focus on important personnel decisions, including the evaluation and removal of ineffective teachers. Reform requires leadership, and the schools are neither selecting nor training for this role.

Principals committed to the status quo are legion; able principals committed to reform are rare. After all, most principals are teachers who were trained in schools of education. The idea that principals should be, or should have been, teachers, is good; but as a stopgap, individuals who are not teachers but managers should be considered for educational leadership. A good principal or superintendent is not necessarily a good teacher, any more than vice versa. Clearly, schools of education are not the place to train principals and other education administrators. Schools of business would do a better job.

Curriculum Reform

How does one improve the curriculum, beyond hiring teachers who are good at what they do and are masters of their subject? Curriculum upgrading involves on one hand, higher content standards, and on the other, higher expectation of students, which means a reversal of grade inflation. There must be consequences for effort and attainment, and consequences for failure to learn. Laggards in turn must have some recourse, whether it be after school, summer school, tutoring, or repetition. There should be consequences for teachers also: pay, preferred assignments.

The traditional structure of separate subjects, not all taken by every student, is obsolete. Chemistry and physics developed independently. Physics evolved through observation of the sun, moon, stars and determination of their regularities, later through examination of the principle of the lever, the screw, the trajectory of projectiles. Chemistry evolved from alchemy, a process of trial and error which did not develop a theoretical foundation until the late 19th century. These subjects, and biology, are still taught in many schools as though they were independent. In fact, physics, typically studied last, if at all, has become the foundation on which science can erect chemistry and biology as well as other natural sciences, such as geology. That is the way it should be taught: first, not last. That is one view; there are others, more traditional. Physics requires math.

In math and science we cannot look back a generation or two as a model for tomorrow. Whatever may have been the appropriate stress on math and science half a century ago, it must be much greater today. Every scientific field has grown; there is more to learn, and the capacity to continue learning after school days are over is as important as what is learned in school. This, and only this, is a plausible argument against stressing just rote facts. But the alternative is an understanding of scientific methods and their logic, not ignorant discussions of science and society. Mathematics, statistics in particular, has also grown in importance for daily life as well as for understanding the sciences. All graduates need a sound foundation in algebra and geometry as a minimum. Scheduling should keep in mind the math requirements of the sciences. Science and math high school teachers should be regarded as peers with college faculty teaching lower division courses in their subjects; there should be closer association between them. Ideally they should be interchangeable in teaching advanced placement courses in high school and freshman courses in college..

The focus of attention may be on math and science, but the field with the largest percentage of teachers who did not major in it is history. This subject presents problems beyond mere numbers. In the sciences there are objective tests of "truth," accepted methods of testing hypotheses. But college majors in history are a diverse group. The traditional bias toward monarchs and wars has been corrected by stress on social, political, and economic forces shaping societies But many college history departments have succumbed to the same temptation to be innovative, creative, new and different, stressing aspects history neglected in the past, history from the perspectives of the lowly, the marginalized and powerless. There is nothing wrong with that as a supplement to traditional history from the viewpoint of the rich and powerful and their interests and accomplishments. But beyond extending the formerly narrow confines of history, they have sought scholarly distinction by rejecting traditional history while inflating their new perspectives into a dominant thesis. Thus some history teachers neglect American history, or degrade it, pursuing instead their pet fashions, themes, isms (ideology is too grand a term for their views). History lends itself to diversity of curriculum content – whose history, when, and from what perspective? All students must be familiar with American history, in particular its founding ideology and the progress made in its realization, and the responsible institutions – what was once called civics. Beyond that, there will be choices. Perhaps some day historians may agree on a basic core which all students should know, but I doubt it.

Social studies is an oxymoron in which teachers vent their favorite themes, biases, and cultural and political views. It could be a great course, but only if taught by real scholars with a wide command of the social sciences and history. There are few such people today, it is an age of specialization. Which social science should be stressed? There is no one right answer; students can't do it all. Most faculty will have earned a college degree in just one social science and are likely to stress that one in their teaching. High schools should have a sequence of topics, each stressing a particular social science and taught by a major in that field. There are other approaches, viewing a major issue from the diverse perspectives of the several social sciences. In social studies there is a further choice between an analytical and a descriptive-empirical approach, both perfectly legitimate. It will be more difficult, probably impossible, to obtain agreement among professionals on the role of values and issues in social studies curriculum content. But the analytical core should be the point of departure. Values should be objectively examined and their implications analyzed. Issues should be subjects of analysis, not promotion. Neither values nor issues should be imposed by the teacher, the school system, the textbooks, or the tests. Teachers have no right to indoctrinate or proselytize. It is not their role.

The curricula in nations whose students lead the world in performance provide one source of guidelines for curricula. But they have national systems of education, whereas in the United States often there is no common curriculum even in same school. Efforts have been made in this country to develop standards in math, history, other fields. Most of these proposed standards were found unacceptable. A full page ad in the Washington Post [18] and no doubt other papers signed by over 200 professional mathematicians and addressed to Secretary of Education Richard Riley denounced recommendations for mathematics education developed under the auspices of the National Science Foundation and endorsed by the Secretary of Education as lacking in mathematical substance. They pointed out that the Expert Panel that made the final decisions included not a single research mathematician and that it was unlikely that it shared the mainstream views of practicing mathematicians and scientists. They found the program, described by its producers as exemplary or promising, was neither, rather deficient in substance and pedagogy. A standard also developed under government agency for history was found so objectionable that the House of Representatives passed a resolution against it almost unanimously.

What was at fault with these and numerous other proposed curricula, is that they were developed under the influence of schools of education and public school teachers, with essentially no input from working professionals or college faculty in the respective fields. Some have been accused of incorporating questionable if not outright unsound methodologies, or of reflecting ideological bias. All this is to be expected at first; the three monopolies dominating public education are on the defensive and seek self-preservation.

Stotsky [19] summarizes the analyses of several coauthors on national and state standards. She reports that academic scholars have been almost totally excluded from influence on standards in science and math; standards de-emphasize learning of detailed facts and concepts; they stress minimal competence but fail to assess high achievement. She finds similar problems with standards in English, especially literature. History is worse, tainted with ideological fads: riddled with multiculturalism, myths and inventions, and convenient omissions [20].

Who is to develop curriculum standards? Not associations of teachers whose students are doing poorly, they are part of the problem; not the Department of Education, nor the National Science Foundation. Independent academic scholars and working professionals must be heard if students are to be prepared for college and for work. They are the ones to recommend what should be taught and learned. Textbooks must be written and adopted that implement their recommendations.

Better teachers must have better tools to work with. Perhaps the most difficult reform is that of textbooks. It requires dumping most of the current stock of simplified texts padded with propaganda parading as learning aids. The task of making them more rigorous and stripping them of irrelevant material cannot be left to the current crop of educators. It must be in the hands of professionals in the field who are not part of the public school system. Adoption of such textbooks requires political changes: decision makers at the top of school systems in large states. As a stopgap, textbooks published in other English-speaking nations could be used in some subjects, especially in math and science. In English, there is no shortage of reading materials; all that needs to be done is to revise reading and writing assignments. Fortunately the publishing industry is faster on its feet than the teacher training industry.

Greater attention must paid to the high proportion of the age group that does not go to college, and to those who never finish high school. This means restoring vocational training in those schools many of whose students will never go to college. Some vocational training now offered in community colleges could also be provided in high schools, although improvements in the academic quality of the curriculum may be a prerequisite. The immediate objection to vocational training or occupational training in high school, and sometimes in community colleges as well, is that during the course of a working life the requirements of jobs and occupations will change. Even if they do not, the demand for specific jobs and occupations may drop or disappear. This is an argument for retraining facilities, not for a college degree. The only generic skills are language and numeracy; all others are specific to jobs and occupations whose future is unpredictable

Reforming failed pedagogy is relatively easy; teaching can be guided by educational results. Methods that work have already been invented. No new methods that don't work, please! It is difficult to deny facts indefinitely. Creativity is great, but no one can be creative without intellectual resources and tools. These are acquired mainly by memorization. Educators have to realize that memory, rote or otherwise, is not a dirty word but an essential tool for acquiring the knowledge and the skills to be creative. Schools whose students fall far short on achievement in basic skills simply have to devote time to learning. If even that does not work, face the executioner.

POLICIES

Information: Standards, Tests and Achievement

Reform of public primary and secondary education across the nation cannot be achieved by the industry of education. It has little interest in doing so, nor the capability. It is threatened by reform, and its lobbies have no interest in reversing the course followed for much of the past century. Its values and goals are in conflict with those of most parents and citizens. Reform must come from outside, over the objection of educational lobbies, unions, schools of education and many teachers, all with some vested interest in the status quo. Standards and tests are Siamese twins. Standards spell out what is to be learned: the curriculum, student attainment, graduation requirements. Curriculum standards have been discussed above. They are of little worth without means to measure student achievement and determine compliance with standards. Tests provide information on performance of students, teachers, schools, on achievement of standards. They can also generate motivation to comply with standards. Achieving standards takes time; the process must start in the first few years of elementary school, not at the high school senior level.

Standards and tests have another purpose: to generate the popular and political pressure to bring about radical change in schools: curricula, teacher capabilities, and student achievement. The influence of parents on curricula and performance is weak or nonexistent. Most parents believe that public schools are not doing a good job, but that the particular school in which their children are enrolled is an exception. What else can they believe, if their children bring back good grades and glowing commendations? The sooner they realize they are being duped the better. Teachers, teachers unions, schools of education are strongly opposed to standards, to standardized tests, most are opposed to tests and to grades as objective measures of student learning (and of teacher performance). Information is needed to empower parents. Without it, local control of schools and education means school self-control and union control.

The first step to generate external pressure for reform is transparency. The provision of information is badly needed, so that schools and teachers may know how they are performing compared to other schools, and compared to some consensus idea of acceptable performance. More important perhaps is the need to inform parents and communities. Parents must know how their children are doing; taxpayers must know how their schools are performing. And they should be made aware of the consequences of school failure. This means standards and tests and reports of test results to the public, to parents, and to students. To achieve transparency there must be national benchmarks at multiple grade levels, in key subjects. No Child Left Behind is a step forward for primary schools, to be extended in time to secondary schools as well. But standards set by each state can be low to meet performance. Eighty seven percent of Tennessee eighth graders were found proficient in math by state standards, but only 21 percent by federal government standards [21]. This will change. Without visibility, standards allow dumbing down to perpetuate school and student failure.

Standards can refer to many different things. At one extreme, national standards impose a national curriculum. Comprehensive national standards can be found in many countries, but literacy and numeracy aside, a single standard is out of the question in the United States, unique in its state and local control of public education. Standards of attainment may be limited to high school seniors, or apply to every school grade. They may have a narrow scope or encompass a wide range of topics. They may aim at minimum competency, a floor, or set goals of achievement appropriate for success in college, in the labor market and in society. Standards are meaningless unless reflected in the subjects taught, the content covered, the textbooks assigned, and in teacher qualifications. Better texts and teachers' guides can be generated quickly. But many of the teachers needed to take advantage of them and to meet standards for students will have to be educated and hired, replacing those committed to failing ways. And who will train the teachers? Not the Old Guard.

There are numerous tests of student achievement, as well as of ability. Tests of ability are useful in admission to magnet schools, to advanced placement courses, and eventually to college. But it is tests of achievement that inform students, parents, teachers, schools, and the public of the contribution of schools to learning. We have little testing of compliance with standards, which would involve both assessment of teacher performance and of content of textbooks. Significant gains in achievement require changes in curriculum and pedagogy. Above all they require able teachers. Too many of the teachers we have are strongly opposed to standards and tests, to changing their ways.

Teachers

Tests start with teacher certification. At present these are on a state basis, with different standards, most of them absurdly low. We do not allow medical schools to decide who is qualified to practice medicine, or law schools to design their own bar exam. Teacher certification should be the function of professionals in the subject to be taught who are independent of the school system. Most states have no teacher certification requirement in specific subject areas for middle schools, 21 have none for high school. Almost all of those that do have loopholes, as evidenced by the frequency of out of field teaching. The requirements themselves in most are undemanding. As to teacher education, 30 states require a major, but most of them accept a minor, and there are ways around both.

Most states use the Praxis test administered by the Education Testing Service for teacher certification. The test for reading and math is said to be at the 8th grade level. Praxis tests for pedagogically correct methodology taught in schools of education, not for would-be teachers' ability to affect student achievement in a subject [22]. Passing scores set by many states are laughably low. A study conducted in 1999 by the Pew Charitable Trusts found that although 29 states in 1999 required that new teachers pass tests on subjects they will teach, all but New Jersey had loopholes.

The No Child Left Behind legislation requires that all teachers be highly qualified; this means a college degree, competency in the subject they teach, and state teacher certification. However, each state is allowed to set its own certification requirements. It is free to adjust requirements to teacher availability, and to certify that those currently teaching a subject are qualified. Parents and taxpayers should be informed of the certification requirements in each state, and of the extent to which teachers old and new meet them. A little transparency here is needed.

The requirement of a major must refer to the department in which the subject is the exclusive commitment, not to a school of education degree. Minors should not be accepted; for one thing, there are no standard definitions. A degree in education should be neither a requirement nor a qualification in any subject. Achievement has declined despite the fact that the percentage of public school teachers with a masters degree (nearly all of which are in education) or education specialist's degree rose from 27 percent in 1971 to 56 percent in 2001 [23]. Once it is clear that graduates of schools of education are at the tail end of the line of applicants, not at the head, enrollments in such schools will fall rapidly. The schools themselves are not going to undertake a radical metamorphosis.

This change in recruitment criteria will not be adopted by current administrators; it must be imposed from outside the industry of public education. Neither can teacher certification standards be left to the public school system or its proxies. Demands for student achievement indirectly upgrade teacher performance; standards will follow.

Efforts by the American Board for Certification of Teacher Excellence to raise standards of teacher qualification are a threat to many in the industry, and have met opposition and even sabotage. The National Education Association called efforts to substitute tests for education school credits demeaning to the teaching profession [24]. The president of the American Association of Colleges of Teacher Education leaked a confidential teacher certification exam being field-tested by the American Board. Professors of education overwhelmingly want less reliance on objective tests and think schools should avoid competition [25]. What all this means is that needed reforms cannot be fully implemented by a faculty that is overwhelmingly opposed to the reforms. That is a reason, apart from quality of teachers, why it is necessary to fill teaching positions with applicants with a background and attitudes different from those currently prevailing, why it is necessary to turn over current faculty as rapidly as possible.

Such a system would greatly reduce the number of qualified teachers, unless there are accompanying changes in salary levels and schedules. In some fields it would take a decade or two even with pay adjustments. It should be possible for individuals to be certified who can demonstrate their mastery of a subject regardless of formal education. That is the advantage of a test over a diploma whose relation to subject mastery is unclear.

A college degree in a subject is not a guarantee of teaching ability. The college diploma itself has been compromised by needs to maintain or increase enrollment and by the shrinking of core curricula in favor of cafeteria style student choice. The GRE or some equivalent should be taken by all would-be teachers. The subject matter component is necessary to judge knowledge. The verbal component is also needed, to provide some minimum assurance of the ability to communicate. The math component is not needed for competence in some majors, and is embedded in the subject matter component for other majors. Such an exam may be taken by applicants who have not majored in the subject they are to teach, even by applicants who did not graduate from college. It is knowledge, not diplomas, that counts. Each state may then set minimum scores for certification. Many states will be under pressure to set low scores because of the shortage of applicants in some areas, but that is an issue for the future. For the present it is enough to advance from the current mostly high-school level to college-level standards for teacher certification.

High School Seniors

State after state has imposed standards and tests to determine whether or not a high school senior will be given a diploma. This has resulted in panic among many teachers, superintendents, and parents. The California State Board of Education found that the prospect of the "sudden death" test had led to considerable improvement in local school curricula, but that nevertheless 20% of seniors were expected to fail [26]. This trend is probably a major reason for the recent turnaround in math SAT test scores, partially reversing decades of decline. As it is, they test for minimal competence, and some states are under pressure to lower the bar. The level of competence tested differs from state to state. Test results are binary: pass/fail. Thus their information value is quite limited. They classify high school seniors into two undifferentiated groups: graduates and non graduates. This approach is not a replacement or a substitute for an honest grading system providing objective information on level of mastery of different subjects. It alone cannot revalue the diploma.

Critics claim that standardized tests measure only the ability to take tests. The implication, obviously false, is that doing well on subject matter tests is unrelated to subject matter mastery. It is true that some who know the subject may not do well in tests. A test is a small sample [27]. But the alternative: a degree in a subject with good grades, is itself the outcome of a series of tests. There is no alternative to tests, though one may argue which is the best test

There is an ethical problem, which is being confronted by delaying enforcement of minimum test scores for high school graduation. Failure can mean many things: this is a student of low ability who should not go to college and perhaps should not make it to a high school diploma; this student fails the test because the curriculum never included courses covered in the test, or this is a student who is able and whose curriculum is appropriate, but who was taught by ill-prepared teachers in key subjects, or taught dumbed-down versions of key subjects, or who was absent much of the time and made little effort. Students failed most often the math component; a high proportion had never taken algebra or geometry.

At this time parents of seniors denied a diploma are more likely to express outrage at the standard and test than at the school system, since they had little forewarning. It is difficult to admit that they have been deceived for twelve years. Parents may have been happy with a curriculum that stressed sports, extra-curricular nonacademic activities [28] because they were unaware of its implication for college admission or job preparation. When first enforced there is bound to be strong opposition, even complaints that minimum standards are too high, because so many students fail. But standards and tests need not serve as a barrier to promotion or graduation; they may simply provide information.

The 12th grade is too late to learn the truth about a student's education, too late to do much about it. Texas, which has required a competency test for high school graduation since the mid 1980s, first tests students in the 10th grade and allows them to retake the test up to 7 times. It has succeeded in substantially narrowing the racial gap in performance [29]. Starting in the earlier grades provides the information, incentives and opportunity to improve achievement, and is much fairer to the student, and to teachers as well. The No Child Left Behind program starts with standards and tests in the early years of school, and plans to advance to secondary schools.

In the long run differences in standards will be reflected in the value of a state's high school diplomas. Interstate competition may tend toward convergence upward rather than downward. With school reform, eventually such tests could become superfluous. One purpose of standards is to revalue the high school diploma. If it were a guarantee of certain basic competencies, not just in linguistic and quantitative skills but in discipline and effort, employers would be more willing to hire high school graduates instead of upgrading their educational requirements, giving preference to those completing an associate or bachelors degree, or even requiring such degrees.

Standards must not exclude room for diversity in curriculum content or in levels of attainment. The extent to which standards concentrate on raising the minimum attainment or on increasing the share of students with higher levels of achievement is open to debate, and to diverse tradeoffs. What is essential is that standards restore some common content and some credibility to the high school diploma. Beyond language and math skills I would add to core standards some mix of history and civics to encourage a sense of community in each new generation. Much of the curriculum could remain open to local choice. Tests in other subjects might be voluntary, serving as information for college admission officers or potential employers. Their value would depend on their rigor. There are strong arguments against national or even state standards of a comprehensive nature. First, needs, interests and possibilities differ, and schools and school districts should retain some flexibility, not constrained by standardized tests. Second, standards once established become bureaucratic or political obstacles to change, and in a dynamic economy and society curriculum should evolve over time.

High school graduation sorts students by achievement; it sorts out some 28% of the age group. (These numbers do not include recipients of GEDs and similar high school-equivalency certificates) Standards for high school graduation also signal prospective employers or college admissions officers. They are a crude sorting. The test seniors must pass to graduate in many states raises the credibility of the diploma.

There is no optimal standard. should it suit the employer, the college admissions officer, the parents, the educational establishment? These vested interests will never agree. The higher the standard, the more valuable the diploma. It provides some information, but not much. Standards for promotion, standards for graduation needs to be supplemented by standardized tests which partition individuals instead of whole classes and schools. They are strongly opposed precisely because they provide calibrated information on individuals. Such tests may signal preparation for college, or for particular jobs and occupations. They are a countermeasure against grade inflation and should help reverse it. There is a tradeoff between standards high enough to be valuable and the failure rate. What is to be done with and for those who can't make them?

The reality is that any state or national standard for high school graduation is bound to be low at first, it is politically impossible to deny a diploma to a significant proportion of a high school senior class. In time, with curriculum reform and higher standards for the preceding 12 years, the minimum standard for graduation can be raised but it can never be high enough to revalue the high school diploma for all. A simple pass/fail breakdown of seniors is not a substitute for an objective grading system as a source of useful information for employers and college admissions officers. If every graduating senior were to take an ACT or a SAT II test, then the score would be a substitute for an objective grading system. The value of the diploma would be related to individual achievement.

Standards must be comparable across the nation, results must be visible. The same applies to standards for certification of public school teachers: they must be upgraded and made visible and comparable across the nation. Meeting those double requirements will take two generations. National standards are appropriate for students, given their great geographic mobility; for teachers, such standards would promote a national market and eliminate any refuge for the incompetent.

Teachers will always object to any test, that's a given. Standardized tests test teachers and schools as well as students. For many years they have complained that the SAT for college admission. forced them to "teach to the test." Now it is also NCLB. Multiple choice is not ideal for evaluating individual students, but there is no other practical way of objectively comparing millions of students. Learning how to take multiple choice tests takes days, not weeks or years. The other objection is the implicit requirement that all students master a minimal national curriculum of literacy, numeracy, and subject matter content. If high school seniors can only read at the basic level, as most do, they will not do well in any written test. If high school teachers neglect the scholastic curriculum in order to teach to the test, as many claim, it doesn't work; SAT scores are down. The idea that rote memorizing long lists of words out of context in high school can compensate for lack of reading in the previous decade is absurd. Besides, it doesn't take any teaching. The value of SAT and ACT is that states cannot lower test standards to meet the achievement levels of their schools. If students are to be prepared to do well in any such test they must start preparing in elementary school.

To increase the performance of high school graduates significantly, the proportion of an age group completing high school must decline initially. For it to be maintained calls for a dramatic change in values and attitudes. The same is true of the proportion entering and completing college. Performance and egalitarianism conflict, and there is no resolution But that is in the short run, because higher standards have been implemented initially at the end of secondary education. They are now being applied from the beginning of elementary education. Some years down the road the proportion of the age group graduating from high school could actually rise, while the value of the diploma itself is restored. It would be based on achievement. Better teaching, in elementary schools as well as high schools, will minimize this decline, but not avoid it.

Higher standards for graduates and college applicants should be accompanied by reforms offering better options for those who don't make it, or are not interested, not necessarily postponing job training to post-high school days. High school counselors, perhaps middle school as well, need to focus less on advising on college applications, more on advising students who will not or should not apply. No doubt counselors are needed with a flexible mind-set and suitable training. The high school seniors going to college will be better prepared, and many colleges will be able to improve their own standards.

NCLB

Reform should start at the bottom, the beginning of schooling. The No Child Left Behind Act has required states to set standards in numeracy and literacy for the first 4 grades. These standards rise yearly for ten years until they attain the desired level of proficiency as determined by the state. Eventually a similar requirement is expected for secondary schools. Students must be tested every year on reading and math. There will be alternatives to failing schools and for failing students: transfers from failing schools to better public schools, tutoring for failing students. Logically and ethically, this should have been the first step; a test for seniors would have been less needed, and should have come last. There is a long way to go. The 2007 National Assessment of Educational Progress found only 31% of 4th graders and 29% of 8th graders proficient in reading.

The legal consequences of failure limit the ability of most states to set high standards at this time. Parents now have reports on elementary school and school district performance. It is reported by student group, so that lags of ethnic minorities cannot be hidden in school and district overall averages. School districts are to hire qualified teachers, but the definition is up to the state at this point, and the directive cannot be made retroactive. New teachers are a tiny proportion of total faculty in any one year.

The NEA strongly objects to the law and many of its provisions, including the testing and the right of students to transfer from failing schools. Three fourths of high school teachers oppose standards and testing in high school and only one quarter support holding all students, teachers, schools to the same standards, whereas parents and the public support both [30]. Elementary school teachers no doubt are also strongly opposed. Monitoring and enforcement are real problems. Underreporting of failing schools is widespread and cheating on student tests by schools and teachers is not uncommon [31].

Independent evaluations are needed early and at several steps along the way to graduation to provide timely information for corrective measures. The two subjects on which information is absolutely needed, and standards specified, are literacy and numeracy. These are the essential tools of learning to deal with everyday needs and to open the door to opportunities to learn in all subjects. Their absence closes almost all doors. For them the complaint that they compel teaching to the test is invalid because that is exactly what they should do. Opposition is just a cover-up for failure. Numeracy does not imply a national standard on mathematical knowledge, only a minimum. States, schools, students should set higher and different targets

Tests can serve three purposes; first, as an indicator of the achievement of an individual in the subject tested; second, as a means of evaluating the performance of a teacher, a school, a school system. Third, testing requirements apply pressure on school systems and teachers to improve their performance in particular directions. They provide information on achievements and deficiencies, without which "solutions" cannot be targeted effectively.. In time they can restore credibility to grades and diplomas in the eye of prospective employers or college admissions officers. They increase the benefits of learning to the student and to the school. As an unintended consequence, they reduce the harassment of high achievers found in many schools [32]. Why such denunciation of "teaching to the test" at the primary and secondary school level? Should not all students master the basics of mathematics as well as reading and writing? One complaint is that standardized tests divert teaching effort from critical thinking, as though mathematics and writing were not excellent ways of teaching and practicing just that? Most humans just don't like to be tested.

There must be accountability - some means of assessing the performance of teachers and schools [33]. This is anathema to most teachers. Performance can mean individual or school achievement of some objective minimum; achievement relative to a higher standard, the judgment of working professionals as to what all students should know; or increases in achievement from one year to the next. The last is particularly important as a measure of teacher effectiveness, whereas achievement at a point in time may reflect class or school composition rather than teacher effectiveness. Students too should be accountable.

If there is to be accountability, standards, tests and evaluation must be independent of teachers, schools, school systems and schools of education. The school system cannot be trusted with assessment because it is held accountable for performance. Independent evaluation is necessary to provide accurate and credible information to parents, students, and eventually, to colleges and employers. It would undermine the incentive, the pressures, for grade inflation, so that grades themselves might regain value as information, and incentives for students to work hard and to do well would be restored. At this point in time most states are unable or unwilling

College

A high quality public school system would automatically reduce if not eliminate many of the problems that colleges face, including remedial course work and high attrition rates. Standards are needed for college, not just in elementary school and for high school graduation. Not just standards, but test results that provide information to students, parents, prospective employers.

Before WWII the Carnegie Foundation for the Advancement of Teaching found little relation between test scores and level of education. Harvard president James Conant wanted to make Harvard more meritocratic. That was the origin of SAT, now taken by most high school seniors [34]. Later the American College Testing Program introduced ACT. SAT tries to measure ability, whereas ACT tries to measure achievement. SAT II is similar to ACT. These are alternative ways of assessing merit and contributing to equality of opportunity.

There are legitimate disagreements over the content of standardized tests, over what they are designed to "measure". The Chancellor of the California University System argues in favor of testing achievement in particular subjects rather than attempting to test ability, which is poorly defined; in favor of SAT II over SAT I. SAT II appears to be a better predictor of college student success. An additional advantage is that it can exercise a healthy influence on high school curricula, assuring that all students are exposed to courses in the core competencies to be tested. But it means a return to sorting largely by socioeconomic status; children of educated and well-to-do parents go to good schools with good teachers, many to private schools, where they learn much more by high school graduation than children of poor and uneducated parents, who mostly attend inferior schools staffed not by the best teachers.

SAT and ACT tell us something about the college freshman class. Such information would not necessarily tell us how well the college is performing, it may merely reflect its admission standards. GREs and other standardized tests taken by college seniors are designed for admission to graduate study. Most students do not take them. Perhaps they or similar tests should be recommended for all seniors, not for admission to graduate schools, but to inform prospective employers of what students know or can do, and to give some indication to high school counselors and seniors of the quality of the college and of particular departments. Such tests would be corrective for grade inflation, restoring some of the value lost to the sheepskin as an indicator of ability and learning.

Looking backward, these tests provide a more finely calibrated ordering of students, schools and inferentially teachers that the pass/fail high school graduation exam. Looking forward, they offer to college admissions officers and to potential employers information far more useful than a high school diploma.

What proportion of an age group should finish college is debatable, as is the purpose of a college education itself. But to the extent that college is a preparation for future employment, it is clear that too many are graduating. A quarter of college alumni polled in 1994, a year after graduation, did not think that their job was related to their major, and this is the key point, nearly half thought that a college degree was not necessary to do their job. Three years later their responses were essentially unchanged [35]. Yet not enough are graduating in some scientific and technical fields which require high academic standards, as described in Chapter 5. We know that some very advanced countries, Germany specifically, manage to meet their higher skill needs with a much smaller proportion of their population going to college.

The catalog of almost any college is riddled with courses that offer entertainment but no knowledge, courses, and majors, that guarantee high grades but offer no job prospects or useful skills. For most students who follow this path of least resistance college is not a good investment but four years lost, at least from the viewpoint of society. Such courses and majors should go. The absence of quality control for high school graduation, and college needs to enroll and retain students, are the basic causes for their creation. There are other reasons, some of them ideological. Reform of pre-college education would prepare more college students to succeed in reasonably rigorous and coherent educational programs for which there is an economic payoff.

The sorting function of high school education is not being well performed; neither is the learning function. The result is that more students have to continue their education post-high school simply so that they may increase their chances of being selected for desired jobs and occupations. And if additional education does not result in sufficient additional learning, then the years of schooling must be extended [36].

Competition: Vouchers and Charter Schools

Many fine plans and programs have failed for lack of implementation or enforcement. The players, teachers and principals in this case, must be motivated or reforms will be ignored. There must be consequences. One alternative is circumvention of the monopoly of public schools by increasing access to private schools on the assumption that greater competition will improve student achievement. The main means is vouchers. The other alternative is to seek improved performance through incentives and penalties within the existing system. That is what standards and compulsory testing are intended to accomplish. The current approaches include charter schools, magnet schools, tracking, advanced placement and home schooling. Vouchers and charter schools represent the revolt of the masses; magnet schools and advanced placement courses reflect the revolt of the classes.

Vouchers

Vouchers represent school choice for students, and an incentive for school improvement. They are the equivalent of anti-trust legislation for business. One argument for vouchers, circumventing public school monopoly, is that they can become effective immediately. But their scope is limited, considering the limited capacity of private schools within commuting distance, as well as their reluctance to enroll all those who might wish to take advantage of vouchers. Private schools are free to accept or reject applicants. This is one reason why high ability students are the biggest gainers. The better schools are reluctant to expand by admitting lower quality students; lower quality schools seek to attract better students who are unlikely to apply. Some private schools may be reluctant to alter the character of their student body. Thus the potential number of direct beneficiaries is limited; the number of indirect beneficiaries, however, is not. The option of transferring to another public school could have a larger and more immediate impact.

Let us be realistic. Public schools account for 90% of enrollments. The capacity of private schools to implement a voucher program is quite limited; even if they were able to increase their enrollments by 50%, that is less than 6% of public school enrollment. Apart from infrastructure capacity, where are the additional teachers? Private schools face the same problem of shortages of able teachers in some fields as do public schools. Vouchers on a significant scale might lead them to draw on the best public school faculty. They are not a solution, merely a threat, a prod, to public schools to shape up or ship out. In the short run the main contribution of vouchers is to magnify incentives for public school reform in line with parental expectations. In the long run, the impact of voucher programs is greater if the vouchers are generous enough to encourage formation of new private schools as well as expansion of existing schools. The size and generosity of voucher programs has not been large enough so far to give an indication of the potential scope of vouchers

Private schools are demonstrably more efficient in converting educational resources into student achievement. Vouchers on the very limited scale on which we have experience have resulted in higher achievement, graduation rates and college attendance [37]. Whether they could maintain that margin were they to become a significant share of enrollment is another question. Efficiency alone is a strong case for vouchers even if beneficiaries were to do no better that similar students not using vouchers. But the public argument for vouchers is that recipients do better, and that the existence or the mere threat of vouchers should improve performance of public schools, whether or not recipients do better.

Private schools have a flexibility, an autonomy, denied to schools that are part of a school system, whether in responding to demand or in generating demand. The biggest advantage of private schools is their ability to circumvent the monopoly of schools of education, teachers unions, and public school boards. They are better able to hire individuals qualified to teach math, science, and other subjects, to correct mistakes in hiring, to adjust pay schedules to reward good teaching. This advantage will only make a difference nationally if private school enrollment grows substantially at the expense of public schools. To make a big difference, competition from private schools must force public school systems to reform their personnel policies on hiring, retention, pay. if they are to retain the good teachers they now have. Private schools also have autonomy with regard to curricula and choice of textbooks often lacking in public schools, where such decisions are often made at the state level. The greater accountability of private schools, more subject to parental influence, enhances the efficiency with which resources are used.

Another explanation for superior academic performance of Catholic schools in particular was noted by Coleman, Hoffer and Kilgore [38]: student behavior. The schools enforced strict disciplinary standards, one reason for high graduation rates and high college attendance rates compared to similar students in public schools.

Competition between private schools also provides greater diversity than an all-public school system. This does not mean that everyone is better off in private schools. There are market failures, bankruptcies. The difference between market failures and public school failures, is that the former tend to be corrected or eliminated, whereas the latter tend to persist..

Voucher programs and proposals are too diverse for simple evaluation. At one extreme is the proposal that every student be eligible for a voucher to any school that will accept the student. This is the recommendation of Milton and Rose Friedman [39], long time conservative proponents of school choice. It may come as a surprise that the proposal of Donald Weiss [40], reformed Marxist, is basically the same. The Friedmans argue in behalf of freedom of choice, Weiss in the name of diversity, to implement a classless society. Most voucher programs seek to provide opportunity for students in underperforming schools, or for low-income students, rather than the universal freedom of choice recommended by the Friedmans and Weiss. Most programs have been means-tested; only students from families at or not far above the poverty level are eligible. Some programs are limited to other public schools. If they are to extend beyond a single school district, their scope is limited by the area size of school districts and resulting commuting time, never mind the ability to cooperate between different bureaucracies. Under the NCLB, students in failing schools can opt to go to other public schools. It is a limited voucher program without vouchers as such. Florida has a program based not on students but on schools. All students in failing schools are eligible for a voucher. This program is similar to charter schools in terms of the students served.

The dollar amount of the voucher, usually a small fraction of the average cost of public school instruction, is so low that many private schools are willing to accept few students, that many charge tuition in addition to the voucher which exceeds the ability to pay of some who would like to take advantage of a voucher option. There is also the issue of religion; most private schools are Catholic, and some states are averse to vouchers for religious schools. (This issue has been clarified by the Supreme Court. As long as the voucher goes to the parents who then redeem it in a religious school, there is no legal problem.) The total number of vouchers available may also be restricted. With so many variables all one can do is indicate the kinds of consequences without knowing their actual magnitude.

Benefits are concentrated on low income and minority students, and especially on high-ability students among them [41]. They are greater if the public school has no tracking. Students of the same background achieve more in private than in public schools; the difference is largest for minorities [42]. Higher income parents can send their children to private schools - a voucher system paid entirely by the parents. They can also choose to live in areas with good public schools. What amounts to the same thing, areas whose population is upper middle income and well-educated will tend to have good public schools, or else. The ability of poor families to exercise choice depends on the size of the voucher. Private schools can accept a limited number of additional students at small additional cost as long as they do not have to expand their physical facilities. But to accept more they have to build or buy more capacity, and the cost per student will be much higher.

The gains are not limited to those who take advantage of vouchers, choice stimulates failing schools to improve performance. Even without any significant use of vouchers, their availability promotes improvement in public schools. A study of the voucher system in Florida finds that schools under threat of vouchers improve their test scores more than those not under threat; the greater the threat, the larger the improvement in scores [43]. Loss of students to other schools is an indictment of the school they leave, and a threat to its administration and faculty. It motivates them to do better.

Vouchers are likely to increase the public school demand for teachers with a high quality college education as a result of the enhanced competition with private schools [44]. Furthermore, they empower parents who in turn can apply pressure to improve curricula and achievement.

There is also the question of eligibility for vouchers. If all students in a public school system are eligible, then private schools will have more choice in terms of student attributes. If only students from failing schools are eligible, private schools may be less willing to accept them.

To concentrate the benefit on those for whom the voucher makes the difference between attending public school or shifting to a private school, there should be an income ceiling on eligibility for vouchers. Eligibility may be means-tested, or the amount of the voucher may be means-adjusted. Means-testing concentrates available funds on those who need them. It is more efficient, but unfair, since well to do families pay more than their share of the taxes supporting public schools. Without means-testing, some who can afford private schools and intend to send their sons there would take advantage of vouchers.

The right to transfer from a failing school under the NCLB legislation refers to other public schools, which are free. Choice between public schools within a school district is more limited an alternative than a voucher system that includes private schools, but would have similar results in terms of demand for able teachers and parental influence. In neither case is transfer compulsory.

Vouchers are voluntary; many of the students who most need them, or their parents, will not use them. Ladd [45] fears that universal vouchers would harm many disadvantaged students. The argument is made that vouchers deprive public schools of some of their best students and most committed parents. No one except the beneficiaries likes to see private schools, or for that matter magnet public schools, draw off many of the best students and most involved parents from under-performing public schools. The assumption behind this argument is that the leavers had positive influence on performance of other students, who are in greater need of help, and of the school. In fact there is no evidence that vouchers result in cherry-picking or loss of positive role models. One reason to leave is that the peer group influence runs in the other direction, and its impact is negative. Even if all this were true, why should anyone be denied opportunity because some do not take advantage? The hypothetical possibility that there might be some losers is no reason why there should not be any gainers. Few outside the industry of education want to foreclose their children any choice.

Critics suggest that students who use vouchers, or the student's families, are different from other students of the same ability and socioeconomic characteristics., perhaps in family values, student motivation. The better performance of voucher recipients compared to similar students who do not opt for vouchers should not be credited to the schools to which they transfer. Peterson et al. [46] studied voucher programs in New York, Dayton and Washington, DC which had several times as many applicants as there were vouchers available. The vouchers were given by lottery, so that there could be no difference between applicants who won and applicants who lost. They found that in each city there were sizeable gains for Afro-American students, but no significant gains for others. However, in each city the cost of the private schools accepting vouchers was not quite half that of the public schools.

A voucher system could be expensive, but only in the short run. It is true that most of the private schools to which students with vouchers transfer spend less per student that the public schools from which students come. Vouchers never amount to anywhere near the average cost of schooling per student in the public school. But costs in schools losing students do not decline in proportion to their loss of enrollment, if they decline at all. Most school costs are fixed; the cost of the building and equipment, its operation and maintenance, are much the same over a wide range of enrollment. So is the cost of the faculty and staff: they are quasi-fixed costs. Class size may decline-another potential benefit of vouchers to students staying put; but costs per student rise. Thus the cost of vouchers to public school systems is mostly a net addition to total costs, at least in the short run. Nor should one compare the amount of the voucher with private school tuition. Schools to which vouchers are paid are likely to experience a drop in cost per student for the same reasons: most costs are fixed. A few additional students may have no perceptible influence on total costs; only as the number increases do additional costs become a consideration. Furthermore, tuition and school costs are not the same thing. The private school may be heavily subsidized – by alumni, churches – and many students may pay less than full tuition – on scholarships based on need. In the longer run, gains in efficiency in public schools should more than compensate for the costs of vouchers whether or not there are changes in scale.

The impact of vouchers depends upon the specifics of the voucher system which in turn affects student demand for vouchers and private schools' willingness and ability to accept students entitled to vouchers. If the voucher amount is large, more private schools will be willing to accept more students. This in turn increases student demand, since they are more likely to be accepted by schools of their choice. If the voucher system is perceived to be permanent, existing private schools may increase their capacity, and new private schools may open. The size of the voucher could affect tuition policies in private schools: will they accept the voucher as payment in full or charge additional tuition? Writing in 1996, Hoxby estimated that a $1,000 voucher would be used by 4 percent of public school students, improving achievement in both public and private schools [47]. Without a means test, much of the voucher money would go to students who would have attended private schools anyway.

Vouchers have been proposed for many decades. The very limited use made of them to date despite wide if not majority public support is an indication of the united opposition of the educational establishment. Teachers unions strongly oppose vouchers for transfer of students to private schools, and on the whole are against private schools altogether. They have few members in private schools and no control over private school staffing, except sometimes indirectly via influence on school accreditation. They feel threatened. Schools of education are in the same boat. Few monopolists welcome competition. Why do teachers unions and schools of education oppose the smallest voucher programs so adamantly? Superintendents should worry, but able teachers should smile. If a voucher program were extensive in scope, union power over hiring, salary structure, seniority rights might be: undermined. Parents would gain more influence. Public schools would be forced to behave like private schools, competing for students and faculty, judged by their performance, differing only in the extent of public subsidy and perhaps in their requirement (hard to enforce) to accept every student.

Charter Schools

Charter schools are a response to school failure rather than to individual student or parent dissatisfaction. Their purpose is to reduce the inequality in educational achievement between schools in a single school district. If a public school fails to attain specified levels of student achievement year after year, it may be turned over to a charter school, which remains a public school but is run as a private institution, with a degree of autonomy not available to public schools. They have one great advantage over public schools: if they do not perform, they can be terminated promptly.

Charter schools can be a rough equivalent of vouchers, for entire schools rather than for individual students. They differ from vouchers in that in most cases their primary beneficiaries are not a matter of individual student or family choice; all students are involved. A second difference is that most of them take over low-performing schools, whereas some voucher programs are available to students in any school. Another important difference between charter schools and vouchers is that most charter schools are new, untried, inexperienced, whereas vouchers go mainly to long-established private schools with a record of performance. One would not expect students to do as well in the average charter school as the same students would do if given vouchers to attend private schools of their choice. But as charter schools gain experience, and as underperforming schools do not have their charters renewed, average gain in performance compared to relevant public schools performance should improve. The greater their autonomy, the better their opportunity.

Charter schools differ widely in the conditions and constraints under which they function - in their freedom from public school bureaucracy and teachers unions. Typically they receive much less taxpayer money per student than public schools. In Maryland, for instance, they were getting less than half as much, until the Maryland State Board of Education ruled that school systems must provide as much money per student as they do for regular public schools. There are differences also in their freedom to hire teachers and to change curricula. Comparing all charters with all public schools is nearly meaningless. What is needed is, first, funding equivalent to that of public schools; second, freedom to hire whatever teachers the school wishes. Freedom to hire implies some flexibility in salary scales, not available to the standard public school. Perhaps it is the freedom to fire that is most important if the charter school is to reshape curricula and to innovate in teaching methods and teaching content.

They are on trial; if they do not improve student achievement their charter may not be renewed. Achievement must be monitored, not just in terms of public schools with comparable students, but in terms of objective standards. They represent an internal threat to the monopoly of public schools and to the jobs of public school teachers and administrators. In combination with the external threat of individual vouchers for private schools, they could in time revolutionize the dysfunctional practices of public school systems.

Forty two states allow charter schools, 3,399 of which were in operation in 2004-'05 in thirty eight states and the District of Columbia. Their enrollment is estimated at 2% of the school-age population and rising fast. How are they performing? It depends on who you ask, and compared to what. An American Federation of Teachers study using a 3% sample concludes that they do not do as well as public schools. The study has been described as "flawed" by the Secretary of Education, and worse by scholarly researchers. The Department of Education itself issued a report finding that they do not do quite as well as public schools in math, but do as well in reading, comparing schools rather than students [48]. However, when scores are broken down by ethnic group, there is no difference in math, and charters may do better than public schools in reading. Since charter schools are typically alternatives to, replacements of, failing schools, doing as well as the average school would be a signal achievement. Caroline Hoxby [49], examining test results in reading and math for 4th grades in charter schools, finds that they outperform comparable public school students in nearly all states. Their advantage is greatest in states where charter schools have been operating the longest. I'll bet on Hoxby.

Greene et al. [50] compared charter schools serving the general population in 11 states, rather than schools targeted on poorly performing student populations. Charter schools outperformed nearby regular public schools in test score improvements over a one-year period in both math and reading. But no generalization is possible, because there is no such thing as a typical charter school. Such schools vary widely in their degree of autonomy with regard to staffing, pay, curriculum, pedagogy, even students, and the environment in which they are placed. Financial resources vary widely between school districts. This very diversity offers opportunities for learning more about which policies work best. Many school districts only grudgingly accept charter schools. They are less threatening than vouchers, since only failing schools are at risk.

Disputes on the achievement of charter schools are pointless. Their very existence is a reprimand. What matters is that they are subject to a Darwinian process. Those that do not perform can be closed down or transferred to a different management. Ideally they should have all the autonomy of a private school that is publicly funded.

Vouchers and charter schools are not a solution but a means of implementing a solution by significantly reducing the number of underperforming teachers and schools, and by applying competitive pressure for improvement on those teachers and schools capable of improvement. That requires charters and vouchers on a much larger scale than currently contemplated. That scale would also apply pressure to reform the salary structure of public schools if they are to attract and retain qualified teachers. Pressure on schools means pressure on teachers unions and school boards. Vouchers and charters on a large enough scale would also reduce the number of public school teachers and the reduction would be predominantly of the less competent teachers. It is one way to accelerate the process of increasing the proportion of teachers competent in the subjects they teach.

Diversity: Tracking, Advanced Placement, and Magnet Schools

The democratic ideal that everyone should have the same education is absurd and harmful. Not all high school graduates will go to college; not all who start will finish. Different individuals will live different lives and do different work and no uniformity of education can prevent that. Individuals are not identical in abilities, interests, goals. Society and economy are highly differentiated and hierarchical, and schools can't homogenize them. Ability is too valuable to be wasted; achievement too important to be neglected. Tracking, advanced placement and magnet schools seek to address these differences.

Vouchers and charter schools make no distinction between students; assuming everyone can learn. Tracking and magnet schools on the other hand are responses to assumed differences in ability to learn. Whereas vouchers and charter schools are the escape route from underperforming public schools, tracking and advanced placement are adjustment to diversity in student ability, achievement, and interest within a school, magnet schools an adjustment within school districts. Tracking is a traditional practice; magnet schools and advanced placement were rare but have multiplied in recent decades. They protect from private school competition for the better students, and help prevent alternatives such as vouchers.

Tracking and Advanced Placement

Tracking may refer to ability, or to objectives. The former differentiates students by course difficulty, the latter by curriculum composition. Long ago it was the practice for cities to have high schools that were college-preparatory, others that were strictly vocational. This is less common today; the vast majority of high schools are allegedly college-preparatory. Tracking now is predominantly on the basis of course difficulty, not educational objectives. There is some self-selection with regard to choice of electives, but admission to honors and advanced placement courses is typically subject to faculty approval.

Tracking in primary school is in terms of learning expectations and level of achievement. In secondary school tracking is also an adjustment to differences in goals and interests, not necessarily based on ability. College preparatory will include advanced placement courses; vocational/technical track can offer a variety of options with differing requirements, most of them not terminal with high school graduation.

Tracking is a means of improving instruction and learning by reducing differences in knowledge and ability within a class. It is an alternative to reducing class size as a means of improving teacher-student interchange. The job of the teacher is made easier. It is often possible to assign teachers to the track in which they do best. It may make better use of the current teaching staff, but is not a means of improving its composition. Without tracking, many classes will include bright students who are bored, and slow learners always lagging behind. Reducing the teaching range is a means of minimizing both. There are teachers who can in a single diverse class challenge the brightest students and simultaneously motivate and teach the laggards. But such teachers are rare, and always will be.

Ability grouping is important in subjects which build up cumulatively, such as math and language. It is less important in subjects that are taught topically, such as geography and history and social studies in the earlier grades. Slavin [51] reviewed and evaluated many studies on the effects of ability grouping in elementary schools. He evaluated a variety of plans, recommending ability grouping for reading and math, including within-class grouping for math and across-grade lines grouping for reading. Students should stay in heterogeneous classes for other subjects. Student assignment to groups should be reassessed often. Grouping has potentially detrimental psychological effects.

Tracking can be viewed as student-centered education, in that it adapts curriculum difficulty and content to student abilities and interests. In high school, choice of electives, including advanced-placement courses, is a form of self-tracking. Since not everyone finishes high school, and many who do never continue their formal education, there is a need for a vocational/technical education track as well as an academic college-preparatory track [52]. Not all students should be expected, and cannot be compelled, to attend a community college for this purpose.

The level of achievement with tracking will be higher on average than in its absence. But tracking has coexisted with dumbing down of texts, curricula, standards. Thus its role as an alternative to vouchers and magnet schools is limited.

The case for tracking in the United States today rests heavily on unwillingness or inability to demand higher achievement from low-achieving students. Such a practice discriminates against high-achieving students, and tracking is one of the ways of correcting for this discrimination. It rests on the assumed dominance of differences in ability in achievement - whether this be IQ or its equivalent, or special abilities such as math or music or language, or learning preferences. The nations whose students score highest in almost every test, or the teachers, students and parents in these nations, assume that achievement depends mainly on effort. Their tracking is vertical rather than horizontal: everyone can do well through high school, but diligence without native talent will not suffice for a career in medicine or mathematics.

Advanced placement courses are piecemeal tracking. As a response to grade inflation and dumbing down of instruction, high school students aiming for better colleges are taking large numbers of advanced placement courses, most presumably college level, but many simply at the level they once reached before the degradation of public schools. Given the problems of staffing with teachers who majored in the subjects they teach, if the best equipped teachers are assigned to such courses, there are negative externalities for students not taking such courses. It is common practice to award extra grade points to students who take such courses. One result is that there are quite a few students who graduate from high school with grade point averages higher than 4.0. This practice cancels out whatever contribution AP courses might have made to dampen grade inflation. It is also unfair to students in a large proportion of high schools, which offer no AP courses.

The quality of AP courses and grades is evaluated by the College Board, which gives and grades exams in AP fields. The results have been reported as passing rates by school and school district, but in the future the College Board will report only the percentage of all high school seniors who passed, whether or not they took AP courses [53]. This makes it more difficult for others to evaluate the rigor of AP courses in a school or district.

In the absence of tracking, everyone completes high school together, which implies simplified content and low standards. The sorting of students who will go on to complete a 4-year baccalaureate, those who elect a shorter job- and occupation-related certificate program, and those who just drop out, is made in a non-systematic manner, by students and their parents, and by colleges and employers, not by high schools.

So much for the positive side. On the negative side, tracking, including AP courses and magnet schools, is likely to increase differences in achievement. It raises the ceiling without necessarily raising the floor. The higher tracks, advanced placement courses, magnet schools are likely to be taught by the best teachers, to the possible disadvantage of other students and schools. They have been adopted as a response to outside pressure, in self-defense, offering higher standards for a few to avoid requiring them for most. Tracking revalues the high school diploma only for a minority. It is not a cure for low standards and undemanding curricula. The absence of the better students from the lower tracks and the magnet schools may lower teacher demands and expectations. College preparatory courses or tracks no longer mean much, since most high school students plan to go to college, and since there are colleges for every level of ability and achievement.

Gamoran [54] distinguishes four characteristics of tracking: its selectivity, its electivity, its inclusiveness, and its scope. Inclusiveness, leaving future options open, raises achievement and reduces inequality; so does mobility in tracking. But he found little effect of selectivity or electivity. Scope - the extent to which students are assigned to the same track across subjects - is less desirable

There is more tracking in the United States than elsewhere. It may reflect differences in ability, but it may also reinforce differences in achievement if not wisely done. It becomes a means of stratification of opportunity [55]. Students placed in lower tracks, often are exposed to a limited curriculum, don't do as well as similar students in untracked schools or in academic tracks [56]. Early placement may tend to perpetuate itself as a result.

Magnet Schools

The term "magnet school" has been applied to a wide diversity of schools, both public and private, with different objectives. I limit the term here to public schools which are selective in admitting students and which are rigorous academically. Some may have the same curricula as other public schools in the district, but impose higher standards of instruction and achievement. Others are specialized, stressing sciences or arts and humanities.

Charter schools aim to reduce inequality between schools in a district; magnet schools do the reverse. Magnet schools are a form of tracking within school districts rather than within schools. They provide greater opportunities for diversity than tracking alone because they do it at the school district level rather than in a single school. Magnet schools are not just those which serve students of high ability; they may be specialized, in the sciences, the arts, languages, technology. The Bronx High School of Science, which churns out Nobel prizewinners, no doubt pays more than the average school, but gets much better faculty, and it is highly selective in students as well as faculty. Magnet schools must be selective; their capacity limits the number of students, and their programs require some selection on the basis of student suitability. They must also be selective in faculty staffing if they are to fulfill their mission. The students in these schools are the gainers. Other students may be losers: of the best teachers, of the stimulus and example provided by able and motivated peers. Many are a rough equivalent of the college preparatory schools before WWII, when most never finished high school and few went to college. Their graduates are not the typical college student, but the equivalent of students when college curricula were far more rigorous that they are today,

Magnet schools and charter schools, like private schools, have limited capacity, and significant expansion might come at the cost of other public schools. Each of these options has a place, but none, nor all combined, can provide a full solution in the near-term future. The ultimate constraint is the supply of capable teachers; the ultimate obstacle is: a) teachers unions; and b) schools of education.

Flight: Home Schooling

Many parents have become critical of the performance of public schools, more parents have developed their own philosophy of education and failed to find schools, public or private, reflecting their philosophy. Home schooling is facilitated by the decline in family size, but limited by the rise in two-worker families. It does tap a reservoir of competent teachers not available as employees in school systems, largely bypassing schools of education, teachers unions, and school boards. Parental motivation is first, a better education for their children, second, concern about irreligious or anti-religion character of public schools, third, the negative social and learning environment in public schools [57].

The National Center for Education Statistics estimated that home schooling accounted for 1.1 million students or 2.2 percent of school-age population in 2003, a substantial increase from the 1.7 percent in 1999. The National Home School Research Institute estimates the number at between 1.7 and 2.2 million, or closer to 4 percent [58]. At this time more students are being home-schooled than are enrolled in charter schools or are receiving vouchers. But there is little prospect that so burdensome a responsibility will be assumed by so many more that it will exert pressure for reform of the public schools. Home schooling does not pose the potential threat to public schools of vouchers or charter schools.

Home schoolers are predominantly middle income, college-educated, professional and technical in occupation, religious and politically conservative [59]. But they are not of one mind. Although they differ ideologically, they share opposition to school dominance in the realm of culture, politics, the economy and family life. They do not seek to reform, only to escape. There are enough to induce the supply of ample teaching resources through the internet (see www.mindsprinting.com), and to generate home schooling organizations that provide educational materials and also help home schoolers to navigate the obstacle courses they face in some states.

Home schooling means smaller classes, at the limit one to one learning situations. But teachers who almost unanimously support smaller classes oppose this logical limit. Their overt opposition, apart from the self-interest in avoiding the secession of the most dedicated parents if not students, is about socialization. Of course home-schooled children are rarely isolated. But many home-schooling parents choose that laborious option partly to avoid the kind of socialization that prevails in many public schools and to some extent in private schools as well. The negative social environment of public schools is one of three leading reasons for home schooling.

Children who are home-schooled outperform students in public schools, and even in private schools. At least this is the common belief. They have parents who are closely involved in their education, and a very favorable teacher/student ratio. Probably they are a cut above the average in ability as well. They win competitions out of all proportion to their numbers. But in fact there are no comprehensive data permitting assessment of their overall performance and in comparison with public schools. Many home-schooling parents are reluctant to participate in surveys.

Home schooling is discouraged by the educational establishment in most states; it is seen as a vote of no confidence. Obstacles in some states range well beyond those necessary to assure states that parents are qualified and that students are learning. Home schooling is the cheapest education available from a taxpayer viewpoint; all it costs is the bureaucracy that creates obstacles and investigators who see to it that it is adequately performed. It increases the supply of teachers at zero salary and reduces slightly the burden on public schools. Parents who want to home school should be encouraged and assisted, not deterred. They continue to pay the taxes that finance public education. If there is a voucher system, they should be eligible recipients. There should be no obstacle to home schoolers in the upper grades participating in public school courses which require equipment not available in most homes, or for which the parents regard themselves inadequate. In fact cooperation is growing, partly as a result of the legal success of home schoolers in establishing their rights. Many home-schooled students now can participate in extracurricular public school activities, take courses part time, especially in science and the arts, and use libraries [60].

The ignorance of public school superintendents about home schooling is appalling. They hold overwhelmingly negative beliefs about the quality of home teachers, home school facilities, time spent in learning, academic standards, student socialization and self-esteem in comparison with public schools. But they are split on the desirability of the low student/teacher ratio in home schools and on the quality of individual learning programs: some think they are far superior to public schools, some think they are greatly inferior.

Home-schooled students should be tested periodically for achievement in key subjects, just as proposed for other students. Neither the tests nor their evaluation should be in the hands of public school bureaucracy. As to parental certification, it must be more flexible than for school teachers. Let achievement substitute for certification. One parent is almost never the sole teaching resource available. Home schooling, like charter schools, survives on the basis of performance.

Summing Up

Charter schools and vouchers on one hand, tracking and magnet schools on the other, improve student achievement, but they cater to different students. Individually they cannot reform public school education; the scale of private and special public schools is too small, and the impact of tracking is too limited. But in combination with national standards duly enforced they have the capability of increasing achievement for all.

Vouchers and charter schools are up front as long as pay scales and teacher qualifications remain as they are. With a market and merit-oriented pay scale, and gradual elimination of the monopoly of schools of education on teaching jobs, vouchers become less important. Tracking diminishes the role of vouchers but does not eliminate it. Vouchers are about teaching performance or curriculum content rather than ability grouping, but they provide an alternative for some, whatever the performance of the public schools. Like magnet schools, they are about choice. Magnet schools and tracking do nothing about public school monopoly but reshuffle students and teachers with the objective of increasing efficiency. Vouchers and home schooling provide independent alternatives to public schools.

There are limits to each policy, especially in the short run. The capacity of private schools to accept public school students is very limited in the short run. It takes time to increase capacity, and assurance that any increase in demand will continue long enough to justify investment in additional plant, equipment, experienced teachers and administrators.. Charter schools face similar problems, although expansion of physical capacity is not the problem as long as they simply take over failing public schools. Home schooling accounts for too small a share of students to contribute to the overall problem, and we don't see any increase large enough to make much of a dent.

All of these policies help improve student performance. They are not alternatives; all can be pursued, depending on local conditions. Vouchers and charter schools also increase the pool of capable teachers by imposing their own standards and evading school of education course and degree requirements. They can be pursued district by district. Major changes in curriculum standards, in teacher certification requirements, in testing and information need to be carried out on a larger scale, at the state and national level

Public education is adamant in opposition to any and all alternatives that encroach on its monopoly. All must be pursued vigorously to apply sufficient external pressure to produce significant leverage for reform in public schools. These alternatives must be supplemented with direct pressure, via standardized tests and other measures to assure transparency, so that many contented parents at last will learn that even their children's' schools fall short. Informed parents will apply pressure for internal reform and seek alternative schooling for their children, perhaps the most effective leverage. Pressure must be backed by threats, and what more credible threat than mass exodus?

The public school system cannot and should not be remade into a private school system with public financing. There is an enduring need for two systems, private schools offering the widest diversity and choice, and public schools assuring opportunity for all and hopefully a common core of critical learning and social values.

The common problem with all of these alternatives is that of a shortage of good teachers. Changes within the public school system: tracking, magnet schools, simply reassign faculty and students; gains in achievement of some students may be at the expense of losses by other students. Vouchers to private schools do expand teaching resources somewhat by circumventing the entry barriers of schools of education and the compressed salary structure one size fits all of public schools. But in some subjects, especially math and sciences, they still face a shortage of potential teachers who have majored in these subjects. Home schooling is the only alternative that can tap a supply of competent teachers not available to schools, but this alternative is very limited in scope. This is not to suggest that these diverse approaches do not offer some net gains in the short run, but that they do not solve the basic staffing problems of education, mainly public, but also private. Any one school district is easy to improve; raid other districts, tap the wide market for talent. But for the system overall, the first option does not exist, the second is limited. To meet the need for better teachers and administrators who will promote reform instead of opposing it is a project for a generation. Reducing the number of schools of education and their output of graduates will accelerate change in composition of public school faculty, but it is still a matter of a generation. There is no instant solution, although that is what people want.

Institutional Changes

School Size

C. Northcote Parkinson wrote numerous satirical essays on administration. In one of them he addressed the issue of committee or cabinet size, arriving at the conclusion that the maximum should be no more than 19-21, because at that size the committee undergoes a fundamental change. The five or so members who really count start meeting with each other in advance, and meetings of the full committee become a waste of time. His satire makes two important points: as size grows, a hierarchy develops inevitably, and the nature of the relation between members mutates. What might have been a community of shared interests and goals becomes simply a network. Similar reasoning applies to class size. With regard to school size, as long as it is small, it is possible for parents to know a large proportion of the faculty, and it is possible for the faculty, principal included, to know most of the parents. Furthermore, any two or three faculty members are likely to have many of the same students, and are able to share their assessments and perhaps to agree on how to deal with particular students. This kind of personal contact, shared knowledge, close communication becomes impossible as the school grows in size. Large schools must have extensive "market" areas, they are no longer community, neighborhood schools. There is weak linkage between school and home. Large schools for this reason are less subject to parental influence. These same considerations apply to problems of discipline and attendance discussed below. Student subcultures hostile to academic learning are more difficult to establish or maintain in small schools and smaller classes.

There are few if any economies of scale in elementary and middle schools, there is no argument for big schools. In large urban areas, the same is true of high schools; but there may be economies of scope: greater diversity of courses, facilities and faculty. It is the shopping mall-cafeteria high school that needs to be large, to accommodate all the courses that have nothing to do with cognitive gain, preparation for college or for work. This curriculum is a problem not a desideratum. Achievement-oriented diversity is attainable by other means: smaller schools specializing in science, or arts, or vocational training rather than shopping mall schools. The distance between schools would be smaller, offering better opportunities for school choice. With vouchers, diversity is also available via private schools.

School Districts

The number of school districts was 117,108 in 1939, 83,718 in 1949, 40,520 in 1959, down to 14,205 in 2004. Meanwhile, public school enrollment almost doubled between 1949 and 2004 (25.1 vs. 48.6 million) [61]. The average size of a school district, in terms of enrollment, has increased nearly twelve-fold. So has the area. The number of schools declined dramatically, in large part because of the near-elimination of the one-room schoolhouse with a single teacher. It is hard to believe that there were sixty thousand such schools as recently as 1949; there were still 366 in 2002.

Let public school districts compete with one another for students as they do for teachers. Inter-district access via vouchers is an alternative to Tiebout strategy of migration. It is true that it is simpler to allow for public school choice within districts than between districts. But schools within a district are less likely to offer a wide range of choice than if they were grouped into a large number of smaller districts. Extensive busing once was designed to integrate schools. The infrastructure is in place, which can now contribute to school choice to accommodate differences in interests, abilities, even learning styles. Such choice also compels schools losing students to assess their performance. Smaller districts mean more local control. They would enhance parental and community influence on school performance; would narrow the distance between members of the district board of education and individual schools, teachers, and parents. Smaller districts would increase competition with adjacent districts, a process likely to improve the quality of schooling [62]. District size is not the only issue; greater district autonomy is necessary, in hiring teachers, in selecting textbooks, and shaping curricula. Without autonomy there can be little parental influence

Some reformers fear that local control of schools will simply mean control by teachers unions, not community or parental oversight. But that is what we have today. If districts are large it is much more difficult for a local community or the parents of students in a particular school to have much influence. In small school districts, parents of students could organize and bring their views to bear on their schools. Isn't that what parent-teacher associations are about? No, PTAs are run by and for teachers. A parents' association is a different animal, that communicates with teachers and administrators but sets its own agenda and arrives at its own views. This is an educated society now. There are many school districts in which the educational achievement of parents at least equals that of teachers.

In middle class neighborhoods, with educated parents who have knowledge and choices, local control is much more subject to the wishes of parents. But in low income areas, where many parents are poorly educated, and there are many single-parent households, parents may not know enough to care or may not be able to organize to bring their views to bear. In such situations, vouchers may not help much – there are few takers. Visibility – information on student and school performance relative to standards and to performance in other districts, might galvanize parental pressure in some cases. In others, if achievement tests prove unsatisfactory, then charter schools and school closures can substitute for parental influence.

There is one problem with small districts: they could increase the disparity in local tax revenue for schools. In any case, whether districts are small or large, there is an important role for the state in equalizing educational resources across districts. Mere equalization will not equate educational opportunities; districts serving poor and minority populations require more resources per student to achieve this goal.

What of school district boards of education? By and large they are part of the problem, not the solution. Whether driven by bureaucratic concerns, or afflicted with ignorance, or co-opted, or converted, they are not a center of power and decision independent of the unions and the schools of education. Like other nonprofit organizations they are not subject to external oversight, there are no stockholders; like other monopolies, they lack the discipline of competition. If all school boards were locally elected and districts were small they could become part of the solution. Perhaps no one should be eligible to be a board member whose children do not go to the district public schools

There is another reason for the local autonomy possible in small districts but unlikely in large districts. At the state level, the National Education Association can bring to bear its huge financial resources to shape educational policy, including textbooks, curriculum, teacher certification [63]. The NEA is the largest "labor union" and perhaps the wealthiest. It is a powerful lobby promoting a political and ideological agenda; schools and minors attending school happen to be its arena of choice. As long as school policy is determined at the state level, NEA money finds it convenient and easy to dominate school systems. It can concentrate its efforts on a few large states. With more local autonomy its leverage would be greatly reduced. Many districts would go their own way, setting examples for others. Decentralization is a strategy of defense against the entrenched educational establishment.

School Day, Year

Since delayed full time work and work income foregone is the largest cost of additional education, the most effective means of increasing the return to education to individuals would be to shorten the time frame. Students can attend college year-round and finish in 3 years already if they choose. What is learned in elementary and secondary school could be learned in considerably less than twelve years [64]. Alternatively, much more could be taught and learned in that time period. The biggest gain in efficiency would be to discourage college enrollment for those who are very unlikely to benefit. That of course would be the most controversial policy; no one can be sure who will benefit, who will not. But life is about probabilities, not certainties. Once high schools are staffed with teachers all of whom majored in their subject and students arrive well prepared in elementary school, the pattern common in the past could be resurrected: occupation-specific training could be restored in every school district so that many students who will never finish college, or perhaps even start, can be prepared for gainful employment. From a national standpoint, the last thing needed is a postponement of entry into the labor force during the next forty years, when the ratio of workers to retirees will be declining dramatically.

A longer school year is expensive: more pay for teachers and staff, in some places the need to install air-conditioning. There are constraints on vacation plans, summer work. But a longer school day need not mean more time in school, simply a: radical reform in use of school time: less sports, social engineering, entertainment, more time on academic subjects. A longer school day also means more homework, which implies cutting down on TV, computer game playing and e-mailing, less time spent on portable phones. Teachers may prescribe, but only parents can enforce a more rigorous regimen.

COSTS OF SCHOOL REFORM AND HOW TO PAY FOR THEM

Instead of concentrating on costs of policies for improving student achievement, one should focus first on the large increase in cost that has taken place during a long period of declining or static achievement which did not include appreciable amounts for vouchers, charter schools, or magnet schools nor large increases in teacher salaries. Rising costs restrict the ability of schools to institute reforms that would improve student achievement.

Schools are suffering from the same disease infecting all sorts of nonprofits, including health care services and philanthropies. Too small a share of resources is devoted to teaching; an excessive and increasing share is absorbed by "overhead" of all sorts: administration, consultation, conferences, "research." Large differences between school districts in share of educational resources devoted to teaching may help explain the lack of relation between spending per student and achievement, as well as large differences in achievement. Each school district, and each school, enjoys a monopoly of students resident in its area; there is little competitive constraint on inefficiency. Public schools have no stockholders And schools pay no taxes.

There have been major changes in the composition of public school employees since 1950. The share of instructional staff has declined from 74 to 68%, but the share of actual teachers has gone down from 70 to 51%. Instructional aides, a mere 1.7% in1969, jumped to 7.8% in 1980 and 11.7% in 2004. Why should competent teachers need so many instructional aides, and what has it gained the students? The other large increase was in guidance counselors, who increased from 0.7% in 1959 to 1.5% in 1980, and 1.7% by 2004. Support staff meanwhile grew from 23.8 to 30.1%. Administrative staff at the school district level has declined as a share of employment, 2.6 in 1949-50 to 1.9in 1969-70, and 1.8% in 2004. [65] But actual numbers more than tripled. With a precipitous decline in the number of school districts, this large increase in numbers seems excessive.

Cut out the waste. One hears this suggestion for paying bills in every proposal involving higher costs. In the case of public schools it is easy to point out the large increase in use of resources, even if we cannot measure the amount with any precision. The real cost per student in public elementary and high schools more than tripled between 1960 and 2004. It rose from 6.2% of median family income in 1960 to 12.5% in 1980 and 17.3% in 2003. It was primarily the result of the rise in the ratio of staff to students, which accounted for 60% of the increase, not to salaries. It cannot be justified in terms of educational performance. Flyer and Rosen [66] also identify unionization in the 1960s and the resulting political process as contributing to cost increases.

What can be done? In which districts? States differ, and so do school districts. More transparency is the initial condition for identifying waste and inefficiency, and to motivate corrective steps. Neither the local school district taxpayer, nor the parent of school children, has any idea how much is being spent on public schools and how the money is being used. Information is now available annually on test scores of elementary schools in every district; these should be compared with budget and staffing data. Local data can be compared with performance statewide and nationally on all counts.

There is a striking difference in current spending per student between states. For 2003-2004 Utah spent $6,110, less than half the amount spent by five other states. The District of Columbia spent $14,827. Yet Utah public school students scored well above the national average in reading, math, science and SATs. A little analysis of spending patterns should reveal opportunities for saving. Although the District of Columbia spends more per student than any state, many of its students have no textbooks. Perhaps this inefficiency has contributed to the shift to charter schools, which are a higher proportion of students than any state, some 20%.

Costs can be kept down by increasing the share of enrollments in private schools, which cost about half as much per student as public schools but on average produce better results. This difference needs investigation. Why do public schools cost so much more than private schools? Unpaid volunteer workers in Catholic schools are part of the explanation, but only part.

As to costs of policy innovations, one must distinguish between the short run, transition cost and the long run cost. Initially almost any significant change involves extra costs, even though it may be cost-saving in the longer run. The largest costs will be those of hiring only middle and high school faculty who majored in the subjects they teach, and the cost of reducing their turnover. It may be fairly high initially, because of a shortage of potential teachers who majored in some fields, particularly math and science. The cost would be outrageous and unacceptable if school systems simply raised salaries across the board. A market -based salary structure is essential to make good teaching affordable for all. Such a structure imposes new responsibilities on principals or school districts which require judgment and competence.

Improving the curriculum includes more teaching in these same fields, therefore more teachers, further increasing the short run cost. But these costs will decline as improved instruction in these fields increases the number of college students majoring in them. The costs in both cases are those of replacing the current salary structure with a market and merit-based structure. Some changes involve permanent increases in costs: employing more teachers in highly paid specialties, longer school years, more tutoring

On the other hand, vouchers could reduce costs substantially. Initially they increase costs because in the very short run the costs of public schools are fixed. But soon enough a large voucher program would reduce public school enrollments, reducing total school costs. Costs per student will fall because private schools are more efficient than public schools, and because the competitive pressure will improve the efficiency of public schools. The same can be said of charter schools; in the long run they should save money, although the case for charter school efficiency compared to schools they replace or compete with is not as clear as in the case of private schools. Magnet schools and tracking have the opposite effect: they help retain students in the public school system, and raise teaching costs.

Increasing federal government funding is pouring money into an insatiable maw; all it will accomplish is increase school costs and college tuition. The problem is not lack of funds, but lack of good managers, teachers and curricula. If we need to pay more to attract good teachers (without rewarding mediocre and poor teachers in the bargain), one answer is not more money, but increased average class size. The large reduction in class size since 1960 coincided with reductions in student achievement. There is no evidence that class size within a wide range makes much if any difference, with the exception of disadvantaged children and in the early grades. Increase class size in middle and high school. We can make do with fewer but better teachers, and larger class size. Teacher quality is far more important than class size.

One source of inefficiency is the unequal distribution of school resources. Our worst schools, many in decaying urban centers, serving largely poor and minority students, cannot compete for good teachers with the present structure of school district financing or salary schedule. Typically these schools are located in districts with a smaller per capita tax base than our better schools. There must be an increase in the share of school financing at the state level, some redistribution of tax revenues from districts that can afford to hire the best teachers to those that cannot. Such redistribution is not simple; there must be decisions on how much needs to be redistributed, oversight so that redistributed funds are used as intended, and care taken to avoid free riders: schools and districts that rely on redistribution to substitute for their own efforts rather than to supplement them.

What few notice is the large improvement in our ability to pay for better education. The ratio of the school-age population, 5-18, to the working-age population, 18-65, has dropped dramatically. These changes are the result of changes in birth rates in the past 65 years, and the large increase in the proportion of women in the work force. Retirement age is likely to rise on the average in the years ahead, further reducing the ratio. In 1960 there were 1.7 employed civilian workers per student in primary and secondary public schools. By 2004 there were 2.7 workers per student: We should be in a much better position to afford good education than we were when the baby boomers were enrolled. It is true that in future decades the growth in retirees will place an additional burden on working taxpayers. But now and for a considerable period in the future, the fiscal situation - the ratio of earners to learners - is much better than it was in previous decades. We can pay for high quality education for all if there is the will.

BETTER STUDENTS AND RESPONSIBLE COMMUNITIES

We have been assuming that the problems with primary and secondary education are the school: curricula, teacher qualification, low expectations. What if they are not, or no more than a response or reflection of the society in which they function? Perhaps students in Japan, Taiwan, Korea, Singapore, the Czech Republic, Finland, Canada are smarter, better motivated, more disciplined. Why should American students fare poorly not just in math and science but also in reading and writing? Grade inflation, social promotion, semi-literate high school seniors cannot be blamed entirely on the school system. It does not function in a vacuum but in a community, a society, which must bear and should assume responsibility but does neither. Imagine the public uproar were ransoms to the self-esteem of students and their parents eliminated, and high standards enforced which deny promotion and high school diplomas to a large share of students: parents with pitchforks and hangman's nooses at the boards of education. Several states have averted this prospect by delaying enforcement of standards, others by lowering the bar they had recently raised. Attacks on the SAT, one of the last holdouts for standards and objectivity in a world steeped in subjectivity and sensitivity, do not come exclusively from the educational establishment which is being graded. They come also from parents of students with elite college admission aspirations, and from colleges stressing admissions criteria other than ability and achievement.

Where is the culture of learning found in nations that consistently score at the top? A survey by the Kaiser Family Foundation found that students ages 8 to 18 spend 6 hours and 43 minutes a day using media, nearly all on TV and other media entertainment [67]. There is a strong inverse relation between TV hours watched and school performance. Yet there are those who believe that all this will change, for the better, once more students have computer screens to hypnotize them: a naive American belief in simple technical solutions. More energy is spent on sports than on studying. Schools should not be child care centers or sports clubs. Not all learning can be entertaining; study is hard work, not fun, nor should it be a matter of choice by those whom we do not allow choice in driving, drinking, voting, and for the same reasons. Americans do not study enough. Students in East Asian nations not only have a longer school day and school year, they do much more homework [68].

Schools cannot shift blame to family and community. They must bear some responsibility for changes in both, which have been part of their intention and commitment for generations. And schools have monopolized the time of students for six to eight hours 180 days a year for thirteen years, plus pre-kindergarten for many. They have had more contact time with students than many parents. They are and must be held accountable in part for the attitudes, values, behavior and achievement of their charges in school and later in life.

Discipline

So far there has been no mention of the discipline problems found in many schools, usually caused by a few which interfere with learning by the many. They are important for learning, but too complex and diverse for brief treatment and beyond my competence, hence excluded from the scope of this book. Many of the behavioral problems are societal, not school problems, dumped on public schools by the policy of compulsory education to age 18 or high school graduation, but not the schools' responsibility. Private schools can discharge disruptive students, public schools often cannot. Lack of discipline is one of the main reasons given for home schooling by parents. But it is also important in teacher turnover. Ingersoll [69] stresses that the teacher supply problem is not primarily a shortage but high turnover. The principal reasons given by teachers who leave their profession are lack of community support 52%; lack of student motivation 38%; student discipline 30%; and inadequate school support 30%. The lack of student motivation and discipline problems are probably closely related. In some cases they may be the fault of the school or the teacher, but to a large extent they are family and community problems and responsibilities.

Part of the problem is a disjunction between the standard classroom and the learning needs and interests of some students. It can be addressed through diversification and specialization of schools and curricula. This is one argument for school choice, including the option of choosing private schools for which diversification is a survival strategy. It is also addressed through special education of students whose abilities do not correspond to the typical classroom curriculum or pedagogy. This is a learning problem, only incidentally and occasionally behaviorally disruptive.

But there are disruptive behaviors not explainable in terms of deficiencies in schools or curricula or pedagogy. They are subcultures, often violent, intimidating, imported to schools from the neighborhood or local society. We should not expect schools to resolve them. There must be an alternative to permission to disrupt the teaching efforts of faculty and the learning process of other students. High schools in addition face the oppositional subculture characteristic of teenagers everywhere. What has changed is the diminished role of parents, family, and community in containing rebellion, in directing it to constructive outlets. As long as children are out of control at home, even if they are not in command at school, the problem of discipline will persist. But blame not the children, they rule by default, they know not what they do.

Discipline is not just the absence of disruption, but focus, concentration, the ability to defer gratification, immunity to peer pressure. Good teachers may be an essential part of the solution, but it cannot be entirely up to them. There are social as well as individual consequences of the current culture of self-indulgence, primacy of rights over obligations, of self-esteem over social concerns. It bears some resemblance to what has been called the culture of poverty [70] present-orientation, self-absorption, materialism and a deconstructionist psychology, attaching little value to work, sacrifice, self-improvement, or service to anyone or anything. We want Ivy League designer labels on lapels, consumer goods in a materialist paradise. But we don't want to pay the price.

Perhaps there can be no dramatic improvement in education in a society one third of whose students are born to single mothers, with many of the rest experiencing parental separation and divorce. Much is made of the increase in single-parent households, and two-earner households. Not mentioned is the large decline in birth rates since the days when schools and students were allegedly better. The parent-student ratio has improved greatly, as has the teacher-student ratio, and that should be a plus. Not all learning is accomplished at school. Many parents can devote more time to one or two children than they could have devoted to four or five. This decline in birth rate largely cancels out the effect of the increase in labor force participation of married women and in the proportion of single-parent families. Children can also learn from older children, information, but more important, the habit of learning, the practice of study. (Perhaps Benjamin Franklin, who had 12 older siblings, had an advantage over the current typical family of two. But that is idle speculation.)

If the culture and society bear much of the blame for a failing system of public education, introducing competition, shifting many students to private schools via vouchers, would be no solution; it would only redistribute the unintended consequences of prevailing values and attitudes

One encouraging note is the experience of a long-term high school teacher who found that the children of the students he had a generation ago, largely minority and poor, are much more serious about school than their parents [71]. The parents when in school put all their pride in their possessions, disdained the academic agenda. Apparently they learned rather late that without the work ethic and useful skills there is no income to sustain the consumer style of life, and that not everyone ends up a millionaire professional athlete or public entertainer. But they did learn, and passed the lesson on to their children.

Apart from family breakdown, the prevalence of automobiles has contributed to the dissolution of neighborhoods, to the loss of community. When cities were compact, high-density, everyone knew several 'next-door' neighbors. Most services and facilities of frequent use were nearby and shared. Now there are few neighborhoods – much of the urban population lives in suburbs – dormitory tracts where people live among strangers. Social contacts, once based on proximity, are now one-dimensional networks linking people who work at the same place, or whose children attend the same school, or who share the same sports, hobbies, other activities. And there is high mobility of residence and school districts. This makes it difficult to organize and sustain community efforts to reform schools.

Smaller schools and school districts can reduce the problem. Anti-learning, anti-school student subcultures are more difficult to establish and maintain in small schools with class sizes on the smaller side. Perhaps more important is the introduction of objective testing in key subjects at every grade level, testing beyond the influence of the teacher, the school, the school district. This should ease the pressure on teachers who have high expectations of their students, and the harassment of high achievers who no longer can be blamed for grade distributions [72].

Responsibility for student behavior cannot be delegated to family and community. Coleman et al attribute the superior performance of private schools, Catholic schools in particular, to strict discipline strictly enforced. Private schools do have the advantage that they have been chosen by parents if not students, that they have the option of dropping unmanageable students, that parents pay for education out of pocket. Public schools could do much more to preserve an environment favorable to learning if they chose, or if they were allowed the means by district and state administrators. Magnet schools do have some discretion on whom they accept as students. Disciplinary problems should not allow a few to interfere with the education of the many, that is the primary concern. What to do about problem students is secondary as long as they are not allowed to degrade learning or to dominate student subcultures.

The problem of discipline is not limited to students. There are teachers who do not choose to show up for class half the time but retain their jobs and pay. I know of schools much of whose faculty is indolent and indifferent to the wellbeing of students. How many schools allow such behavior I have no idea, very few I hope and expect. Nor do I know whom to blame beyond teachers: principals, superintendents, unions?

Unfortunately significant change is generational. It is taking that long to inform and energize the public to demand reform. Let us not delude ourselves into thinking that legislation alone can do the job. The demand for educational reform must be maintained, for it will take decades to bring about major improvements in public school faculty and revolutionize the curriculum and pedagogy. Will it require some traumatic event or turn of events to bring it about? Meanwhile most of the reforms suggested are largely means of redistributing scarce resources.

Chapter 8

OCCUPATIONAL PRESTIGE OF TEACHING

How to attract able and well-prepared individuals into high school teaching? It will take time in the best of cases — a generation or two. As indicated previously, not enough college students have been majoring in some scientific fields to supply the needs of the economy and of schools, even with a substantial pay increase. How do we persuade abler students to teach in elementary schools? How will we persuade more majors in fields other than education to enter high school teaching? Pay isn't everything. It alone will not buy the occupational prestige needed to attract more and abler college graduates into teaching.

In many other countries, teachers, high school teachers especially, are held in great regard. Their status is comparable to college professors in this country. No wonder students do better than ours. Nations whose students do best are distinguished not by high salaries but by high standards for teachers. The fact that high school completion was the exception and college attendance rare elsewhere until very recently may be a factor. But history and culture may be a more important explanation. Our tradition is the frontier, a nation of immigrants. We never looked up to an aristocracy; we never had one. Many of those we admire were self-made. We valued enterprise and hard work more than intellect and higher learning. Many of our presidents before the twentieth century were high school dropouts or less. Education was not the main path to success. Conditions have changed, people are becoming aware of the importance of education for individuals and for the society. The widespread concern with the status of our schools and colleges is one result. In time this revaluation of education in the public mind should upgrade the status of teachers.

FAVORABLE JOB MARKET

The good news is that the rapid aging of primary and secondary school faculty is an opportunity to change its composition rapidly. The constraint, as mentioned earlier, is not the demand for teachers, but the limited supply of teachers with majors in math and the sciences. If changes in curriculum needed for the current century are made, then the shortage in these subjects will be greatly increased. Stopgap measures: foreign teachers, part time teachers including graduate students and retirees, would help accelerate a change in composition of faculty and weaken the powers of bureaucracy. A sense of urgency also would contribute to appreciation and respect for those who teach. The obstacles are the certification requirements serving as protective tariffs for schools of education and their graduates.

The other good news is that schools, school districts, teachers unions are not going to have a choice. Their ability to impose school of education study requirements on majors in other subjects is rapidly diminishing. The number graduating with degrees in education is far too small to meet the needs of the immediate future. For the past twenty years only some 106 thousand bachelors degrees in education have been awarded annually, far below the number in the 1970s. Higher standards for teacher certification will reduce the proportion of these graduates who will enter and remain in teaching, and likely will further reduce the number of education majors in the future. Only elementary schools will still have faculties mainly with degrees in education.

HIGHER PRESTIGE FOR TEACHERS

Raising teacher pay is unlikely to affect occupational prestige. Pay at least in the early years of teaching may be adequate in comparison with other college graduates, and prestige is higher than pay would indicate. But this is for teachers drawn predominantly from the bottom quarter of college graduates. If new teachers were to come largely from the top quarter, and elect to make teaching a career, then pay must increase, and somehow so must the prestige of public school teaching. And that cannot be bought, it must be earned. The prestige of an occupation is not determined by its typical income or educational attainment.. The fact that the majority of public school teachers now have masters degrees (preponderantly in education) does not appear to have boosted prestige; it is irrelevant for teaching performance or student achievement and it is not required for beginning teachers or for most teachers. Occupation has a greater effect on prestige than pay, or is more closely correlated with it.

Why should a college professor teaching math or English to freshmen have so much more prestige that a teacher of the same subjects to these same freshmen a year earlier, when they were high school seniors?. It is not the difference in pay. The assumed difference in education between a bachelors in education versus a PhD in the subject taught may seem important, and no doubt it is. But it is merely an indicator of a difference in occupations. One is a teacher, the other a mathematician or writer whose job happens to be employed teaching at the college level. College faculty draw distinctions between institutions: community colleges, four year colleges, and universities, which themselves are evaluated in a status hierarchy; between faculty teaching undergraduate and graduate courses; between teaching faculty and faculty engaged in research. Prestige among faculty is associated with research, publications, expertise in a field of knowledge, more than with teaching The prestige hierarchy among college faculty is related to standards for employment, to the difficulty of obtaining a job. There is no shortage of applicants.

Prestige applies both to jobs and to occupations. The occupation of the college professor is mathematics or history or economics. His or her job happens to be teaching. Occupations that require considerable training tend to be lifelong attributes of an individual, who may change jobs several or many times. For the majority of elementary and secondary school teachers, their job is also regarded as their occupation. Pay is an important consideration in choosing between jobs, but much less so in choosing occupations.

When a high school diploma was regarded as a terminal degree, this difference in status between high school and college teachers made some sense. Now most high school students are expected to go on to college, and in fact most do. There is no longer any justification for the great divide between high school and college faculty. But as long as secondary school faculty are seen as products of schools of education, the divide cannot be bridged. Once all high school faculty earn degrees in the subjects they teach, and once those who continue for a masters degree also specialize in their subjects, the divide should diminish if not disappear. The additional education would be perceived as relevant, and would be expected to improve teacher performance and student achievement. The teacher might be viewed as a scientist or historian, who is teaching the subject, but might be practicing it elsewhere. An experienced high school teacher should be able to teach the college freshman class in his subject. Perhaps with colleges relying more on part time faculty, occasionally he might. With upgrading of the high school curriculum, college faculty might occasionally teach high school seniors. Association between the two faculties within disciplines is now almost totally absent. The gap should be narrowed and bridged. There might be less remedial course work in college and a lower dropout rate

If high school teachers were viewed first as experts in math, chemistry, history, whatever field of knowledge, second as teachers in that field, they would be held in higher regard. This is not just a matter of perception; it should be a matter of fact. Teaching positions in middle and high schools should be limited to majors in the fields in which they teach (or in some cases, closely related fields with common core of knowledge). Experienced teachers lacking the requisite degree would be replaced slowly. Many have acquired the knowledge needed since graduating from college; others might be required to upgrade their subject matter skills

The lack of occupational alternatives for many public school teachers with college degrees in education affects their earnings and their status. There are many public school teachers presumably trained to be principals and superintendents, but not prepared for professional jobs in the subjects they teach. There is little doubt that the near-monopoly that schools of education and teachers unions have on public school teaching jobs contribute to lower status, quality, and possibly earnings as well. Friedman [1] asked professional workers whether or not they regarded elementary and secondary school teachers as professionals, and reports one response: "Because of their union-like behavior, lack of peer review, self-discipline, and accountability within the teaching ranks, it is very difficult for the public to view them as professionals." Friedman sees this perception that teachers are only semi-professionals as a fundamental handicap in attracting well-qualified individuals into teaching. The growth of professionally oriented alternatives to the NEA and the AFT is an encouraging development. So are the requirements of No Child Left Behind legislation for measuring student achievement and standards for teacher qualification. Public perceptions of school performance in their school district will influence their attitude toward teachers. So will higher standards for teacher qualification.

If most teachers had degrees in the subjects they teach, they would have greater occupational mobility. It is math and science teachers who experience the highest turnover. There is a price to pay for quality teaching: starting pay must reflect the market; pay increases must reflect merit as well to keep turnover of good teachers within reasonable limits.

The stress has been on secondary school teaching. Elementary schools also have a problem of staffing and achievement, but their shortcomings are more about pedagogy and curriculum than about mastery of subject matter. They do not need a bachelors degree in the subject they teach, almost any subject will do except education. Such a background would enhance their status and increase their occupational options. If their degree is not in psychology, then they should earn some credits from a department of psychology stressing child psychology and learning theory.

The status of a teacher in the eyes of the community is affected by the institution of employment as well as by the occupation. Most of us agree that education is critically important and that its condition needs improvement. But assignment of importance to an institution does not translate automatically into respect and reward for those who do its work:. A poor opinion of public schools lowers the regard with which public school teachers are held. It is another circle which needs converting from vicious to virtuous. Higher standards, higher achievement, would enhance the status of all teachers. Magnet schools are magnets for teachers as well as students. Charter schools could follow in their steps. Somehow we need to convert individual concerns into community effort and support for those doing a difficult job and doing it well.

The problem of mediocre prestige of teaching is more fundamental, a characteristic of a society that respects doers, achievers, practical pursuits, and does not view teaching in these terms. Most people view education as an obstacle that must be surmounted in order to succeed in the job market rather than as a valuable activity in itself. The pursuit of knowledge is for the nerd. Community perceptions of the key role of the occupation, the difficulty of the work involved in teaching, the consequences of failure, need enhancement. Viewing the teacher as a chemist or mathematician, a writer or artist who is teaching in his field cannot but help.

Concerns about college admission have multiplied; they represent a heightened awareness of student achievement and its consequences. Many parents and students experience anxiety verging on panic over the college admissions game. The process is far more competitive in their eyes than in the past. Admission to the "right' college is considered more important than it was to previous generations. There is a somewhat mistaken view that this decision may determine the student's entire future. This perspective is an overdue realization that formal education has obtained a monopoly on access to more desirable jobs and occupations, which it did not have within living memory. Parents, if not their immature offspring, have to be more concerned about the quality of their children's public school education than they ever were in the past. The parental goal of higher educational attainment for their children has been achieved by and large. What matters most in the future is quality, not years. Good schools, good teachers cannot but reap the benefits of parental concern and appreciation.

The prestige of high school teaching should creep up somewhat relative to that of many occupations of college graduates in the future for a simple reason: it does require a college education, preferably somewhat different from that currently prevailing, but a diploma nonetheless that is relevant and necessary for their work. A large share of college graduates, on the other hand, will have to make do in jobs and occupations for which a college education is not necessary, nor was it expected in the past. Teaching has the further advantage that it is a major occupation whose workers readily acquire the equivalent of tenure or lifetime employment security. What is taught may change slowly over time, but public school systems do not move or shut down. In a world of jobs more mobile and transient than ever, job stability and security should gain favor. It is an industry little threatened by declining demand, technological change or by outsourcing. Employer-contributory pension plans and health insurance should be safe while other industries default or cut back on theirs It is also an occupation that is found in every town of any size; offering a range of geographical choice matched by few other occupations. As state after state relaxes the monopoly of schools of education and their proxies, the teachers unions, over hiring and conditions of employment — in particular market pay and merit pay — teachers mobility is enhanced and teachers are bound to be viewed more favorably than they are viewed now.

Occupations have been ranked by socioeconomic status as well as by prestige. Although the two are correlated, they are different. Both have a role in decisions to enter teaching, and to leave teaching. The traditional correlates of socioeconomic status were educational attainment and income. These still matter, but other considerations will gain in importance. The great compression of educational attainment: most are completing high school, the majority starting college, soon one third completing college, means that educational attainment is less important than in the past as an indicator of status. There is rapid increase in postgraduate education and degrees, but most of these advanced degrees are closely related to particular occupations, unlike a "college diploma", hence it is the occupation rather than the educational attainment that is the primary influence on status.

While inequality in educational attainment has been greatly reduced, the reverse has happened with regard to earnings and income. Thus income has increased its differentiating role relative to education. But income is even more weakly related to occupational prestige than education.

CHANGING DETERMINANTS OF STATUS

Occupation has become a more uncertain determinant of status or prestige than in the past. A century ago, most people had a rough idea of what people in other occupations did. Traditional occupations are entrenched in family names: Farmer, Baker, Smith, Cooper, Carver, Weaver, Miller, Sawyer, Forester, Hunter, Fisher. These are the occupations from which we derived our status, self-esteem, identity, by which we described ourselves, and many still do, in their obituaries, for dramatic changes in occupation have been concentrated in a single lifetime. Rare are the seniors whose children have followed in their occupational footsteps.

In the past, there was a great divide between white collar and blue collar jobs. Now, most jobs are white collar, blue collar jobs are a small and declining share of the total, hence the distinction must be among white collar jobs rather than between blue and white collar. One rarely speaks of blue collar and white collar workers any more. The blue collar worker was not just someone working with his hands - surgeons and dentists were not so classified - but also someone of limited education and skill. Today that worker will often have had some college, wear a white collar. Some of the remaining blue collar jobs have radically altered their modus operandi, with complex instruments and machinery manipulated by workers whose blue collar jobs are more like the engineer or airplane pilot than the ditch digger. Educational attainment also distinguishes the modern from the traditional blue collar worker: farmers, laborers on average have not only completed high school, they have some college experience. As the more skilled blue collar artisan of old becomes the technician of today, his collar color changes at least in the public eye.

Gradually new occupations have proliferated, whose activities are abstract or unknown to most people, and the numbers employed in them multiplied, so that most of us have only a vague idea where to "rank" them. Is a computer programmer a new go-fer or a Bill Gates? Managers are everywhere, but what exactly do many of them manage, and what does that mean? Many people find it hard to describe to others exactly what they do - paper work of one kind or another, communications, coordination - but of what, for what purpose? They have no subsistence value; nor does the stranger understand their contribution to the general welfare. There is little concrete in communications, information coordination, data manipulation. Occupations have multiplied in number and become ever more specialized in response to growing complexity of technology and of institutions and organization. Old occupational titles have experienced inflation: secretaries and clerks have becomes executive aides, who have become assistant managers, who are now vice presidents Today a baker could be titled a fermentation specialist; a blacksmith a sidereal engineer. New occupational titles and the work involved are too unfamiliar for consensus ranking, or for ranking at all. The status structure has become multidimensional and intransitive. The status hierarchies of the past are in shambles.

Then what is to distinguish one occupation, one job from another in terms of a status hierarchy? The studies on the subject provide us with averages, no more. People are not of one mind on work preferences; some like pressure, others hate it; some like company, others prefer working alone. Some prefer dealing with people, others with things, or facts or ideas. Individual perceptions of their own jobs and occupations may be quite different from those of others. Those for whom differences in earnings are not the main concern will seek jobs and occupations on the basis of idiosyncratic personal likes and dislikes. There would be as many hierarchies as there are differences between individuals. Many like teaching who do not enter or remain in the teaching profession for reasons of income or entry barriers unrelated to ability to teach imposed by the education industry. Those barriers must go. What remains as a deterrent is the working environment in our worst schools: students who are unruly, who do not study, who place no value on learning. Good teachers can do only so much; these are problems of the larger society.

Perceived status of a job or occupation is a factor in attracting workers. Teacher recruitment however is not just increasing entry; it is also, perhaps more important, reducing attrition in the early years It is job satisfaction that matters most in retaining them. Only after employment does job satisfaction come into play. Job satisfaction is a matter of individual preferences and working environment. It is not closely related to either prestige or pay. The principal factor in satisfaction is autonomy. What is the prospect of increased autonomy? Charter schools and magnet schools offer enhanced autonomy for a few. Smaller school districts would enhance autonomy on a local basis. A shift from primary concern with process to stress on results by whatever means is a very liberating movement for the individual teacher. Relief from the oppressive burden of detailed state and district regulations, prescribed pedagogy, freedom to choose textbooks and other learning materials should come as a byproduct of stress on student achievement. (But student mobility and transition from lower to higher grades limit the autonomy of individual teachers and schools.) Griffin [2] and Wise [3] propose increasing the attractiveness of teaching by converting it from a job to a professional career. One step is additional formal training and more rigorous certification standards. Another is formalization of the role played informally by experienced teachers, as mentors to new teachers and teachers in training, as advisers on curriculum, teaching practices, school organization, community relations. My reaction is that job description in most professional occupations is not hierarchical. Only large organizations provide such opportunities, and in education they are technical and administrative rather than classroom teaching. Good principals and district superintendents will provide such responsibilities to qualified teachers; it is better not to convert this process into a bureaucratic hierarchy. Pay increases for good experienced teachers are called for, not new titles and jobs. There is no evidence that formalization would increase the attraction of teaching to college students, or increase retention of teachers.

Additional teacher education has not been reflected in improved student achievement nor has it enhanced teacher prestige. When schools face great difficulty in attracting and retaining teachers is no time to raise the bar by increasing educational requirements. It is a good time to change such requirements, to attract more and better teachers. Enhancing the status of teachers via more education may come later, provided the additional education clearly contributes to performance.

IDENTITY AND WORK

With the disparity between the distribution of jobs and occupations on one hand and the multitude of degree holders on the other, jobs and careers will decline as the central component of individual identity and self-respect. Our society has long been work-oriented; people in the past derived their identity from their work. What the employed individual sees as the value of work, others see as the prestige of an occupation. A high proportion of English family names are occupational names, more than in any other language. This is unusual. Many traditional societies hold labor, in particular manual labor, in low regard. The Hindu caste system honors priests and scholars, to a lesser degree warriors, but downgrades other occupations. The Romans valued agriculture, politics and war, placing much less value on learning, for which they turned to the Greeks. The Athenians had low regard for specialization, which they relegated to slaves; free citizens were amateurs, dilettantes, not technicians. In sports they honored the amateur, not the professional. Even in modern continental Europe we will not find identity and status so heavily based on work and occupation. Workers in France demand long vacations — 6 weeks — shorter hours, and tolerate double-digit unemployment for years in a row. Many of the unemployed seem content to live in leisure for the duration of their social safety net. Other West European countries are of much the same mind.

The role of occupational prestige in the labor market is an attribute of the work ethic long prevalent in the land. But a growing share of the population no longer believe in gratification deferment, an essential component of the traditional work ethic. Individualism, once the pursuit of gain, of achievement, has mutated into the pursuit of pleasure as an end in itself, a cult of consumption with immediate gratification,. what Lasch called "The Culture of Narcissism" [4].

In the not so distant past, opportunity was quite limited. Success was an individual achievement, a win against the odds. Today there may not be equality of opportunity, whatever that means. If it means equally supportive parents, it will never happen. But there is opportunity so ample that success loses some of its significance as individual achievement. Everyone can go to college. Ample opportunity personalizes failure; it can no longer be so easily blamed on others, on circumstances, it becomes the individual's own responsibility. The structure of success remains hierarchical. There is little realization of the psychological trauma resulting from equal opportunity in a world of unequal outcomes. The normal reaction is to disconnect individual values and goals from the positional struggle. A job, an occupation becomes only a means of financing one's own life style, not the primary source of status or self-esteem. Leisure is the principal resource available to nearly all. Increased life expectancy means that many will spend a year in retirement for every two years in the workforce. Future orientation is shifting from career to the retirement years, their needs and uses.

The United States, once production and future-oriented, is described today as a consumer society, present-oriented. This shift is indicated by the breakdown of the family as a dominant institution, by the decline of household saving to close to zero despite rising incomes and lower tax rates, despite fewer children to support in the middle years and to rely upon in later years, despite two-worker families, by record individual bankruptcies during the boom of the late 1990s. More and more Americans are deriving their identity, their sense of self-esteem, from their consumption, their possessions, their life style, not from their work or occupation. As size of families drops, size of houses doubles, both size and number of cars increases. Workers may face a choice between consumption and leisure which reduces income available for consumption. Elimination of compulsory retirement has not resulted in much increase in average age of retirement despite a large increase in life expectancy after age 65.

Why is popular culture shifting from production orientation and occupational status to leisure orientation and consumer values? For the childless, a much larger share of the population than in the past, more time and income for disposal could be a factor. For the far-sighted, the expectation of many years in comfortable retirement with time on one's hands might be important.

We should change family names from Smith, Brewer and Baker to Player, Golfer and Tourist. This is likely to be a permanent change - too many will always be educated for jobs that require education, hence in time learn to expect dissonance between education and work outcomes. Education itself becomes acceptable as a time-intensive consumer good rather than as an investment. Disappointed expectations for education, occupation and income divert the search for identity from one's job and occupation to leisure time activities.

Teaching should grow in attraction as consumption replaces work as the foundation of identity and self-esteem. There are two kinds of consumption: income-intensive and time-intensive. If consumption means buying another dozen pairs of shoes, an original work of art, a car than can go 150mph, or designer labels of any kind, the consumer needs lots of cash (or credit). If consumption means participating in sports, reading, watching TV, participating in chatter at a neighborhood café, the consumer needs lots of time, little or no money. A teaching job is near-ideal in providing opportunities for time-intensive consumption: long summer vacation, several shorter breaks during the school year, the possibility of teaching part time or part year, of leaving and returning. The job does not change much from one year to the next, there is no career track to derail. For the consumption-oriented, in particular those who prefer time-intensive consumption, the advantage of teaching, of a teaching career, should rise substantially relative to almost all other occupations.

The irony of the moment is that the decline of the work ethic in favor of the ethic of consumption and pleasure is also the debasement of achievement. This is a culture that always valued doing, and learning by doing, above. knowing. But in the last two or three generations it has been 'educated' to value personal opinion above informed judgment, belief as a substitute for fact, entertainment above achievement. The nerd, the geek, is a term of derision. Only a fundamental shift in the perceived value of knowledge can promote both teaching and learning. It must come from teachers and schools, and will take a generation to begin changing the culture of the day. It must come from teachers and administrators trained in disciplines that honor reason, fact, objectivity, and truth above pleasure, personal opinion and self-esteem. And it must come from society. Hopefully the urge to excel, to surpass, and the passion for change and novelty will remain part of consumerism in the meantime.

Culture changes, sometimes from one generation to the next. The "roaring twenties" ended abruptly with the great depression and the second world war. The return of cultural narcissism in the 1960s may have run its course. Future historians may conclude that the events of September 11, 2001 marked a boundary between cultures. Public schools have contributed to current cultural devaluation of learning and exaltation of self; they could also contribute to reverse current attitudes and practices. But it takes at least 30 years for a new generation to grow up with a different ordering of values and begin to make its influence felt.

Cultural change is under way, if Sorokin [5] was correct. He described a repetitive oscillation between sensate, ideational and idealistic culture patterns in world history. Half a century ago he foresaw the disintegration of the sensate culture then prevailing and the beginning of idealistic and ideational revival. But his patterns are centennial, we cannot wait but must improve the performance of the next generation.

VALUES AND INSTITUTIONS

To enhance the status of teaching we need to restore public belief that public schools, and their teachers, are doing a good job. But the perception cannot precede the achievement, it must follow. High achievement cannot be reconciled with egalitarian constraints on what is taught, how it is taught, and on what is expected of students. As long as high school graduation remains an entitlement it cannot be viewed as an achievement, nor can it gain respect. Neither can the schools or the teachers that graduate semi-literates.

The widespread public concern with the performance of our public schools is an indicator of the value the public places on education and on the institutions that provide it. It is inevitable that the public will value those schools that do an excellent job - the high tuition in good private schools, and their many applicants, are evidence of that. Teachers in such schools will also be highly regarded. If the status of teachers is low, it is not the occupation that is held in poor regard, it is the performance of its firms, the public schools, and its employees. Reform the public school system to achieve high performance, and high respect must follow for its teachers.

How to improve the prestige of teaching? Ultimately it is up to good teachers school by school, district by district. Elevating respect for teaching as a means of attracting good teachers is not possible; causation must run the other way. What can be done is to eliminate all existing barriers to hiring good teachers, in particular the protective tariffs represented by school of education requirements, and to install a system of incentives and rewards instead of security and solidarity. Reform of the curriculum will follow, but it cannot be done in a day.

REFERENCES

1. INTRODUCTION

[1]   Young, M. (1994). *The Rise of Meritocracy.* New Brunswick, NJ: Transactions Publishers, pp. 69-75.

[2]   National Center for Education Statistics. (2005). *Digest of Education Statistics 2004.* Washington, DC: U. S. Government Printing Office, Table 36.

[3]   Butts, R. F. (1955). *A Cultural History of Western Education - Its Social and Intellectual Foundations.* New York: McGraw-Hill Book Company, pp.569-584.

[4]   National Center for Education Statistics. (2007). *Digest of Education Statistics 2006.* Washington, DC: U. S. Government Printing Office, Table 50.

[5]   *Ibid.,* Table 41.

[6]   Gonzales, P., Guzman, J. C., Partelow, L., Pahlke, E., Jocelyn, L., Kastberg, D., & Williams, T. (2004). *Highlights from the Trend in International Mathematics and Science Study: TIMSS 2003.* Washington, DC: National Center for Education Statistics.

[7]   Vogel, G. (1997). "U.S. Kids Score Well in Primary Grades". *Science* 276 (13 June), p.1642.

[8]   Holden, C.(2000). "Asia Stays on Top, U.S. in Middle in New Global Rankings." *Science* 290 (8 December), p. 1866.

[9]   Centre for Educational Research and Innovation. (2003). *Education at a Glance 2003.* Paris: Organization for Economic Co-operation and Development, Tables A4.1, A5.2, A6.1, and A6.2. *Op. cit.* (2006) Tables 2, 5.

[10]   Lemke, M., Sen, A., Pahlke, L., Miller, D., Williams, T., Kastberg, O., & Jocelyn, L. (2004). *International Outcomes of Learning in Mathematics Literacy and Problem Solving: Pisa 2003 Results from the U.S. Perspective.* NCES 2005-003).:Washington, DC.: U.S. Department of Education, National Center for Education Statistics:.

[11]   Rotberg, I. C. (1998). "Interpretation of International Test Score Results." *Science* 280 (15 May), pp. 1030-1.

[12]   Vogel, G.(1998). Northern Europe Tops in High School." *Science* 279 (27 February),: p. 1297.

[13]   National Center for Education Statistics. (2007). *Op. cit.,* Table 153.

[14]   Centre for Educational Research and Innovation. (2003) *Op. cit.,* Table A7.1

2. PROBLEMS OF HIGH SCHOOL TEACHER SUPPLY

[1]   National Center for Education Statistics. (2004). *Digest of Education Statistics 2003*. Washington, DC: U. S. Government Printing Office, Table 66.

[2]   National Center for Education Statistics.(2007). *Digest of Education Statistics 2006*. National Center for Education Statistics. Washington, DC: U. S. Government Printing Office, Table 66.

[3]   *Loc. cit.*

[4]   Murname. R. J., Singer, J., Wilson, J. B., Kemple, J. J. & Olsen. R. J. (1992). *Who Will Teach? Policies that Matter*. Harvard University Press: Cambridge: pp. 59-61, 64.

[5]   Flyer, F. & Rosen, S. (1997). "The New Economics of Teachers and Education." *Journal of Labor Economics* 15 (1), pp. S104-S139:S134-136.

[6]   Sowell, T. (2003). "Another Grand Fraud." *Washington Times* April 5, p. A11.

[7]   National Center for Education Statistics. (2007). *Op. cit.*, Table 41.

[8]   Butts, R. F. (1955). *A Cultural History of Western Education Its Social and Intellectual Foundations*. New York: McGraw-Hill Book Company, p. 468.

[9]   Nakao, K. & Treas. J.(1994). "Updating Occupational Prestige and Socioeconomic Scores: How the New Measures Measure Up." *Sociological Methodology* 24, pp. 1-72: 18.

[10]   National Center for Education Statistics. (2007). *Op. cit.*, Tables 8 and 376.

[11]   *Ibid.,* Table 66.

[12]   Hanushek, E. A. (1986). "The Economics of Schooling: Production and Efficiency in the Public Schools." *Journal of Economic Literature* XXIV (3), pp. 1141-77: 1161, 1167.

[13]   U. S. Census Bureau (2004). *Statistical Abstract of the United States 2003*, Washington, DC: U. S. Government Printing Office, Table 315. For data on the 1960s and 1970s, see various issues of *Employment and Earnings*, published by the Bureau of Labor Statistics

[14]   Hauser. R. M. & Warren, J. R.(1997). "Socioeconomic Indexes for Occupations: A Review, Update and Critique." *Sociological Methodology* 27, pp.177-298: 188-190, 211-214.

[15]   Butts, R. F. & Cremin. L. A.(1953). *A History of Education in American Culture*. New York: Henry Holt and Company, pp. 449-453

[16]   Murnane, R. J. et al (1991). *Op cit.*, p. 9.

[17]   Fletcher, M. A.(2003). "As High School Exit Exams Cost Diplomas, Anger Arises." *Washington Post* May 31, pp. 1, 24.

[18]   Ingersoll, R. M. (1999). "The Problem of Underqualified Teachers in American Secondary Schools." *Educational Researcher* 26 (2), pp. 26-37.

[19]   Corcoran, S. P., Evans, W. N., & Schwab, R. M. (2004). "Changing Labor Market Opportunities for Women and the Quality of Teachers, 1957-2000." *American Economic Review* 94 (2), pp. 230-235. See also Corcoran. S. P., Evans, W. N., & Schwab., R. N. (2004). "Women, the Labor Market, and the Declining Relative Quality of Teachers." *Journal of Policy Analysis and Management* 23 (3), pp. 449-4470.

[20]   Gross. M. L. (1999). *The Conspiracy of Ignorance - the Failure of American Public Schools*. New York: Harper Collins Publishers, pp. 43-45.

[21] Hoxby, C. M. & Leigh, A. (2004). "Pulled Away or Pushed Out? Explaining the Decline of Teacher Aptitude in the United States." Unpublished paper.

[22] Hoxby, C. M. (1996). "How Teachers and Unions Affect Education Production." *Quarterly Journal of Economics* 11 (3), pp. 671-718.

[23] Peltzman, S. (1993). "The Political Economy of the Decline in American Education." *Journal of Law and Economics* 36 (1), Part 2, 331-370.

3. QUALITY OF EDUCATION AND EGALITARIAN VALUES

[1] Gatto, J. T. (1992). *Dumbing us Down - the Hidden Curriculum of Compulsory Schooling.* Philadelphia: New Society Publishers, pp. 317-329.

[2] National Center for Education Statistics. (2007). *Digest of Education Statistics 2006.* Washington, DC: U. S. Government Printing Office, Table 102. There are claims that this figure is too low, and too high. The evidence favors a lower estimate. Fall enrollments decline steadily from the 9th to the 12th grade. Recently the ratio of seniors, not all of whom graduate, to 9th graders has been roughly 72%. It was over 80% in the 1980s, and dropped below 70% in the 1990s.

[3] Graham, P. A. (1995). "Assimilation, Adjustment, and Access: an Antiquarian View of American Education." In D. Ravitch & M. A. Vinovskis (Eds.), *Learning from the Past- What History Teaches Us about School Reform* (pp. 3-22). Baltimore: Johns Hopkins University Press.

[4] Gross, Martin L. (1999). *The Conspiracy of Ignorance - the Failure of American Public Schools.* Harper Collins Publishers: New York: 71-89, 104-128. See also Hirsch, Eric D., Jr. (1996). *The Schools we Need - and Why we Don't Have them.* New York: Doubleday, pp. 48-68.

[5] Machlup, Fritz.(1962). *The Production and Distribution of Knowledge in the United States.* Princeton: Princeton University Press, p.133.

[6] Angus, D. & Mirel, J. (1995). "Rhetoric and Reality: The High School Curriculum" In D. Ravitch & M. A. Vinovskis (Eds.), *op. cit.,* (pp.295-328): 301-312. See also Powell, A. G., Farrar, E., & Cohen, D. K.(1985). *The Shopping Mall High School-Winners and Losers in the Educational Marketplace.* Boston: Houghton Mifflin Co., pp. 8-65.

[7] Angus, D. and Mirel, J. (1995). *Op. cit.,* pp. 312-319.

[8] *Ibid., pp.* 302, 320

[9] Nappi, C. R. (2001). "Local Illusions". *Wilson Quarterly Review,* 2001 (Autumn), pp. 52-59.

[10] Mare, R. D. (1981). "Trends in Schooling: Demography, Performance, and Organization." *The Annals, American Academy of Political and Social Science* 453 (January), pp. 107-9, 115.

[11] Stotsky, S. (1999). *Losing our Language-how Multicultural Classroom Instruction is Undermining our Children's Ability to Read, Write and Reason.* New York: The Free Press, pp. 11-21.

[12] Gatto, J. T. (1992). Op. cit., 13.

[13] Sowell, T. (1993). *Inside American Education - the Decline, the Deception, the Dogmas.* New York: The Free Press, pp. 74-82.

[14] Schmidt, W. H., McKnight, C. C., Houang, R. T., Wang, H. C., Wiley, D. E., Cogan, L. S. & Wolfe, R. G.(2001). *Why Schools Matter - A Cross-National Comparison of Curriculum and Learning*. San Francisco: Jossey-Bass, pp. 76-163.

[15] *Ibid,* pp. 300-1

[16] Schmidt, W. H. et al. (2001). *Op. cit.* pp. 260-295.

[17] *Ibid.*, p 356.

[18] Schmidt, W. H. et al.(1996). *Characterizing Pedagogical Flow - An Investigation of Mathematics and Science Teaching*. Dordrecht: Clair Academic Publishers,, pp. 39-67. See also, Porter, A. (1989). "A Curriculum out of Balance". *Educational Researcher* 18 (5),pp. 9-15.

[19] Flanders, J. R.(1987). "How Much of the Content in Mathematics Text-books is New?" *Arithmetic Teacher* 35 (1), pp.18-23. See also Porter, A. (1989). *Op. cit.*

[20] *Mathematically Correct*: www.ethnomath.org

[21] Steen, L A. (2003). "Math Education at Risk". *Issues in Science and Technology*, (Summer), pp 79-81.

[22] Mervin, J. (1998). "U.S. Tries Variations on High School Curriculum". *Science* 281, 20 July, pp.161, 163.

[23] Chiappetta, E. L, Sethna, G. H., & Fillman, D. A. (1991). "A Quantitative Analysis of High School Chemistry Textbooks for Scientific Literacy Themes and Expository Learning Aids." *Journal of Research in Science Teaching,*, 28 (10), pp.939-951.

[24] National Center for Education Statistics. (2007). *Op. cit.*, Tables 121, 139.

[25] Pene, M. & Moran, R. (2005). *NAEP 2004 Trends in Academic Progress: Three Decades of Student Performance in Reading and Mathematics*. U.S. Department of Education, National Center for Education Statistics. Washington, DC: U. S. Government Printing Office, pp.16-25.

[26] National Center for Education Statistics. (2007). *Op. cit,*, Table 132; National Center for Education Statistics.(2004). *Digest of Education Statistics 2003*. Washington, DC: U. S. Government Printing Office, Table 127.

[27] The report, "Social Studies Textbook Review July 2002", Texas Public Policy Foundation, is available on the web: constitution.org/tx/textbook/compilation-textbookfactualerrors

[28] Nash, G. B.(1995). "American History Reconsidered: Asking New Questions about the Past." In D. Ravitch & M. A. Vinovskis (Eds.), *Op. cit.*, (pp. 135-163).

[29] Sewall, G. T. (1996). "The Postmodern Schoolhouse." In K. Washburn & J. F. Thornton.(Eds.), *Dumbing Down - Essays on the Strip Mining of American Culture*, (pp. 57-67); New York: W. W. Norton & Co., pp.:58-60

[30] Archibald, G. (2003)."Textbooks Flunk Test - Dumbing Down, PC Distort U. S. History, Critics Say." *Washington Times,* March 28, pp. A1, A6.

[31] Angus, D. L. & Mirel, J. E. (1993). "Equality, Curriculum, and the Decline of the Academic Ideal: Detroit 1930-1968." *History of Education Quarterly* 33 (2), pp. 177-207.

[32] Angus, D. & Mirel, J.E. (1995).*Op. cit.*, pp. 312-19.

[33] Powell, A. G., Farrar, E., & Cohen, D. K. *(1985). The Shopping Mall High School - Winners, and Losers in the Academic Marketplace*. Boston: Houghton, Mifflin Co., pp. 8-65.

[34] Leo, J. (2005). "The Parent Trap." *US News & World Report,* October 2.

[35] Loveless, T. (2001). "The Parent Trap". *Wilson Quarterly Review* (Autumn),.pp. 6-42.

[36] Rosenbaum, J. E.(2001). *Beyond College for All - Career Paths for the Forgotten Half.* New York: Russell Sage Foundation, pp. 38-40, 93–98.

[37] Stotsky, S. (1999). *Op. cit.*, pp. 57-124.

[38] *Ibid.*, p. 149

[39] Powell, A. B. & Frankenstein, M. (1997). *Ethnomathematics - Challenging Eurocentrism in Mathematics Education.* Albany, NY: State University of New York Press. See also Ascher, M. (1991). *Ethnomathematics - A Multicultural View of Mathematical Ideas.* Pacific Grove, CA: Brooks/Cole Publishing Company.

[40] *Ibid,* pp. 193-200.

[41] Anderson, S. E (1997). "Worldmath Curriculum: Fighting Eurocentrism in Maths.." In A. B. Powell & M. Frankenstein (Eds.), *op. cit.*, (pp. 291-306), p. 293.

[42] Murray, C. (2003). *Human Accomplishment.* New York: HarperCollins Publishers.

[43] Baumeister, R. F., Campbell, J. D., Krueger, J. J., & Vohs, K.D. (2003). "Does High Self-Esteem Cause Better Performance, Interpersonal Success, Happiness, or Healthier Lifestyles? *Psychological Science in the Public Interest 4 (1)*, pp. 1-44.

[44] Twenge, J. J. (2000). "The Age of Anxiety? Birth Cohort Change in Anxiety and Neuroticism 1952-1993." *Journal of Personality and Social Psychology* 74 (6), pp. 997-1021. Twenge, J. J. (2006). *Generation Me. Why Today's Young Americans are more Confident, Assertive, Entitled and more Miserable Than Ever Before.* New York: The Free Press. At first she concluded that decline in social connectedness associated with the breakup of the traditional family was a major factor. More recently she has come to believe that the preaching of self-esteem in schools, which suffers rapid deflation when colliding with reality, was also important.

[45] Sowell, T. (1993). *Op. cit.* pp. 47-52,66-9; Sewall, G. T. (1996). *Op. cit.,* pp. 57-67.

[46] Zaslavsky, C. (1991). "World cultures in the maths class" 307-20. In A. B. Powell & M. Frankenstein, *op. cit.*, pp. 325-6.

[47] Higher Education Research Institute.(2004). *The American Freshman: National Norms for Fall 2004.* Los Angeles: UCLA Graduate School of Education and Information Studies.

[48] Higher Education Research Institute.(1999). *The American Freshman: National Norms for Fall 1999.* Los Angeles: UCLA Graduate School of Education and Information Studies.

[49] U.S. Department of Education, National Center for Education Statistics. (2003). *Remedial Education at Degree-Granting Postsecondary Institutions in Fall 2000.* Washington DC: pp. 17-19.

[50] Shettle, C., Roey, S., Mordica, J. et al. (2007). *America's High School Graduates - Results from the 2005 High School Transcript Study.* Washington, DC: National Center for Education Statistics, pp.12, 13. See also Woodruff, D. J. & Ziomek, R. L. (2004). "High School Grade Inflation from 1991 to 2003." ACT research report, March 2004.

[51] Finder, A. (2006). "Schools Avoid Class Rankings, Vexing Colleges." *The New York Times* March 5. AP (2006) "Admissions Boards Face 'Grade Inflation'" *The New York Times* November 18.

[52] Gouras, M. (2004). "Honor Roll is Suspended in Nashville - State Privacy Laws Lead District to Abandon Awards - and Others May Follow". *Washington Post* January 25, p. A13.

[53] Birk, L. (2003). "Grade Inflation: What is Really Behind all those A's?" *Harvard Education Letter* (online), May 2003.

[54] Stotsky, S. (1999), *Op cit.*, p. xi.

[55] Vonnegut, K. J. (1961) "Harrison Bergeron" *Fantasy and Science Fiction Magazine*, Oct. 1961.

[56] Fogel, R. W.(2000). *The Fourth Great Awakening and the Future of Egalitarianism.* Chicago: The University of Chicago Press, pp.5, 6.

[57] Anderson, S. E. (1997). *Op. cit.*, p. 294.

[58] Gardner, H. & Hatch, T. (1989). "Multiple Intelligences Go to School: Educational Implications of the Theory of Multiple Intelligences." *Educational Researcher* 18 (8), pp. 9-15.

[59] Gottfredson, L. (2004). "Schools and the g Factor." *Wilson Quarterly* Summer, pp. 35-45.

[60] Scheffler, S. (2003). "What is Egalitarianism?" *Philosophy and Public Affairs* 31 (1), pp. 5-39. See also Dworkin, R. (2003). "Equality, Luck and Hierarchy". *Philosophy and Public Affairs* 31 (2), pp. 190-198.

[61] Ueda, R. (1995). "Ethnic Diversity and National Identity in Public School Texts." In D. Ravitch & M. A. Vinovskis (Eds.), *op. cit.* (pp. 113-134). Nash, G. B. (1995). "American History Reconsidered: Asking New Questions about the Past." In D. Ravitch and M. A.Vinovskis (Eds.). *op. cit.* (pp 135-163).

[62] Sowell. T. (1993). *Op cit:.* pp. 48-53, 67

[63] Powell, A.G., Farrar, E. & Cohen, D. K. *(1985). The Shopping Mall High School - Winners, and Losers in the Academic Marketplace.* Boston: Houghton, Mifflin Company, pp. 8-65.

[64] Barzun, J. (1959).*The House of Intellect*, New York: Harper & Brothers Publishers, pp. 33-4.

[65] Barzun, J. (1959). *Op. cit,.* pp. 33-4, 71.

[66] Eakman, B.K. (1998). *Cloning of the American Mind - Eradicating Morality Through Education.* Lafayette, LA: Huntington House Publishers. See especially Chapter 8,

[67] Weiss, D. (1993). *The specter of capitalism and the promise of a classless society.* Atlantic Heights, NJ: Humanities Press International Inc.

[68] Boehm, C. (1997). "Impact of the Human Egalitarian Syndrome on Darwinian Selection Mechanics". *The American Naturalist* 150 Supplement July 1997: S101-121.

[69] Fogel, R. W. (200). *Op. cit,* pp. 176-235.

[70] *Ibid.*, pp. 15-43.

[71] Harris, L. (2004). *Civilization and its Enemies - the next Stage of History.* New York: Free Press, pp. 43-4, 94, 132.

[72] Rayner, K., Foormon, B. R., Perfetti, C. A., Pesetsky, D., & Seidenberg, M. (2001). "How Psychological Science Informs the Teaching of Reading". *Psychological Science in the Public Interest* 2 (2), pp. 31-74: 31-4.

[73] Gatto, J. T. (1992). Op cit,, p. 13.

[74] Lyon, G. R., Chief, Child Development and Behavior Branch, National Institutes of Health. (1998). *Overview of Reading and Literacy Initiatives.* Statement to the Senate Committee on Labor and Human Resources, April 28 1998: p. 3.

[75] Department of Education, National Center for Education Statistics.(2005). *2003 National Assessment of Adult Literacy - A First Look at the Literacy of America's Adults in the 21st Century.* Washington, DC: Institute of Education Sciences.

[76] Gatto, J. T. (2000). *The Underground History of American Education - a Schoolteacher's Intimate Investigation into the Problem of Modern Schooling.* New York: Oxford Village Press, p. 65

[77] Stotsky, S. (1999). *Op. cit., pp. 3-17.*

[78] Miller, G. A. "The Challenge of Universal Literacy." *Science* 241 (9 September), pp.1293-9.

[79] Fondacaro, R. & Higgins, E. T. (1985). "Cognitive Consequences of Communication Mode: a Social Psychological Perspective" In D. R. Olson, N. Torrance, & A. Hilyard (Eds.), *Literacy, Language, and Learning - On the Nature and Consequences of Reading and Writing.*(pp. 75-101). Cambridge: Cambridge University Press.

[80] Shaywitz, B. A., Shaywitz, S. E. et al. (2004). "Development of Left Occipitotemporal Systems for Skilled Reading in Children after a Psychologically-based Intervention." *Biological Psychiatry* 55 (9), pp. 926-933.

[81] Scribner, S. D. (1997). "The cognitive consequences of literacy" pp. 160-89 In E. Tobach, R. J. Falmagne, M. B. Parlee, L. M. W. Martin, & A. S. Kapelman (Eds.). *Literacy Mind and Social Practice - Selected Writings of Sylvia Scribner* (pp. 165-169, 183). Cambridge, UK:: Cambridge University Press. See also Scribner, S. D. (1997). "The Practice of Literacy",190-205 In E. Tobach et al, *op. cit.*:(190-205): 192. For a more extensive discussion see Scribner, S. D. & and Michael Cole. M. (1981). *The Psychology of Literacy.* Cambridge: Harvard University Press.

[82] Olson, D. R. (1991). "Literacy as Metalinguistic Activity." In D. R Olson, N. Torrance & A. Hilyard (Eds.), *op. cit.* (251-270).

[83] Scholes, R. J. & Willis, B. J.(1991). "Linguists, Literacy, and the Intentionality of Marshall McLuhan's Western Man." In D. R. Olson, N. Torrance & A. Hilyard (Eds.), op. cit., (215-235).

[84] Goody, J. & Watt, I. (1963). "The Consequences of Literacy." *Comparative Studies in Society and History* 5 (3), pp. 304-345. Narasimhan, R. (1985)."Literacy: its Characterization and Implications, 177-197 In D. R. Olson, N. Torrance & A. Hilyard (Eds.), *op cit.*, (177-197):177, 181.

[85] Porter, A. (1989). "A Curriculum out of Balance". *Educational Researcher* 18 (5), pp. 9-15.

[86] Borba, M. (1997). "Ethnomathematics and Education." In A. B. Powell & M. Frankenstein. *Ethnomathematics - Challenging Eurocentrism in Mathematics Education,* (261-272):268. Albany, NY: State University of New York Press.

[87] Ravitch, D. (1995). "The Search for Order and the Rejection of Conformity: Standards in American Education." In D. Ravitch & M. A. Vinovskis (Eds.), *Learning from the Past -What History Teaches us about School Reform,.* (pp. 167-190):182. Baltimore: Johns Hopkins University Press. Schlafly, P. (2006) "Education Experts Wrong; Parents Right." *Washington* Times September 27: A18

[88] Beyer, B. K. (1992). "Teaching Thinking: an Integrated Approach." In J. W. Keefe & Walberg, H. J. (Eds.). *Teaching for Thinking,* (pp. 93-109):97. Reston, VA: National Association of Secondary School Principals.

[89]   Keefe, J. W. (1989). "Thinking about the Thinking Movement." In J. W. Keefe & H. J.
       Walberg (Eds.), *op cit.*, (pp. 19-28). Perkins, D. N. & Salomon, G. "Are Cognitive
       Skills Context-Bound?" *Educational Researcher* 18 (1), pp.16-25.

[90]   Presseisen, B. Z (1987). "Thinking Skills in the Curriculum.", 1-13 In J. W. Keefe &
       H. J. Walberg (Eds.), *op. cit.*, (p.12).

[91]   Nisbet, R. E., Fong, G. T., Lehman, D. R., & Cheng, P. W. (1987). "Teaching
       Reasoning". *Science* 238 (30 October), pp. 625-31.

[92]   Darling-Hammond, L., Griffin, G. A., & Wise., A. E. (1992). *Excellence in Teacher
       Education: Helping Teachers Develop Learner-centered Schools.* Washington, DC:
       National Education Association, pp. 9-27.

[93]   Fleming, N. (2001) *How do I Learn Best?* Christchurch, New Zealand.

[94]   Scribner, S. & Cole, M. (1973). "Cognitive Consequences of Formal and Informal
       Education." *Science* 182 (9 November), pp. 553-9.

[95]   Stebbins, L., St. Pierre, R. G., Proper, E. C., Anderson, R. B., Cerva; T. R.; Kennedy,
       M. M. Project Officer. *Education as Experimentation: A Planned Variation Model
       Volume IV-A, An Evaluation of Follow Through et al Evaluation of Follow Through,*
       Abt Associates, Cambridge, MA 1977: xxii-xxiv,- 129-167.

4. COLLEGE EDUCATION

[1]   Barzun, J. (.1959). *The House of Intellect.* New York: Harper & Brothers Publishers,
       98-9.

[2]   National Center for Education Statistics.(2007). *Digest of Education Statistics 2006.*
       Washington, DC: U. S. Government Printing Office, Table 8.

[3]   *Ibid.* Table 9. National Center for Education Statistics. (1973). *Digest of Education
       Statistics 1972,* Washington, DC: U. S. Government Printing Office, Table 14.

[4]   U. S. Census Bureau. (1977}. *Statistical Abstract of the United States 1976.*
       Washington, DC: U. S. Government Printing Office, Table B-12 National Center for
       Education Statistics.(1993). *Digest of Education Statistics 1992.* Washington, DC: U.
       S. Government Printing Office, Table 364.

[5]   Taubman, P. & Wales, T. (1972). *Mental Ability and Higher Educational Attainment in
       the 20th Century - A Technical Report Prepared for the Carnegie Commission on
       Higher Education.* National Bureau of Economic Research Occasional Paper 118.

[6]   National Center for Education Statistics.(2007). O*p. cit.*, Table 176.

[7]   Brewer, D. J., Gates, S. M., & Goldman, C. A. (2002). *In Pursuit of Prestige - Strategy
       and Competition in U.S. Higher Education.* New Brunswick: Transactions Publishers.
       See also Clotfelter, C. T.(1999). "The Familiar but Curious Economics of Higher
       Education: Introduction to a Symposium." *Journal of Economic Perspectives* 13 (1),
       pp. 3-12.

[8]   Atkinson, R. (2001-2). "Achievement versus Aptitude in College Admissions." *Issues
       in Science and Technology* Winter, pp. 31-36.

[9]   Menand, L. (2001). "College: The End of the Golden Age". *The New York Review of
       Books* October 18, pp. 44-7.

[10]   Bromell, N. (2002). "Summa cum Avaritia" *Harpers* 304 (1820), pp.71-6.

[11] Yardley, J. (2001). "Harvard's high-grade inflation". *Washington Post* December 10, p.
      C2. Of the Harvard Class of 2001 91% graduated cum laude, versus. 51% at Yale, 44%
      at Princeton

[12] Johnson, V. (2003). *Grade Inflation - A Crisis in College Education.* New York:
      Springer-Verlag, p. 207.

[13] *Ibid.*, p.192

[14] Trout, P. (1999). "Professors in the Dock". *Washington Times*, February 24, p. A17.

[15] Menand. L. (2001). *Op. cit.*, pp. 46-47.

[16] MacDonald, H. (1996). "Writing Down Together." In K. Washburn & J. F. Thornton
      (Eds.). *Dumbing Down - Essays on the Strip Mining of American Culture* (pp. 88-96).
      New York: W. W. Norton & Company,

[17] Goldberg, S. (1996). "The Erosion of the Social Sciences". In K. Washburn & J. F.
      Thornton (Eds.), *op cit.*, pp. 97-113.

[18] D'Souza, D.(1991). *Illiberal Education - The Politics of Race and Sex on Campus.*
      New York: Free Press, pp. 59-93, 157-193, 194-228. See also Sowell, T. (1993). *Inside
      American Education.- the Decline, the Deception, the Dogmas.*: New York: Free Press,
      New York pp. 202-231.

[19] National Center for Education Statistics. (1991). *Digest of Education Statistics 1990.*
      Washington, DC: U. S. Government Printing Office, Table 279.

[20] Sowell, T. (1993). *Op. cit.*, pp.132-173.

[21] Levine, M. L. (2005). College Graduates Aren't Ready for the Real World. *The
      Chronicle Review of Higher Education*, 51 (24).

[22] National Center for Education Statistics. (2001). *Op cit.* Table 385

[23] Kane, T. J. & Rouse, C. E. (1995). "Labor-Market Returns to Two- and Four-Year
      College". *American Economic Review.* 85 (3), pp. 600-614: 610-11

[24] Kane, T. J. & Rouse, C. E. (.1999). "Community College: Educating Students at the
      Margin between College and Work." *Journal of Economic Perspectives* 13 (1), pp. 63-
      84. Hoachlander, G., Sikora, A., and Horn, L. (2003). "Community College Students:
      Goals, Academic Preparation and Outcomes." *Education Statistics Quarterly 5 (2).*

[25] Twitchell, J. R. (2004). "Higher Ed, Inc." *Wilson Quarterly* Summer, pp. 2004, 46-59.

[26] Winston, G. C. (1999). "Subsidies, Hierarchies and Peers: The Awkward Economics of
      Higher Education." *Journal of Economic Perspectives* 13 (1), pp. 13-36.

[27] Boyer, E. L. (1990). *Scholarship Reconsidered - Priorities of the Professionals.*
      Carnegie Foundation for the Advancement of Teaching,. New York: Jossey-Bass, New
      York, pp.12, 44, Appendix Tables A-23, A-26.

[28] Bishop. J. (1991). "Achievement, Test Scores, and Relative Wages." 146-186 In M. H.
      Kosters (Ed.). *Workers and their Wages - Changing Patterns in the United States.*
      American Enterprise Institute Press, Lanham, Md. Distributed by University Press of
      America, 1991

[29] Blackburn, M. L. & Neumark, D. (1995). "Omitted-Ability Bias and the Increase in the
      Return to Schooling." *Review of Economics and Statistics* 77 (2), pp. 217-230: 228.

[30] Kane, J. T. & Rouse, C. E. (1995). *Op cit*

[31] 31. Wilkinson, B. W.(1966). "Present Values of Lifetime Earnings for Different
      Occupations." *Journal of Political Economy* 74 (6), pp. 556-572.

[32] Grogger, J. & Eide, E. (.1995). "Changes in College Skills and Rise in the College
      Premiums". *Journal of Human Resources* XXX (2), pp. 280-310.

[33] Rumberger, R. W. & Thomas, S. L. (1993). "The Economic Returns to College Major, Quality, and Performance: A Multi-level Analysis of Recent Graduates." *Economics of Education Review* 12 (1), pp. 1-19.

[34] National Center for Education Statistics. (1991). *Digest of Education Statistics 1998*. Or 1990 Washington, DC: U. S. Government Printing Office *Op. cit.* Table 279. Or 2 2006

[35] *Ibid.*, Table 176.2006

[36] National Center for Education Statistics. (1999). *Digest of Education Statistics 1998*. Washington, DC: U. S. Government Printing Office. Table 386. National Center for Education Statistics. (2003). *Digest of Education Statistics 2002*. Washington, DC: U. S. Government Printing Office, Table 387.

[37] Reynolds, J., Stewart, M., MacDonald, R. & Sischo, L. (2005). *Have Adolescents Become too Ambitious? U.S. High School Seniors' Career Plans, 1976 to 2000*. Department of Sociology, Florida State University.

[38] Yin, S. (2003). "The Road not Taken." *American Demographics*, 29 (9), p 13.

[39] Kennedy, D. (2001). "College Science: Pass,, no Credit." *Science* 293 (31 August), p. 1557.

[40] Holden, C. (1995). "Is it Time to begin Ph.D. Population Control?' *Science* 270 (6 October), pp. 123-128. Bhagwati, J. & Rao, M. (1996). "Too Many Scientists." *American Enterprise* January-February, pp. 1 71-72.

[41] Lemieux, T. (2006). "Postsecondary Education and Increasing Wage Inequality." *American Economic Review* 96 (2), pp. 195-199.

[42] Becker, G. S. *(1975). Human Capital - A Theoretical and Empirical Analysis, with Special Reference to Education*. New York: National Bureau of Economic Statistics, pp. 157-166.

[43] Dale, S. B. & Krueger, A. B. (.2002). "Estimating Payoff to Attending a More Selective College." *Quarterly Journal of Economics* CXVII (4), pp.1491-1527.

[44] Hunter, J. E. (1985). "Cognitive Ability, Cognitive Aptitudes, Job Knowledge, and Job Performance" *Journal of Vocational Behavior* 29, pp. 340-362. See also Cawley, J., Heckman, J., Lochner. L. & Vtlacil, E. (2000). "Understanding the Role of Cognitive Ability in Accounting for the Recent Rise in the Economic Return to Education." In K. Arrow, S. Bowles & S. Durlau (Eds.), *Meritocracy and Economic Inequality* (230-265). Princeton: Princeton University Press.

[45] Jaeger, D. A. & Page, M. E. (1996). "Degrees Matter: New Evidence on Sheepskin Effects in the Returns to Education." *Review of Economics and Statistics* 78 (4), pp. 733-740.

[46] 45. Durant, Will. & Ariel. (1968). *The Lessons of History*. New York: Simon and Schuster, p. 77.

[47] 46. Freeman, R. B. *(1976). The Over-Educated American*. New York: Academic Press.

[48] 47. Berg, 1. E. *(1970). Education and Jobs: The Great Training Robbery*. New York: Praeger Publishers.

[49] 48. Rumberger, R. W. (1987). "The Impact of Surplus Schooling on Productivity and Earnings." *Journal of Human Resources* XXII (1), pp. 24-50: 34.

[50] 49. Murphy, K.M. & Welch, F. (1993). "Occupational Change and the Demand for Skill, 1940-1990. American Economic Association *Papers and Proceedings*. 83 (2), pp. 125-126.

[51]   50. Hecker, D. E. (1992). "Reconciling Conflicting Data on Jobs for College
        Graduates." *Monthly Labor Review* 115 (7), 3-11. Tyler, J., Murnane, R. J., & Levy. F.
        (1995)."Are more College Graduates really taking 'High School' Jobs?" *Monthly
        Labor Review* 118 (12), pp. 18-27. Hecker, D. E.(1995). "College Graduates in High
        School Jobs: A Commentary." *Monthly Labor Review* 118 (12), p. 28.

[52]   *Economist* (2003)."Money Back." June 21, p.46.

5. CONSEQUENCES FOR THE ECONOMY

[1]   National Center for Education Statistics. (2007). *Digest of Education Statistics 2006.*
        Washington, DC: U. S. Government Printing Office, Tables 282, 287, 288.

[2]   Hecker, D. E. "Occupational Employment Projections to 2014.". *Monthly Labor
        Review* 127 (2), pp. 70 -100: 82-5.

[3]   Barber, E. G. & Morgan, R. P. (1987). "The Impact of Foreign Graduate Students on
        Engineering Education in the United States." *Science* 236 (3 April), pp. 33-37

[4]   National Science Board. *Science & Engineering Indicators - 2006*, Arlington, VA:
        National Science Foundation Appendix Table 2-33.

[5]   *Ibid.,* Appendix Table 2-33.

[6]   Mashelkar, R. A. (2005). "India's R&D: Reaching for the Top." *Science* 307 (4
        March), pp.: 1415-1417. See also Waldman, A. (2004). "Indians Go Home, but Don't
        Leave U.S. Behind". *New York Times* July 24.

[7]   Boyer, E. L (1990). *Scholarship Reconsidered - Priorities of the Professionals.* New
        York: The Carnegie Foundation for the Advancement of Teaching & Jossey-Bass, p.
        17.

[8]   National Science Board. *Science & Engineering Indicators - 2004*, Table 3-23

[9]   National Science Board (2006). *Op. cit*, 2006, Table 3-20, Appendix Table 3-18.

[10]   Van Opstal, D. (2001). "The Skills Imperative: Talent and U.S. Competitiveness."
        Issues in Science and Technology 17 (1), pp. 51-58.

[11]   Thompson, P. & Fox-Kean, M. (2005). "Patent Citations and the Geography of
        Knowledge Spillovers: A Reassessment." *The American Economic Review* 95 (1), pp.
        450-460, and Henderson, R., DAM Jaffe and Trajtenberg, M. (2005). "Patent Citations
        and the Geography of Knowledge Spillovers: a Reassessment: Comment," *The
        American Economic Review* 95 (1), pp. 461-464.

[12]   National Science Board (2004) *Op. cit.,* Appendix Table 2-37.

[13]   National Science Board (2006). *Op. cit.* Appendix Table 6-6.

[14]   Dohm, A. and Schniper, L. (2007). "Occupational Employment Projections to
        2016.".*Monthly Labor Review* 130 (11), pp. 86-125: 107-109.

[15]   Nakamura, H. (1964). *Ways of Thinking of Eastern Peoples.- India, China, Tibet,
        Japan.* Honolulu: The University of Hawaii Press

[16]   National Science Board. (2006). *Op. cit.* Appendix Table 4-42.

[17]   *Ibid.,* Appendix Table 4-4. National Science Board (2004) *Op. cit.* Appendix Table 4-3.

[18]   National Science Board (2006). *Op. cit.* 2006, Appendix Table 4-43.

[19]   U.S. Bureau of the Census.(2007). *Statistical Abstract of the United States 2007.* Table
        795. U.S. Bureau of the Census. (1995). Table 992.

[20] National Science Board (1991), Appendix Table 6-21. National Science Board (2006). Appendix Table 6-12.

[21] Friedman, T. L. (2005). *The World is Flat - A Brief History of the Twenty-first Century*. New York: Farrar, Straus and Giroux, p. 30

[22] 22. National Science Board (1980). Appendix Table 1-19. National Science Board (2004). Appendix Table 6-4.

[23] Bix, A. S. (2000). *Inventing Ourselves out of Jobs? America's Debate over Technological Unemployment 1929-1986*. Baltimore: the Johns Hopkins Press.

[24] Jacob, M. (1997). *Scientific Culture and the Making of the Industrial West*. New York: Oxford University Press, 105-108.

[25] Lewis, B. (2003) *The Crisis of Islam - Holy War and Holy Terror*. New York: The Modern Library, pp.114-116.

[26] Lewis, B. (2003). *Loc. cit*

[27] Schumpeter, J. A. (1939). *Business Cycles - A Theoretical, Historical and Statistical Analysis of the Capitalist Process*. New York: McGraw-Hill Book Company, Inc., pp. 164, 168, 325--448, 753-793.

[28] Bhagwati, J., Panagariya, A. & Srinivasan, T. N. (2004). "The Muddles over Outsourcing". *Journal of Economic Perspectives* 18 (4), pp. 93-114.

[29] Hewell, P. A. (1987). "The Deskilling Controversy". *Work and Occupation* 14 (3), pp. 323-346.

[30] Friedman, T. I. (2005). *Op. cit.*, pp. 289-290

[31] Levin, H. M. & Russell Rumberger, R. (1987). "Educational Requirements for New Technologies: Visions, Possibilities, and Current Realities". *Educational Policy* 1 (3), pp. 333-354.

[32] Capelli, P. (1993). "Are Skill Requirements Rising? Evidence for Production and Clerical Jobs." *Industrial and Labor Relations Review* 46 (3), pp. 515-530.

[33] Howell, D. & Weiler, S. S. (1998). "Skills-Biased Demand Shifts and Wage Collapse in the United States: A Critical Perspective." *Eastern Economic Journal* 24 (3), pp. 343-366.

[34] Bills, M. & Klenow, P. J. (2000). "Does Schooling Cause Growth?" *American Economic Review* 90 (3), pp. 1160-1183.

[35] Hanushek, E. A. & D. Kimko, D. D. (2000). "Schooling, Labor-Force Quality, and the Growth of Nations". *American Economic Review* 90 (3), pp. 1184-1208.

[36] Hirsch, F. (1976). *Social Limits to Growth*. Cambridge, MA: Harvard University Press.

[37] U.S. Department of Education. (2006). *Digest of Education Statistics* 2005, Washington, DC: U. S. Government Printing Office, Table 246.

[38] Becker, W. E. & Kennedy, P. E. (2005). "Does Teaching Enhance Research in Economics?" American Economic Association *Papers and Proceedings* 95 (2), pp. 72-178.

[39] Boyer, E. L. (1997). *Scholarship Reconsidered - Priorities for Professionals*. The Carnegie Foundation for the Advancement of Teaching. New York: Jossey-Bass, pp. 11-12, Appendix A, Table A-1.

6. Simple 'Solutions'

[1]   Ehrenberg. R. G., Brewer, D. J., Adam Gamaran, A. & Willms., J. D. (2001). " Class Size and Student Achievement". *Psychological Science* 2 (1), Supplement pp. 1-30. See also: Hanushek, E. A. (1999). "The Evidence on Class Size".(pp 131-168). In S. E Mayer & P. E. Peterson (Eds.). *Earning and Learning - How Schools Matter* (pp 131-168). Washington, DC:. Brookings Institute Press, New York: Russell Sage Foundation See also Mosteller, F.(1999). "How does Class Size relate to Achievement in School?" In S. E. Mayer & P. E. Peterson (Eds). *Op. cit.*, (pp. 117-129).

[2]   Ferguson, H. F. & Ladd, H. F. (1996). "How and Why Money Matters: an Analysis of Alabama Schools." In H. F. Ladd (Ed.). *Holding Schools Accountable -Performance-Based Reform in Education* (pp. 265-298).Washington, DC: The Brookings Institution, 279-80, 288-9.

[3]   Hallinan, M. T. & Sorensen, A. B. (1985). Ability Group Size, and Student Achievement." *American Journal of Education 94 (1), pp. 71-89*

[4]   National Center for Education Statistics. (2003). *Digest of Education Statistics 2002*. Washington, DC. Table 70. National Center for Education Statistics (2006). *Digest of Education Statistics 2005*. Washington, DC., Table 68.

[5]   Greenwald, R., H., Hodges, L. V. & Leine, R. D. (1996). "The Effect of School Resources on Student Achievement" *Review of Educational Research* 66 (3), pp. 361-396.

[6]   Hanushek, E. A. (1996). "A More Complete Picture of School Resource Policies". *Review of Educational Research* 66 (3), pp.397-409. Hanushek, E. A. (1996). "School Resources and Student Performance." 43-73 In G. Burtless (Ed.). *Does Money Matter? The Effect of School Resources on Student Achievement and Adult Success. (43-73)*. Washington, DC: Brookings Institution Press.

[7]   Blau, F. D. (1996). "Symposium on Primary and Secondary Education". *Journal of Economic Perspectives* 10 (4), pp. 3-8.

[8]   Childs, T. S. & Shakeshaft, C. (1986). "A Meta-Analysis of Research on the Relationship between Educational Expenditures and Student Achievement." *Journal of Education Finance.* 12 (2), pp.249-263.

[9]   Cordes, C. & Miller, E. (Eds.). (2000). "Fool's Gold: A Critical Look at Computers in Childhood." Alliance for Childhood, College Park, MD. See info@allianceforchildhood.net

[10]   National Center for Education Statistics. *Digest of Education Statistics 2005*. Washington, DC, Table 415.

[11]   Centre for Educational Research and Innovation. (2003). *Education at a Glance 2003*. Paris: Organization for Economic Co-operation and Development, Tables A4.1, A5.2, A6.1, and A6.2.

[12]   Temin, P. (2002). "Teacher Quality and the Future of America" *Eastern Economic Journal* 28 (3), pp. 285-300.

[13]   Rumberger, R. W. (1987). "Impact of Salary Differentials on Teacher Shortages and Turnover: the Case of Mathematics and Science Teachers." *Economics of Education Review* 6 (4), pp. 389-399.

[14]   Neal, D. (1997). "The Effects of Catholic Secondary Schooling on Educational Achievement". *Journal of Labor Economics* 15 (!), Part 1, pp. 98-123.

7. MULTIPLE RESPONSES TO COMPLEX PROBLEMS

[1]   Schlafly, P. (2005). "Changes Beyond Opening Dates." *Washington Times* August 17, p. A15.

[2]   Holland, R. (2005). "Virginia Teachers Joining a Nationwide Declaration of Independence." Arlington, VA: Lexington Institute.

[3]   Gross, M. L. (1999). *The Conspiracy of Ignorance - the Failure of American Public Schools*. New York: Harper-Collins Publishers, p. 68.

[4]   Kozloff, M. A. (2001). *Necessary Conditions for Fundamental Reform of Schools of Education*. unpublished paper, July.

[5]   Gross, M. L. (1999). *Op cit*, pp. 175-184.

[6]   Zoch. P. A. (2001). "Our Uneducated Educators". *Wilson Quarterly Review*. Autumn, pp. 60-68. "Hoe to be Top." (2007). The Economist October 20:, pp. 80-81.

[7]   Gross, M. L. (1999). *Op cit*, p.175.

[8]   Ballou, D. & Michael Podgursky, M. (1995). "Recruiting Smarter Teachers." *Journal of Human Resources* XXX (1), p.335.

[9]   Coulson, A. J. (1999). *Market Education - The Unknown History*. New Brunswick: Transactions Publishers, pp.146-8

[10]   Hanushek, E. A. (1986). "The Economics of Schooling: Production and Efficiency in the Public Schools." *The Journal of Economic Literature* XXIV (3), pp. 1141-77. 1167.

[11]   Greenwald, R., Hodges, L. V. & Richard D. Leine, R. D. (1996). "The Effect of School Resources on Student Achievement" *Review of Educational Research* 66 (3), pp. 361-396.

[12]   Dillon, S. (2005). "Students Ace State Tests, but Earn D's from U.S." *New York Times* November 26.

[13]   Zoch, P. A. (2001). "Our Uneducated Educators." *Wilson Quarterly Review,* Autumn, pp. 60-68.

[14]   Schmidt, W. H. & Mary M. Kennedy, M. M. (1990). *Teachers' and Teacher Candidates' Beliefs About Subject Matter and About Teaching Responsibilities*. East Lansing, MI: National Center for Research on Teacher Education, Research Report 90-4.

[15]   Levine, A. E. (2005). *Educating School Leaders*. Washington , DC: Education Schools Project.

[16]   Hess, F. M. & Kelly, A. P. (2005). "Textbook Leadership? An Analysis of Leading Books Used in Principal Preparation*" Papers and Studies*, Program on Education Policy and Governance at Harvard University.

[17]   Hess, F. M. & Kelly. A. P. (2005) "The Accidental Principal." *Education Next,* Summer, pp. 34-41.

[18]   "Mr. Secretary, We Ask that you Withdraw your Premature Recommendations for Mathematics Instruction." *Washington Post*, November 18, 1999, p. A5.

[19]   Stotsky, S. (2001). "Preface." In S. Stotsky (ed.). *What's at Stake in the K-12 Standards War - A Primer for Educational Policy Makers* (xiii-xxiii).New York: Peter

Lang. Barzun, J. (1959). *The House of Intellect*. New York: Harper & Brothers Publishers,

[20] Stern, S. M. (2001). "Why the Battle over History Standards?". in S. Stotsky (Ed.). *What's at Stake in the K-12 Standards War - A Primer for Educational Policy Makers* (149-168). New York: Peter Lang.

[21] Dillon, S. (2005). "Students Ace State Tests, but Earn D's from U.S," *New York Times* November 26.

[22] Izumi, L. T. & Evers, W. M. (Eds.) (2002). *Teacher Quality*. Stanford, CA: Hoover Institute Press, p. 50. See also Gross, M. L. (1999). *Op cit*, pp. 90-97. National Center for Education Statistics. (2006). *Digest of Education Statistics 2005*. Washington, DC: U. S. Government Printing Office, Table 66.

[23] Angrist, J. D. & Guryan, J. (2004). "Teacher Testing, Teacher Education, and Teacher Characteristics. *American Economic Review* 94 (2), pp. 241-246.

[24] Mathews, J. (2002). "Education Effort Meets Resistance.". *Washington Post*, June 10, p. A8.

[25] Evers, W. M. & Walburg, H. J. (Eds.) (2002). *School Accountability*. Stanford, CA: Hoover Institute Press.

[26] Fletcher. M. A.(2003). "As High School Exit Exams Cost Diplomas, Anger Rises." *Washington Post* May 31, p. A1.

[27] Koretz, D. M. (2002). "Limitations in the use of Achievement Tests as Measures of Educators' Productivity." *Journal of Human Resources* 37 (4), pp. 752-777.

[28] Loveless, T. "The Parent Trap." (2001).*Wilson Quarterly Review* Autumn. pp.36-42

[29] Chavez, L. (2000). "Boost for Education Reform." *Washington Times* January 13, p. A13.

[30] Broder, D. S. (2005). "Split over Schools: Parents and Teachers Disagree on Reforms." *Washington Post* June 23, p. A27

[31] Coulson, A. J. (1999). *Op cit*, pp. 191-5. Archibald, G. (2004). "Failing Schools Underreport - States Fear Takeover under Education Act." *The Washington Post* January 14, pp. A1, A8.

[32] Bishop, J. H. (1999). "Nerd Harassment, Incentives, School Priorities, and Learning." In S. E. Mayer & P. E, Peterson (Eds.). *Earning and Learning - How Schools Matter* (pp. 231- 279). Washington, DC: Brookings Institute Press, New York: Russell Sage Foundation.

[33] Ravitch, D. (2002). "Testing and Accountability Historically Considered." In W. N. Evers & H. J. Walberg (Eds.) (1995). *School Accountability*.(pp. 9-21). Stanford, CA: Hoover Institute Press.

[34] Lemann, N. (1995). "The Structure of Success in America". *Atlantic Monthly*. August, pp. 41-60. See also Lemann, N. (1995). ":The Great Sorting". *Atlantic Monthly*. September, pp. 84-100.

[35] National Center for Education Statistics. (2001). *Digest of Education Statistics* 2000,. Washington, DC: U. S. Government Printing Office, Table 385; 35.National Center for Education Statistics (2003).*Digest of Education Statistics 2002*. Washington, DC: U. S. Government Printing Office, Table 387.

[36] Weiss, A. (1983). "A Sorting-cum-Learning Model of Education." *Journal of Political Economy* 91 (3), pp. 420-442.

[37] Peterson, P. E. (1994). "Vouchers and Test Scores." *Policy Review* 93, January-February 1999: -14.

[38] Coleman, J. R., Hoffer, T. & Kilgore., S. (1982). *High School Achievement - Public, Catholic, and Private Schools Compared.* New York: Basic Books, pp.189-94, 97-102

[39] Friedman, Milton and Rose. *(1990).* Free to Choose - A Personal Statement. San Diego: Harcourt Brace Ivanovich, pp.158-171

[40] Weiss, D. (1993). *The Specter of Capitalism and the Promise of a Classless Society.* Atlantic Height, NJ: Humanities Press International Inc., pp.131-158.

[41] Epple, D. & Romano, R. E. (1998). "Competition between Private and Public Schools, Vouchers, and Peer-Group Effects." *American Economic Review* 88 (1), pp.33-62.

[42] Neal, D. (2002). "How Vouchers Could Change the Market for Education". *Journal of Economic Perspectives* 16 (1), pp. 25-44.

[43] Greene, J. P. & Winters, M. A. (2003). "When Schools Compete: The Effects of Vouchers on Florida Public School Achievement." Education Working Paper 2, Manhattan Institute.

[44] Hoxby, C. (2002). "Would School Choice Change the Teaching Profession?" *Journal of Human Resources* 37 (4), pp. 646-891.

[45] Ladd, H. F. (2002). "School Vouchers: A Critical View*". Journal of Economic Perspectives* 16 (4), pp. 3-24: 6-8, 18-21.

[46] Peterson, P. E., Howell, W. G. Patrick Wolf. J. & Campbell, D. E. (2003). "School Vouchers: Results from Randomized Experiments." In C. M. Hoxby (Ed.). *The Economics of School Choice* (pp.107-144). Chicago: The University of Chicago Press.

[47] Hoxby, C. M. (1996). "The Effects of Private School Vouchers in Schools." In H. K. Ladd (Ed.). *Holding Schools Accountable - Performance-Based Reform in Education* (pp. 177-208). Washington, DC: The Brookings Institution:.200-202.

[48] National Assessment of Educational Progress (2006). *The National Report Card - Results of the 2005 Trial Urban District Assessment for Grades 4 and 8.* Washington, DC: Department of Education.

[49] Hoxby, C. M. (2004). *Achievement in Charter Schools and Regular Public Schools in the United States: Understanding the Difference.* Cambridge: Harvard University & New York: National Bureau of Economic Research.

[50] Greene, J. P., Foster, G. & Winters, M. A.(2003). "Apples to Apples: An Evaluation of Charter Schools Serving General Student Populations." Education Working Paper no. 1, Manhattan Institute

[51] Slavin, R. E. (1987). "Ability Grouping and Student Achievement in Elementary Schools: a Best-Evidence Synthesis" *Review of Educational Research* 57 (3), pp. 293-336.

[52] Powell, A. G., Farrar, E. & Cohen, D. K. (1985). *The Shopping Mall High School-Winners and Losers in the Educational Marketplace.* Boston: Houghton Mifflin Company, pp. 118-133.

[53] Mathews, J. (2005). "At 50, AP Test is still Changing." *Washington Post*, January 26, p. A10.

[54] Gamoran, A. (1992). "The Variable Effects of High School Tracking." *American Sociological Review* 57 (6), pp. 812-828.

[55] Rosenbaum, J. (1976). *Making Inequality - The Hidden Curriculum of High School Tracking*: New York: John Wiley & Sons, pp. 29-80.

[56] Darling-Hammond, L. (1995). "Equity Issues in Performance-Based Assessment." In M. T. Nettles & A. L. Nettles (Eds.). *Equity and Excellence in Educational Testing and Assessment.*(pp. 89-114). Boston: Kluwer Academic Publishers, pp.100-01.

[57] Stevens, M. L. (2001). *Kingdom of Children - Culture and Controversy in the Homeschooling Movement.* Princeton: Princeton University Press, p. 17.

[58] Smith, M. (2004). "Trend even stronger than figures show." *The Washington Times* August 23, p. B4. See also Gross, J. (2003). "Dissatisfied with Schools, More Parents Turn to Home." *New York Times* November 10.

[59] Mayberry, L., Knowles, J. G., Ray, B. & Marlow, S. (1995). *Home Schooling - Parents as Educators.* Thousand Oaks, CA: Kirwan Press, Inc., pp. 29-44, 101.

[60] Mayberry op cit. pp.17-18, 70-73

[61] National Center for Education Statistics U.S. Department of Education. (2007). *Digest of Education Statistics* 2006, Tables3, 84..

[62] Peterson, P. E. (1999). "School Reforms: How much do they Matter?" In S. E. Mayer and P. E, Peterson (Eds.). *Earning and Learning - How Schools Matter* (pp. 105-115). Washington, DC: Brookings Institute Press, New York: Russell Sage Foundation, p. 114.

[63] Harmer, D. (1994). *School Choice-Why you Need it - How you Get it.* Washington, DC: Cato Institute, pp. 58-64

[64] Machlup. F. (1962). *The Production and Distribution of Knowledge in the United States.* Princeton: Princeton University Press, pp. 130-134,.

[65] National Center for Education Statistics. (2006). *Digest of Education Statistics* 2006, Washington, DC: U. S. Government Printing Office, Table 77.

[66] Flyer, F. & Rosen, S. (1997). "The New Economics of Teachers and Education". *Journal of Labor Economics* 15 (1 Part 2), pp. S104-S139.

[67] Edwards, E. (1999). "Plugged-in Generation." *Washington. Post* November. 18, p. A1

[68] Walberg, H. (2001). "Do Americans Study Enough?" *Hoover Institution Weekly Essay*, July 23.

[69] Ingersoll, R. M. (2001). "Teacher Turnover and Teacher Shortages: an Organizational Analysis. *American Educational Research Journal* 38 (3), pp. 499-534: 520-523.

[70] Banfield, E. C. (1970). *The Unheavenly City - The Nature and Future of our Urban Crisis.* Boston: Little, Brown.

[71] Welsh, P. (2004). "When the Street and the Classroom Collide." *Washington Post* June 20, pp. B1, B4.

[72] Akerlof, G. A. & Kranton, R. E. (2002). "Identity and Schooling: Some Lessons for the Economics of Education.". *Journal of Economic Literature* 40 (4), pp. 1167-1201: 1173-6.

8. OCCUPATIONAL PRESTIGE OF TEACHING

[1] Friedman, S. J. (2000). "How much of a Problem? A Reply to Ingersoll's Problem." *Educational Researcher* 29 (5), pp. 18-20.

[2] Wise, A. E.(1992). "The Case for Restructuring Teacher Preparation." 43-52 In L. Darling-Hammond, G. A. Griffin & A. E. Wise. *Excellence in Teacher Education:*

Helping Teachers to Develop Learning-Centered Schools. (Pp. 43-52). Washington, DC: National Education Association.

[3]   Griffin G. A. (1992). "Learning from the 'New' Schools: Lessons for Teacher Education." 29-42 In Linda Darling-Hammond, Gary A. Griffin and Arthur E Wise op. cit.

[4]   Lasch, C. (1978.). *The Culture of Narcissism - American Life in an Age of Diminishing Expectations.* New York: W.W. Norton & Company Inc., pp. 52-70.

[5]   Sorokin. P. (1957). *Social Change and Cultural Dynamics - a Study of Change in Major Systems of Art, Truth, Ethics, Law and Social Relationships.* Boston: Porter Sargent Publisher, pp. 699-704.

INDEX

H

J

K

L

T